Managerial Effectiveness

McGRAW-HILL SERIES IN MANAGEMENT

Keith Davis, Consulting Editor

ALLEN   Management and Organization

ALLEN   The Management Profession

BENNIS   Changing Organizations

BERGEN AND HANEY   Organizational Relations and Management Action

BLOUGH   International Business: Environment and Adaptation

BOWMAN   Management: Organization and Planning

BROWN   Judgment in Administration

CAMPBELL, DUNNETT, LAWLER, AND WEICK   Managerial Behavior, Performance, and Effectiveness

CLELAND AND KING   Systems Analysis and Project Management

CLELAND AND KING   Systems, Organizations, Analysis, Management: A Book of Readings

DALE   Management: Theory and Practice

DAVIS   Human Relations at Work

DAVIS AND BLOMSTROM   Business and Its Environment

DAVIS AND SCOTT   Human Relations and Organizational Behavior: Readings and Comments

DeGREENE   Systems Psychology

DUNN AND RACHEL   Wage and Salary Administration: A Systems Approach

FIEDLER   A Theory of Leadership Effectiveness

FLIPPO   Principles of Personnel Management

GOLEMBIEWSKI   Men, Management, and Morality

HARBISON AND MYERS   Management in the Industrial World

HICKS   The Management of Organizations

JOHNSON, KAST, AND ROSENZWEIG   The Theory and Management of Systems

KAST AND ROSENZWEIG   Organization and Management: A Systems Approach

KEITH AND GUBELLINI   Business Management

KOONTZ   Toward a Unified Theory of Management

KOONTZ AND O'DONNELL   Principles of Management

KOONTZ AND O'DONNELL   Management: A Book of Readings

MAIER   Problem-solving Discussions and Conferences: Leadership Methods and Skills

MAYER   Production Management

McDONOUGH   Information Economics and Management Systems

McNICHOLS   Policy Making and Executive Action

MINER   The Management of Ineffective Performance

MUNDEL   A Conceptual Framework for the Management Sciences

PETIT   The Moral Crisis in Management

PIGORS AND PIGORS   Case Method in Human Relations

PRASOW AND PETERS Arbitration and Collective Bargaining: Conflict Resolution in Labor Relations

READY   The Administrator's Job

REDDIN   Managerial Effectiveness

SALTONSTALL   Human Relations in Administration

SARTAIN AND BAKER   The Supervisor and His Job

SCHRIEBER, JOHNSON, MEIER, FISCHER, AND NEWELL Cases in Manufacturing Management

STEINER   Managerial Long-range Planning

SUTERMEISTER   People and Productivity

TANNENBAUM   Control in Organizations

TANNENBAUM, WESCHLER, AND MASSARIK   Leadership and Organization

VANCE   Industrial Administration

VANCE   Management Decision Simulation

Managerial Effectiveness

William J. Reddin

DEPARTMENT OF BUSINESS ADMINISTRATION
UNIVERSITY OF NEW BRUNSWICK
CANADA

McGraw-Hill Book Company

New York   St. Louis   San Francisco   Düsseldorf   London
Mexico   Panama   Sydney   Toronto

Managerial Effectiveness

Library of Congress Catalog Card Number 77-99202

51358

1 2 3 4 5 6 7 8 9 0   MAMM   7 9 8 7 6 5 4 3 2 1 0

This book was set in News Gothic by Monotype Composition Company, Inc., and printed on permanent paper and bound by The Maple Press Company. The drawings were done by B. Handleman Associates, Inc. Paul B. Poss supervised the production.

This book is dedicated to R. E. Tweeddale, Deputy Minister,
Economic Growth, Province of New Brunswick, Canada, who
supported the 3-D Program from its infancy to its maturity.

Preface

The aim of this book is to make managers and the organizations they work in more effective. The book allows the manager to make a value analysis of himself in the organization. It also gives him direct advice on how to improve his own effectiveness and that of others.

It has been difficult for me to write this book as I had so much unlearning to do. I set myself the task of producing a simple, conceptual frame for managers. I wanted to "tell it like it is" and not favor one point of view over another. First I had to drop the notion of an ideal style; then I realized that flexibility must be balanced with resilience; then I recognized that the total situation must be accounted for; then I saw that managerial effectiveness had to be the central value. I did not start squarely at any of the points, though to have done so, in particular concerning effectiveness, seems so obvious to me now. Effectiveness is the central issue in management. It is a manager's job to be effective. It is his only job. He may be a managing director, plant manager, R&D manager, government officer, or military general—the central issue is always the same.

The structure of the theory and the book show clearly what I think the limiting factor on effectiveness really is. It is not knowledge, intent, or lack of external persuasion. The main limiting factor is a behavioral one. Managers need to learn how to manage social systems and how to manage themselves in them. Managers generally know what actions will improve things, but they often don't take them. There is a tremendous gap between what managers know about being effective and what they actually apply. This book tries to explain and close the gap.

Many managers will be surprised at the prominence given to theory. Some may wonder if this is another long-hair theoretical textbook or whether it is in fact a guide to action. This book and the theory itself are meant to be both theoretical and practical. There is nothing more practical than a good theory properly applied or so costly as a poor theory applied inappropriately. The effectiveness potential of sound behavioral theory for managers is only now beginning to be fully realized. It has been seen by some as the opposite to action, yet we could design no bridges, radios, or even egg timers without it. Only a poor theory leads to idle speculation, in-action, or impractical proposals. A sound theory shows clearly how things are related and how and when the relationship changes. Sound manage-ment theories are intended to clarify, not to mystify. They are designed to make sense out of what may appear to be a confusing situation. They show relationships not previously identified and hence lead to actions that would not otherwise be considered. They provide positive, direct guides to action. Useful theory is a reality in the physical sciences. It will become so in the social sciences of which management is an applied branch.

The simple point is that we can build bridges, but we are not sure about building organizations. We can predict what will happen to a beam under stress but not what will happen to a manager under stress. However, our knowledge will continually improve. Universities, at some time in the future, will teach courses in "management styles" or "situational manage-ment" with the same precision and the same guides to immediate, proven application as we now teach courses in concrete structures. The pro-fessional manager as a social engineer will emerge as a reality, as has emerged the professional engineer. It is true that at this point in develop-ment much of management is still an art. The man who has learned from his errors may still be ahead of the one who has learned from his books. At one time this statement was true of medicine, but the thought of a self-trained doctor today is not attractive. So too it will be with managers. Intuition will never cease to be useful, but the scientific approach will continue to assume more and more importance.

The book has developed naturally from the background notes used in the managerial-effectiveness seminar. This seminar is designed to improve effectiveness by enabling managers to apply the 3–D Theory to their work situation.

I have used reference sparingly. They are used either to buttress a key theoretical point or simply to provide a guide for those interested in further reading. The references concerning ideal style are an example of the former and those concerning technology demands, an example of the latter. It would have been a simple matter to surround the descriptive chapters on style and flex with references, but there seemed little point in so doing.

The 3—D Theory had its beginnings on the table napkins of the high table at McConnell Hall at the University of New Brunswick. Neil MacGill, the philosopher, was the professional cynic while Toby Graham, the historian and retired British artillery officer, was the generalist. I argued with them during soup and on, sometimes, to coffee. They still think I am quite confused about the whole issue, so I am anxiously awaiting their own theories; both may produce one. One of them has already threatened me with the 4—D Theory and suggested that with this book, I may both publish and perish.

In addition to the University of New Brunswick Library, this manuscript has seen the inside of many hotel rooms and some wide-open spaces as well. Parts were written in Mauritius, Dublin, and Nairobi. However most of it was written in my somewhat primitive cabin on the shores of Grand Lake in New Brunswick where I have loons, chipmunks, racoons, squirrels, and skunks as regular guests, indoors and out, and a Faustian fireplace for the ten-below nights.

William J. Reddin

Acknowledgments

I want to acknowledge the important contributions to basic theory made by Jim McNaughton, Greg Muirhead, Rick Simms, and Keith Stewart.

Also to those who provided opportunities to test the application of the 3–D Theory: Reg Tweeddale, Derek Oland, Les Kirkpatrick, Dick Toner, Blake McCullogh, Arnie Patterson, Derm Barrett, Harold McIntyre, Richard Hacon, Patrick Kehoe, Bill Morrow, Doug Parks, and Dermot Egan.

My special thanks to D'Arcy Cartwright, Patrick Kehoe, and Alec Irvine for their numerous detailed suggestions and to Peter Firlotte and Jim Kinder, who came to the University of New Brunswick and read the final draft manuscript. Their comments were directly helpful in making this a more useful book for managers.

Also to those who each commented on several chapters: Remy Gagne, Ian Harlock, Jock Jardine, Hugh Marlow, David Robertson, Ken Rowell, Don Simmons, Romi Szawlowski, Raymond Tremblay, and Bill Jenkins.

Also to those who provided helpful ideas on various parts of the book: Dick Bird, Ross Darling, Toby Graham, Jock Jardine, Terry Lawson, Harry Holman, Ed Maher, Rene Martinet, Vance Mitchell, Frank Ryder, Dick Sullivan, Don Veale, and Fred Ward, who contributed to Chapter 14.

And to Jean Hossack and Valerie Richardson, who between them typed all my drafts with care.

Finally I would wish to acknowledge my debt to the thousands of executives in more than a dozen countries who made the book more useful. Their demand for practicality, usefulness, and evidence served to identify the weak point, the impractical conclusion, or the personal bias.

William J. Reddin

Contents

Preface   vii
Acknowledgments   xi

Part 1   KEY CONCEPTS

1   What Is Managerial Effectiveness?   3
2   An Outline of the 3-D Theory   11
3   What Is a Basic Style?   19
4   Is There an Ideal Style?   35
5   What Is Style Flex?   51

Part 2   SITUATION

6   Five Situational Elements   61
7   Technology Influences Style   69
8   Organization and People Influence Style   89
9   Common Situational Problems   115
10   Situational Dynamics   127
11   Situational Sensitivity   139
12   Situational Management Skill   159
13   Situational Management Techniques   169
14   Situational Theory   181

Part 3   STYLES

15   Separated—Deserter—Bureaucrat   205
16   Related—Missionary—Developer   215

17   Dedicated—Autocrat—Benevolent Autocrat   221
18   Integrated—Compromiser—Executive   229
19   The Management—Style—Diagnosis Test   237

Part 4   FLEX

20   High Flex—Flexibility—Drift   253
21   Low Flex—Resilience—Rigidity   261

Part 5   MANAGERIAL EFFECTIVENESS

22   How to Set Objectives   275
23   How to Become More Effective   287

Part 6   ORGANIZATIONAL EFFECTIVENESS

24   How to Develop Organizational Effectiveness   299
25   An Organizational Effectiveness Program   317

APPENDIXES

A   The 3-D Concept Dictionary   327
B   Bibliography   331

Index   341

Part 1
KEY CONCEPTS

The manager has the task of creating a true whole that is larger than the sum of its parts, a productive entity that turns out more than the sum of the resources put into it.

PETER F. DRUCKER

Life is not long, and too much of its must not pass in idle deliberation how it shall be spent.

SAMUEL JOHNSON

The great end of life is not knowledge but action.

THOMAS HUXLEY

Chapter One

WHAT IS MANAGERIAL EFFECTIVENESS?

There is only one realistic and unambiguous definition of *managerial effectiveness*. Effectiveness is the extent to which a manager achieves the output requirements of his position. This concept of managerial effectiveness is the central issue in management. It is the manager's job to be effective. It is his only job. Managerial effectiveness has to be defined in terms of output rather than input, by what a manager achieves rather than by what he does.

Results, not Personality

Effectiveness is not a quality a manager brings to a situation. To see it this way is nothing more than a return to the now discarded trait theory of leadership which suggested that more effective leaders had special qualities not possessed by less effective leaders. Effectiveness is best seen as something a manager produces from a situation by managing it appropriately. It represents output, not input. The manager must think in terms of performance, not personality. It is not so much what a manager does, but what he achieves. As an extreme example:

> A manager's true worth to his company may sometimes be measured by the amount of time he could remain dead in his office without anyone

noticing it. The longer the time, the more likely it is that he makes long-run policy decisions rather than short-run administrative decisions. The key decisions in a company are those with long-run effects and may refer to market entry, new product introduction, new plant location, or keyman appointments. The man making these decisions should not get involved, as can happen, with employee parking lot practices. If he does, he has not decided on the output measures of his job nor has he the skill or opportunity to create conditions where only policy issues reach him.

Effectiveness Standards and Objectives

Every managerial job has *effectiveness standards* associated with it. They may not be written down or even known, but they are always there. These are the standards by which the performance of the manager in the job may be judged. Preparing and using such written standards has cured numerous management ills simply because the true reason for each manager's existence is investigated, discussed, and ultimately agreed on by the manager himself and by his superior.

Effectiveness standards are easily prepared. A typical key opening heading is, "This manager is performing effectively when this happens. . . ."

Initially the answers sometimes are: "My superior says he likes my work," "There is no conflict," "I get raises," "I put in a good day's work," and "Letters and requests are handled promptly." All five of these answers may or may not lead to, or result from, managerial effectiveness, and none reflect output. Managers need to rewrite the answer to the basic question several times before they are satisfied with it.

Effectiveness standards carried to their logical conclusion lead to *management by objectives*. This is nothing more than designing an organization around the outputs of managers' jobs rather than the inputs.

There should be quantification in terms of percentages, dollars, or employees. Time bounds should be set. When this is done the effectiveness standards are transformed to objectives.

When managers write their own effectiveness standards and develop their objectives, a great many things can happen.

A division manager and seven branch managers in a Canadian electrical utility decided to write their effectiveness standards and establish objectives. It was not difficult to convince these men, who were all engineers, that standards and their measurement were important. They saw quickly that a manager's performance was measurable but that no data were available to do it. This led to a redesign of many accounting and recording procedures so that ultimately all of them had a clearly quantified output objective for measures on a weekly, monthly, quarterly, or annual basis. Their interest in effectiveness standards led to a fundamental redesign of part of the total accounting system in the utility and centered around output measurement rather than input control. The measurement system pursued aggressively by these managers led to greatly decreased direct labor costs.

Many managers are held back from focusing on effectiveness because of the way their position is defined. Job descriptions and position descriptions do not usually aid in increasing effectiveness.

JOB DESCRIPTIONS INHIBIT EFFECTIVENESS

The source of much of the problem surrounding effectiveness is found in the way job descriptions are written. Lengthy job descriptions or crash programs to write or update them usually indicate very little. As Parkinson (158) has pointed out, the last act of a dying organization is to issue a revised and greatly enlarged rule book. This observation may hold as well for crash programs to write job descriptions.

Many, if not most, managerial jobs are defined in terms of their input and behavior requirements by such phrases as:

He administers
He maintains
He organizes
He plans

Naturally managers never refer to job descriptions like these. Once made, they are not too useful as an operating guide. They are often proposed initially by those who want to use a seemingly scientific technique to justify a widespread change in salary differentials or change in the organization structure. They are often a negative influence as they focus on input and behavior, the less important end of the manager's job. Some managers focus on their job input by saying, "I manage 200 people," rather than in terms of output, "I am responsible for expanding products A and B at 6 to 10 percent a year, using my existing resources."

EFFICIENCY

Job descriptions often lead to an emphasis on what could be called managerial efficiency: the ratio of output to input. The problem with this is that even if both input and output are low, efficiency could still be 100 percent. In fact, a manager or department could easily be 100 percent efficient and 0 percent effective. The efficient manager is easily identified. He prefers to:

EFFICIENCY VERSUS EFFECTIVENESS		
Do things right	rather than	Do right things
Solve problems	rather than	Produce creative alternatives
Safeguard resources	rather than	Optimize resource utilization
Follow duties	rather than	Obtain results
Lower costs	rather than	Increase profit

Job descriptions lead to the kind of thinking on the left side; effectiveness standards lead to that shown on the right.

POSITION DESCRIPTIONS ALSO INHIBIT EFFECTIVENESS

Some organizations have a predominance of descriptions which focus on a manager's position in the organization, such as:

He reports to
He authorizes
He coordinates
He approves

This kind of description can be important to the military in wartime, when changes in command can take place in seconds. Position descriptions, focusing as they do on structure, spring from and reinforce the bureaucratic style. Many senior military officers who participate in managerial training are surprised to see evidence mount up that they are bureaucrats and that they work essentially for a position-description framework with little attention to output.

> One such officer, a general, was the director of a large military command in peacetime. He found that in situational training exercises he first looked for rules to guide him and then for approval of his action by his superior. He frequently used "I submit" as a verbal prelude to an argument. There was little doubt that this style was appropriate for his peacetime job. He had no real output measures to guide him. He was subject to tight control from above. His job, in fact, was equivalent to the principal of a technical college: maintaining a going concern, which processed raw recruits at one end; changing them to a trained force; and then improving this level of training and readiness, representing the other end, until their retirement at age forty-five or fifty.

Position descriptions without objective standards of output associated with them can lead to the maintenance of managers who are not contributing to their organization in any useful way.

Three Kinds of Effectiveness

Managerial effectiveness is not always clearly understood, and in order to be most effective themselves, managers should learn to distinguish sharply between *managerial effectiveness, apparent effectiveness,* and *personal effectiveness.*

APPARENT EFFECTIVENESS

It is difficult if not impossible to judge managerial effectiveness by observation of behavior alone. The behavior must be evaluated in terms of whether or not it is appropriate to the output requirements of the job. For example, the following qualities, while important in some positions, may, in others, be irrelevant to effectiveness:

Usually on time
Answers promptly
Has tidy desk
Makes quick decisions
Good at public relations

These characteristics usually give an air of apparent effectiveness in no matter what context they are used. Unfortunately apparent effectiveness may or may not lead to managerial effectiveness.

> Charles Smith was an independent consultant in Australia with four employees. He was first in and last out each day. He virtually ran everything and ran everywhere. In a business which usually makes low demands for immediate decisions, he always made them on the spot. "Do it now" was his catch phrase. Very intelligent, active, optimistic, and aggressive— his job input was enormous. His staff turnover in one year, however, was 100 percent and he sometimes signed contracts which he had no possibility of meeting.
>
> If his business were to fail, the casual observer might well say, "It was not because of Charlie," thus showing the confusion over the important difference between apparent effectiveness and managerial effectiveness.

PERSONAL EFFECTIVENESS

Poorly defined job outputs can also lead to what might be called "personal effectiveness," that is, satisfying personal objectives rather than the objectives of the organization. This is particularly likely to occur with ambitious men in an organization which has only a few clearly defined management-output measures. Meetings with these men are riddled with hidden agendas (27) which operate below the surface and lead to poor decision making.

> In a three-day corporate strategy laboratory conducted for a Toronto consumer-goods firm, one of the four vice-presidents present initiated a series of proposals for reorganization and argued for them with great force. While all had some merit, it became clear as he described them that most would not lead to greatly improved team effectiveness. Other team members saw quickly that all these proposals were aimed, to some extent unconsciously, at improving the vice-president's power and prestige. This issue was confronted for several hours and the team members, many of whom previously had similar intentions to those of the vice-president, finally decided to turn their attention away from improving their personal effectiveness to improving their managerial effectiveness and, therefore, total team effectiveness. The top-management structure was modified but in keeping with market, consumer, competitive, and organizational needs, not personal needs.

LEADER EFFECTIVENESS THEORY

A leader is not really a manager in the formal sense. He is someone seen by others as being primarily responsible for achieving group objectives. His effectiveness is measured by the extent to which he influences his followers to achieve group objectives. It is popular to view leadership effectiveness as something akin to "the degree to which the leader gets his own way." This is not leadership effectiveness but personal effectiveness. As this book is written for managers the term "manager" rather than "leader" is used throughout. Practically all has application to the leader as well as the manager however. When used outside the business situation the theory is referred to as the 3-D Theory of Leadership Effectiveness.

EFFECTIVENESS IS REWARDED

A well-designed organization usually ensures that managerial effectiveness, and only managerial effectiveness, leads to personal rewards. While organizations do vary in the extent, speed, and accuracy of rewards for effectiveness, there can be little doubt that, in the long run, the effective manager is the rewarded one. The rewards are usually concrete in terms of salary, level of position, and advancement rate. Other rewards more important to some are fulfilled ambitions, assured security, self-actualization, personal satisfaction or happiness, or simply survival. This book is designed to show managers how they can be more effective and thus obtain the rewards that being so brings.

The 3-D Concept Dictionary

At the end of each chapter the concepts introduced in it are defined in alphabetical order. In addition, the titles of associated concepts are grouped together. The 3-D Concept Dictionary at the end of the book lists all the concepts alphabetically.

New Concepts Introduced

APPARENT EFFECTIVENESS   LEADER
MANAGERIAL EFFECTIVENESS (E)   LEADER EFFECTIVENESS
PERSONAL EFFECTIVENESS

Apparent Effectiveness The extent to which a manager gives the appearance of being effective.

Leader A person seen by others as being primarily responsible for achieving group objectives.

Leader Effectiveness The extent to which the leader influences his followers to achieve group objectives.

Managerial Effectiveness (E) The extent to which a manager achieves the output requirements of his position. Scaled from 0 to 4.

Personal Effectiveness The extent to which a manager achieves his own private objectives.

Make a model before building.

A. N. WHITEHEAD

To think is to live.

CICERO

Chapter Two

AN OUTLINE OF THE 3-D THEORY

By learning to apply the 3-D Theory, any manager can learn to become more effective. It was designed with that single specific purpose in mind.

At the heart of the 3-D Theory is a very simple idea. It was discovered in a long series of research studies conducted by psychologists in the United States. They discovered that the two main elements in managerial behavior concerned the task to be done and relationships with other people. They also found that managers sometimes emphasized one and sometimes emphasized the other, and that these two elements of behavior could be used in small or large amounts. For instance, a manager could be very much task-oriented or only a small amount. Also, both behaviors could be used together (the 3-D term is integrated style), task could be used alone (dedicated style), relationships could be used alone (related style), or each could be used to only a small degree (separated style). The four basic styles are arranged as shown in Exhibit 2.1. The TO and RO along the sides stand for Task Orientation (TO) and Relationships Orientation (RO) respectively. These four basic styles represent four types of behavior. Not all types of managerial behavior will fit neatly into these four types, but they are very useful as a general framework. A clear set of indicators and characteristics for each type has been developed which enables each style to be fully understood. The separated style is described in Chapter Fifteen.

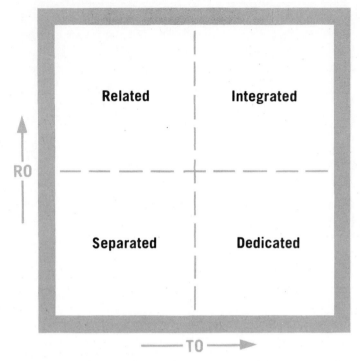

Exhibit 2-1   Four basic styles. There are four basic styles of managerial behavior.

As an example some indicators of the separated style are:

Cautious—careful—conservative—orderly
Prefers paper work—procedures—facts
Looks for established principles
Accurate—precise—correct—perfectionist
Steady—deliberate—patient
Calm—modest—discreet

No One Style Always Effective

Further researches conducted at several universities clearly established that any of these four basic styles of behavior could be effective in certain situations and not effective in others. None are more or less effective in themselves. Their effectiveness depends on the situation in which they are used. This means that each one of the four basic styles has a less effective equivalent and a more effective equivalent, resulting in eight managerial styles:

BASIC STYLE	LESS EFFECTIVE MANAGERIAL STYLE	MORE EFFECTIVE MANAGERIAL STYLE
Integrated	Compromiser	Executive
Dedicated	Autocrat	Benevolent autocrat
Related	Missionary	Developer
Separated	Deserter	Bureaucrat

For instance, when the high Task Orientation of the dedicated basic style is used inappropriately, the popular as well as 3-D name given to it is "autocrat." When used appropriately, the name used instead is "benevolent autocrat."

These eight managerial styles then are not eight additional kinds of behavior. They are simply the names given to the four basic styles when used appropriately or inappropriately. By the use of both the basic and managerial styles, 3-D distinguishes sharply between behavior and the effectiveness of behavior.

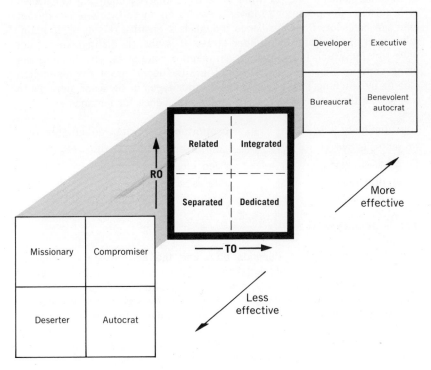

Exhibit 2-2 Adding the third dimension. Any of the four basic styles may be more or less effective.

These eight managerial styles can be arranged around the four basic styles by using a third dimension of effectiveness as shown in Exhibit 2.2. The four basic styles are in the center, the four less effective equivalents at the front, and the four more effective equivalents at the rear. The third dimension is effectiveness. One of the contributions of 3-D is that it gives this term a clear, usable definition. Managerial effectiveness is measured by the extent to which a manager achieves the output requirements of his position. Clearly managers must understand, and then work to achieve, the outputs, not the inputs, of their jobs. The introduction of 3-D training associated with management by objectives ensures that they do. The managers involved play a large part in setting these output requirements.

Style Flex

If any one of four styles may lead to higher outputs, then *style flexibility* is clearly a skill most managers would want to acquire. It is the skill to use a variety of styles to match a variety of situations. Style flexibility needs to be distinguished sharply from *style drift,* that is, changing one's own style to keep the peace or to lower pressure on oneself; this is clearly not effective behavior. *Style resilience* though is a positive quality. It is maintaining an appropriate style under stress; it is sharply distinguished from *style rigidity,* which is maintaining an inappropriate style. The dividing line along some of these is clearly thin. The 3-D Theory makes the distinction clearer by teaching how to recognize all four types of behavior and how to use two of them. Some indicators of style resilience for instance are:

Low ambiguity tolerance	(comfortable in structured situations)
Power sensitive	(control oriented)
Firm belief system	(fixed ideas)
Inner directed	(interested in self)

Three Managerial Skills

Well, if effectiveness depends on using the appropriate behavior to match the situation, what skills besides style flexibility will an effective manager have? He must know how to read a situation (situational sensitivity), and he must have the skill to change the situation if it needs to be changed (situational management skill). An effective manager, then, needs not simply an ability to use a high or low Task or Relationships Orientation, or any particular style but these three: situational sensitivity skill, style flexibility skill, situational management skill. The acquisition of these three skills is usually called experience. Some very young managers have them to a high degree while much older managers have hardly acquired them in even minimal amounts.

The Situation

Clearly the "situation" is very important for a manager to consider. Up to now this term has been used without too much explanation. Just what is it? How can it be broken down into manageable units in order to observe or change it? The 3-D Theory breaks the situation into five elements which contain all aspects of it: organization, technology, superior, coworkers, subordinates.

Organization, short for organization philosophy, is all those influences on behavior that come from outside the manager's work itself and from outside his department or division. Organization philosophy is usually reflected in systems design, in operating procedures, and in who does and does not get promoted. It is an expression of "How we do things around here." A manager in a firm staffed heavily by engineers may have quite different demands on his behavior than one in a firm staffed by accountants. In the same way, the organization philosophy behind a government department is often quite different from the military. These differences are real, and understanding how they operate is important to managerial effectiveness.

The second element, *technology,* is how work can be done. Some technologies need a dedicated style of management, some separated, and so on. For instance, if the work a manager is doing has these elements, he should use the dedicated, highly Task Oriented style:

Subordinates have to put physical effort into their work
The manager knows more about the job than the subordinates
Unscheduled events are likely to occur
Directions must be given
The subordinates' performance is easily measurable

Analysis of work along these lines can help managers to decide which style to use. It is particularly helpful for a manager when he is moving into a new position or when he is redesigning the technology of his department.

One of the helpful analytical tools provided by 3-D is the *flex map.* This map enables managers to get an actual picture of the situation they are in or might soon encounter. From this picture they can more easily decide what action they should take. It is also useful for counseling. The heart of the flex map is the *basic-styles diagram.* On this may be drawn the manager's range of style and one or up to all five of the situational elements.

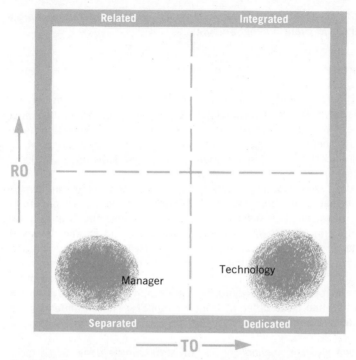

Exhibit 2-3 Something is not right here. The manager who is separated cannot satisfy the dedicated demands of the technology.

To take a simple example. Suppose a particular technology demanded dedicated behavior from the manager, yet the manager could only use the separated style. This situation could be shown as Exhibit 2.3. The shape on the left depicts the range of behavior of the manager. The shape on the right depicts the range of demands of the technology, which is extremely dedicated. Clearly this situation is a poor one. The manager cannot use the style the technology demands. He has two alternatives, increase his flexibility or change the technology. Only if he does one or both of these will the two shapes intersect. The intersection shows the area in which he can operate and in which the style demands of the technology can be satisfied. The 3-D Theory teaches him how to do each and how to decide which to try first. More important, it teaches him to recognize the situation to begin with. Flex maps can help managers really think about what is going on and how they might improve things.

3-D Training

What kind of training must the 3-D Theory lead toward? First the manager must be taught the theory. Then he must be taught to read situations to answer the question, "What does it take to be effective here?" He must be taught to increase his range of style behavior and his skill in changing situations.

In management team training the central question is still, "How can we increase effectiveness?" The team equivalent to managerial style flexibility is *flexible job trading*—rearranging the technology and decision structure of the department to improve effectiveness. This kind of incisive thinking and willingness to take action can be developed among any group of managers. To help create these conditions, such programs start at the top. Example is still the best teacher.

Every man is in certain respects
a. like all other men.
b. like some other man.
c. like no other man.

CLYDE KLUCKHOHN AND HENRY A. MURRAY

The applied psychologist has usually been able to formulate at least rough laws governing the particular behaviors in which he is interested.

KENNETH W. SPENCE

Chapter Three

WHAT IS A BASIC STYLE?

There has been a great deal of research into styles of managers and recently some clear patterns have emerged. It is now reasonable to see managers as being one or another of four basic styles. This chapter will review key research findings which led to their discovery. Every experienced manager will know of other managers who fit each of the four styles. Some managers will recognize themselves.

What Is a Manager?

When looking at leadership research and managerial behavior itself, it is best to agree first on just what a manager is.

A *manager* is a person occupying a position in a formal organization who is responsible for the work of at least one other person and who has formal authority over that person. Persons whose work he is responsible for are his *subordinates*. A person he works with, who is neither his superior, nor a subordinate, is a *coworker*. The person responsible for the manager's work is his *superior*. So the difference between being a manager, subordinate, coworker, and superior is essentially based on where the power lies, or who has the responsibility and authority. Obviously, most of us in our work life are all four of these at one time.

THE TRAIT APPROACH   For centuries effective managers have been described and sometimes measured in terms of a list of personal qualities or traits that all effective managers were thought to possess. Traits such as judgment, integrity, and energy appeared often on such lists. The appeal of this approach is that it is easy to understand, appears sensible, and is widely used. It has also been found useful in describing the qualities required for particular jobs.

The weaknesses of the trait approach are that there is no agreement on the best traits that fit all situations, that there is no evidence that one group of traits predict effectiveness generally, and that there are now well over a thousand different traits to deal with (22).

For these reasons, the trait approach is now becoming less popular with social scientists. It seems likely, however, that as a single sound theory becomes established, sets of traits will become useful but with an important difference. The traits will not be drawn at will from a list of qualities but will be a set of interrelated ideas associated with a comprehensive theory. It is not the idea of traits that is wrong but rather the absence of a theory to show which traits are important for particular managerial situations.

Leadership Research

This book, and this chapter in particular, builds on the work of many others. Some of the many well-known social scientists identified with formal leadership research include Barnard, Davis, Simon, Fiedler, Mayo, Roethlisberger, Likert, Dickson, Blake, Gardner, and the staff of The Tavistock Institute of London. All these people have focused on leadership and human relations in business and industry. Others, like Hemphill, Thelen, Rogers, and Cantor, have been especially concerned with leadership in the classroom. Social change and leadership in the community have been the main concern of such scientists as Lewin, Merton, Deutsch, Chein, Festinger, Lippitt, and French.

Key Leadership-research studies, of direct concern to us here, have been conducted at Ohio State University, University of Michigan, and Harvard University.

OHIO STATE: LEADERSHIP FACTORS

The most extensive and rigorous leadership studies in the world were done under Carroll Shartle's direction at Ohio State in the late 1940s and early 1950s (170). The work has culminated in a series of monographs published by the Bureau of Business Research at Ohio State. The central finding of these studies was that leadership behavior could be usefully classified into two independent factors called *initiating structure* and

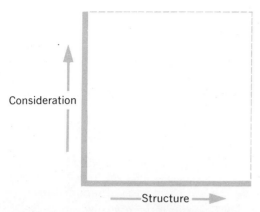

Consideration

——Structure ——▶

Exhibit 3-1 Ohio State leadership factors. This was an important finding resulting from more than $500,000 worth of research.

consideration (174). Initiating structure concerns planning as well as organizing work and tasks. Consideration has to do with maintaining relationships. These two types of behavior are useful to understand, as they help to explain much managerial behavior. In a study of aircrew commanders, for instance, Halpin and Winer (82) found that the structure and consideration behavior variables could account for 83 percent of the differences observed in leader behavior.

These two factors are described as independent because the extent to which a manager uses one of them does not help to predict the amount of the other he is using. This is a vital point for it means that a manager may be using much of both, little of both, much of one and little of the other, or any combination in varying degrees of these two factors.

Because of their independence, the factors may be drawn at right angles, as shown in Exhibit 3.1. A manager's behavior can be represented by any point in the enclosed area. Variations on this basic idea developed by Ohio State are used by many social scientists who are involved in studying leader behavior.

UNIVERSITY OF MICHIGAN: STYLE CONTINUUM

Starting in 1947, the University of Michigan's Survey Research Center conducted extensive leadership studies. A great variety of organizations were studied, including the head office of an insurance company, maintenance-of-way sections on a railroad, an electricity company, an automobile manufacturer, a tractor company, an electrical appliance manufacturer, and two agencies of the federal government (78, 108). A central idea that developed from the Michigan studies was the *Michigan style continuum.*

Employee-   Production-
centered   centered

Exhibit 3-2   Michigan style continuum. Some managers see this as a tightrope and think the midpoint
is a compromise.

Exhibit 3.2 suggests that leader behavior can usefully be viewed as
moving from an employee-centered extreme to a production-centered
extreme. Notice that this approach is radically different from that of Ohio
State. As with the Ohio studies, the two basic ideas of task and relationships are indeed present but the relationship between them is different.
The Michigan continuum suggests that the more employee-centered a manager behaves, the less production-centered he behaves. Ohio State does
not hold this view as it suggests that a manager may be high or low on
both at the same time. The reader might pause and consider which of
these two approaches he thinks fits his own view of managerial behavior.
It is quite impossible to hold them both simultaneously.

In recent years Michigan has modified its view and now sees production-centered and employee-centered more as independent variables rather
than as on a continuum (107). Thus the Michigan position now approaches
that of Ohio State.

HARVARD: GROUP-LEADER TYPES

Bales, of Harvard University, has done much work in the study of small-
group behavior. Most groups studied were experimental groups of college
students, and no manager, as defined, was included in the experiment. In
spite of limitations on the applicability of his findings, his work produced
some results remarkably similar to those of Ohio and Michigan.

He and others found that in small groups two quite different kinds of
leaders would emerge. One kind they called the *task leader,* characterized
by those who talk more and who offer suggestions; and the other kind they
called the *socioemotional leader,* represented by those who make it easier
for others to talk and who offer psychological support. A group member
must be either one or the other; never both. The task leader and the socioemotional leader are two different species, who may therefore be represented as shown in Exhibit 3.3.

THEY POINT TO THE SAME THING   To date, most leadership research has been based on one or the other of these three studies. They
represent the core of current thinking. While they differ on many points,

Exhibit 3-3 Harvard: group-leader types. There are always the two of them in a group.

the essential similarity in all of them is the identification and emphasis on what might be called the task and relationships variables. They are generally talking about the same kind of behavior, as demonstrated in Exhibit 3.4.

That task and relationships capture fundamental measures of managerial behavior is fairly obvious. The two distinct elements of any manager's job are the task to be done and the human relationships skills he needs to see that the task is accomplished. In some jobs, of course, there is no task in the usual sense; the manager's job is primarily to maintain good relationships. This job would be described as having a high relationships component and a low task component.

It follows that a really useful managerial-style model should or even must be built on these two central ideas. Several models, in fact, started this way, and so will the 3-D Theory.

THE DIFFERENCES RESOLVED

These three sets of findings suggest three different kinds of relationships between task and relationships. Are they independent of each other or are they continuous or are they separate? While the consensus is clearly moving toward that of Ohio State, the three views expressed in Exhibits 3.1 to 3.3 can be conveniently represented together to show their essential similarities, (143) (Exhibit 3.5). Within broad limits they seem to point to the same thing.

The two terms which best capture this clear common thread of research are:

	Task	Relationships
Ohio State	Structure	Consideration
Michigan	Production-centered	Employee-centered
Harvard	Task leader	Socio-emotional leader

Exhibit 3-4 Two common ideas. Research results that look different have common threads.

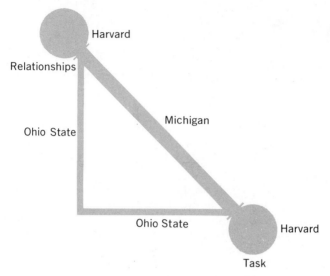

Exhibit 3-5   An integration of Ohio-Michigan-Harvard. It all depends on the way you look at it.

Task Orientation (TO)   The extent to which a manager directs his own and his subordinates' efforts; characterized by initiating, organizing, and directing.

Relationships Orientation (RO)   The extent to which a manager has personal job relationships; characterized by listening, trusting, and encouraging.

These definitions are close to those for initiating structure and consideration of Fleishman (58). Notice that they represent two completely different kinds of behavior. A manager who is using one kind of behavior may or may not be using the other. At any one time, a manager's behavior may consist of any combination or degree of these two. Taken together they comprise his basic-style behavior. The importance of job knowledge and technical skill has not been missed. Implicit in Task Orientation is job knowledge or technical skill. It is difficult to imagine a manager lacking such skill and being able to make any kind of attempt at initiating, organizing, and directing his own work, let alone that of others.

PUTTING TO AND RO TOGETHER

Because of the independence of TO and RO, scales representing these qualities are drawn at right angles to each other, as shown in Exhibit 3.6. In this diagram, TO is represented on the horizontal axis on a scale of

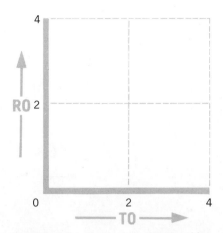

Exhibit 3-6   Task and Relationships together. These two scales can make measurement easier.

0 to 4, and RO is represented on the vertical axis on a scale of 0 to 4. A scale score of 0 would indicate an absence of the orientation; a scale score of 4 would indicate a maximum amount. Thus, scores below two are below average for the managerial population as a whole and scores above two are above average. The scale of 0 to 4 has no magic in it; it was chosen for convenience. The range is meant to cover the range of behavior that is characteristic of modern managers. An RO of zero, then, does not mean no RO at all—that would be hard to imagine. It simply means so little as to be in the lowest few percent of managers.

BASIC-STYLE POINT   The amount of TO and RO a manager is using at a particular time can be represented by two numbers, each between 0 and 4. The first represents the amount of TO he is using, and the second, the amount of RO he is using. Thus 3.0, 3.0 would indicate a fairly high degree of both TO and RO while 0.5, 0.5 would indicate a low degree of TO and RO.

FOUR COMBINATIONS   If the TO and RO scales are each cut into two equal parts, four basic styles can be represented (Exhibit 3.7). These could be labeled according to the diagram: "high TO and high RO," "High TO only," "High RO only," "Low TO and low RO." These labels are unwieldy and for convenient usage must be shortened. This problem brings us to the question of style terminology.

STYLE TERMINOLOGY

The majority of managerial-style models use some kind of labels to make clear the kind of behavior being described. (The "autocrat" and "demo-

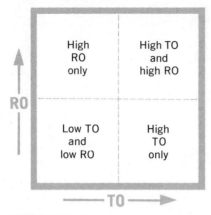

Exhibit 3-7 Four types of behavior. Cutting the two scales into two produces four types.

crat" labels are examples of widely used labels.) There is a variety of terminology available such as style letters, style numbers, and style names.

The *style-letters* terminology has been used by McGregor (140) in labeling the two types of his X and Y Theory. The labels themselves are neutral but may be chosen, as is the X-Y terminology, to convey some form of conflict or opposition. In the Western world, partly because of our use of plane geometry, X-Y conveys something slightly different from A-B or P-Q.

Style numbers have been used by Blake and Mouton (23) in their five-type *managerial-grid theory*. The numbers they use are not intended to be neutral, and 1,1 is generally considered to be not as good as 5,5, and 5,5 not as good as 9,9. Style names are used by virtually everyone else.

Style naming was used for the basic terminology of 3-D because names relate 3-D directly to other theories using names and because names like "deserter," "developer," and others can convey style qualities.

All the labels, once understood, can limit distortion of what is being conveyed by the style name and can have a highly personal emphasis and impact. This is particularly useful in management development programs. Names, in addition, can avoid the black and white extremes of numbers or letters. The important point is, however, that whether names, numbers, or letters are used, most management theorists are talking about the same kind of thing. Managers need not be confused by labels.

3-D Basic Styles

The style labels used in 3-D are shown in Exhibit 3.8. The labels "integrated," "dedicated," "related," and "separated" (25) form the 3-D basic styles, and were chosen to avoid the suggestion that some styles are much

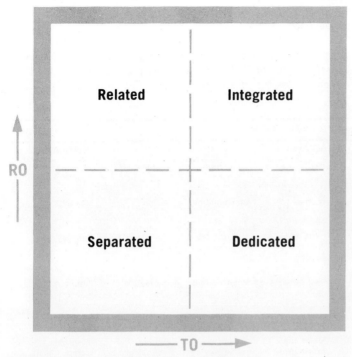

Exhibit 3-8 The 3-D basic styles. The heart of 3-D.

better than others. The *integrated* style, with high Task Orientation and high Relationships Orientation, is so named as it describes managerial behavior which combines TO and RO. The *dedicated* style describes managerial behavior with high Task Orientation but low Relationships Orientation—that is, behavior which is dedicated to the job. The *related* style having high RO alone is related to subordinates. The *separated* style is a basic style with both low Task Orientation and low Relationships Orientation. This style, then, is separated from both TO and RO.

It is important to remember that the four basic styles are a convenience and not a fact. The lines separating the four styles do not really exist; they were drawn to make it easier to talk about behavior. No one, therefore, is pigeonholed when called "related" or something else. The term, as with any style label, means more like that style than like any other style—only that.

How to Appraise Basic Style

Here, in summary form are the indicators of the four basic styles. Studying the first twenty-three sets will result in a very clear idea of what each basic style is and how it differs from the other three basic styles. These indicators may be used as a convenient reference to facilitate style appraisal. All of them must be considered as general at best. They will not all apply in every or even any case and some overlap. They help to convey the idea of each style; they do not define it. They prepare the way for the next chapter which relates the idea of basic styles to that of effectiveness.

Basic-style indicators

	SEPARATED	RELATED	DEDICATED	INTEGRATED
(1) Interactional mode	Correcting	Accepting	Dominating	Joining
(2) Mode of communication	Written	Conversations	Verbal directions	Meetings
(3) Direction of communication	Little in any direction	Upward from subordinates	Downward to subordinates	Two-way
(4) Time perspective	Past	Unconcerned	Immediate	Future
(5) Identifies with	Organization	Subordinates	Superior and technology	Coworkers
(6) System emphasis	Maintains procedural system	Supports social system	Follows technological system	Integrates sociotechnical system
(7) Judges subordinates on	Who follows the rules?	Who understands people?	Who produces?	Who wants to join the team?
(8) Judges superior on	Brains	Warmth	Power	Teamwork
(9) Committee activity	Clarifying, guiding, and channeling	Supporting, harmonizing, and coaching	Initiating, evaluating, and directing	Setting standards, testing, and motivating
(10) Work suited for	Administration, accounting, statistics, and design	Managing professionals, training, and coordination	Production and sales management	Supervising interacting managers
(11) Work not suited for	Nonroutine	Low personal contact	Low-power	High-routine
(12) Employee orientation	Security	Cooperation	Performance	Commitment
(13) Reaction to error	More controls	Pass over	Punish	Learn from
(14) Reaction to conflict	Avoids	Smothers	Suppresses	Utilizes
(15) Reaction to stress	Withdraws and quotes rules	Becomes dependent and depressed	Dominates and exploits	Avoids making decisions

	SEPARATED	RELATED	DEDICATED	INTEGRATED
(16) Positive source of control	Logic	Praise	Rewards	Ideals
(17) Negative source of control	Argument	Rejection	Punishments	Compromise
(18) Characteristic problem of subordinates	Lack of recognition	Lack of direction	Lack of information	Lack of independence
(19) Punishments used	Loss of authority	Loss of interest by manager	Loss of position	Loss of self-respect by subordinate
(20) Undervalues	Need for innovation	Needs of organization and of technology	Subordinates' expectations	Need for independent action
(21) Main weakness	Slave to the rules	Sentimentality	Fights unnecessarily	Uses participation inappropriately
(22) Fears about himself	Emotionality, softness, and dependence	Rejection by others	Loss of power	Uninvolvement
(23) Fears about others	System deviation, irrationality	Conflict	Low production	Dissatisfaction
(24) Reddin more effective style equivalent	Bureaucrat	Developer	Benevolent autocrat	Executive
(25) Reddin less effective style equivalent	Deserter	Missionary	Autocrat	Compromiser
(26) McGregor (140) equivalent	—	—	Theory X	Theory Y
(27) Zaleznik and moment (194) equivalent	Rational—procedural	Maternal—expressive	Paternal—assertive	Fraternal—permissive
(28) Blake (23) equivalent	3.3	3.7	7.3	7.7
(29) Brown (32) equivalent	Laissez faire plus strict autocrat	Incompetent democrat plus genuine democrat	Incompetent autocrat	Benevolent autocrat

	SEPARATED	RELATED	DEDICATED	INTEGRATED
(30) Jennings (103) equiva- lent	Abdicrat plus bureaucrat	Democrat	Autocrat	Executive plus neurocrat
(31) Walling equiva- lent	Objective thinker	Friendly helper	Tough battler	—
(32) Davis (42)	Custodial	Supportive	Autocratic	Collegial
(33) Horney (91)	Moving away (detached)	Moving toward (compliant)	Moving against (aggressive)	—

Capsule Basic Styles

The first twenty-three indicators lead directly to these capsule descriptions of each of the basic styles.

THE SEPARATED MANAGER

The separated manager is one who is very concerned about correcting deviations. He tends to write more than talk and partly because of this has relatively little personal communication in any direction. His time perspective tends to be with the past and "how we did it last time." Thus he identifies with the organization as a whole rather than with individual members of it. Because of his desire to keep things on an even keel he takes great interest in the rules and procedures and naturally judges others on how well they adhere to them. He values intellect in his superior but not necessarily in others. In committees he tends to use a subdued parliamentary style and attempts to clarify positions, guide others to work through the agenda, and channel all communications through the chair. He is obviously well suited to work in administration, accounting, statistics, or engineering design. He avoids nonroutine work because he does not enjoy it. His employees value security. When things go wrong his usual reaction is to propose more controls. This also helps to depersonalize future conflict which he avoids if he can. When faced with conflict or other kinds of stress situations he tends to withdraw and quote rules and procedures. He values logic and rationality and is amenable to being influenced by it. The emphasis on logic can sometimes give way to argument, particularly if the problem could have been solved by relationships skills which he does not see as relevant. His subordinates often believe that he does not recognize them or their accomplishments enough. He sees them less as people and more as parts of his work system. Because of this he tends to punish by removing some of the authority previously given. He undervalues the need for innovation and is generally seen as a slave to the rules. The greatest fear he has about himself is that he might let emotion, softness, or dependence on others influence his judgment. His greatest fear of others is that they might act irrationally and in some way violate the established system.

THE RELATED MANAGER

The related manager is one who accepts others as he finds them. He enjoys long conversations as a way of getting to know others better. Because of this he tends to obtain a lot of useful information from his subordinates. He is not too concerned with time and this in part allows him to get to know others better, particularly subordinates with whom he identifies. He sees organizations primarily as social systems and judges his subordinates on how well they understand others. He judges superiors on the warmth they show to subordinates. In committees he supports others, harmonizes differences, and coaches others to give their best. He is particularly suited for managing professional workers, for some kinds of training and development work, and for coordination positions where the low power of the position tends to demand a related style if effectiveness is to be achieved. He finds it very unpleasant to work with little contact with others. If he finds himself in such a job, he may redesign it so that he can have high contact even though this could lead to decreased overall effectiveness. His subordinates cooperate well with each other partly because of his example and partly because he tends to pass over errors and smother conflict with pleasantness. When facing stress he tends to become dependent on others and depressed. His positive source of influence is likely to be praise while his negative source of influence tends to be the rejection of the individual as a worthy person. While his subordinates like working for him their characteristic problem is lack of direction from him. The punishment he most often uses is loss of interest by him. While he values people highly he tends to undervalue the importance of the organization and its technology. One of his weaknesses is sentimentality and a personal fear is of being rejected by others. The thing he most fears in others is conflict.

THE DEDICATED MANAGER

The dedicated manager tends to dominate others. He gives many verbal directions to subordinates. His time perspective is immediate and when he has the choice he prefers to "do it now." He identifies with superiors and with the technical system of the firm. When possible he emphasizes the demands of the technological rather than the human system. He judges subordinates on the degree to which they produce and superiors on their skill in using power. He plays a very active part in committees and initiates, evaluates, and directs a great deal. He is well suited for some kinds of production management where directions are needed, and also for sales management. He does not work too well in situations where he has only a little power because he then cannot simply tell people what to do. His subordinates soon learn that performance is the thing that counts and punishment can be expected if they are in error. He deals with conflict by suppressing it and deals with other stressful situations by domination. He believes that rewards are a good way to influence others or to be influenced himself. And he also believes that punishments are the best way to stop people from doing things they should not, and the most severe punishment is loss of position. His subordinates often complain about lack of information. He tends to forget they exist as independent entities and does not give enough value to their individual expectations. His main weakness is that he argues with others when matters could be solved another way. He emphasizes the sound use of power so much that the loss of it is what he fears most. His biggest fears about others is that they will not produce.

THE INTEGRATED MANAGER

The integrated manager likes to become a part of things. He is essentially a joiner and he takes great pains in getting appropriately involved with individuals or groups over work. He likes to communicate with others in group settings and uses meetings frequently. Through them he can obtain the two-way communication he prefers. His orientation is always to the future. Because he has no real concern for power differentials he identifies strongly with coworkers and emphasizes teamwork. He uses teamwork and other methods to integrate individual needs with technological needs. He naturally judges subordinates on their willingness to join the team. He judges his superior on his skill in teamwork. In committee activity he tends to be active in setting team performance standards, testing the team members for their commitment and purpose, and motivating them. The work he is most suited for is the management of interacting managers. The work he is least suited for is that with a high component of routine. His employees are usually fully committed and involved, and this is facilitated in part by his intention of learning from errors rather than punishing them. He is interested in investigating the cause of conflict rather than avoiding, smothering, or suppressing it. In highly stressful situations he tends to postpone making decisions. He tends to control others by proposing common ideals or settling for a compromise. Because of his integrated style and emphasis on the group, his subordinates often feel a lack of independence. Because of his use of ideals to motivate, the punishment he can best use involves loss of self-respect in the person punished. He sometimes undervalues the need for independent action and sometimes uses participation inappropriately. His grestest fear about himself is that he might become uninvolved. His greatest fear about others is that they might become dissatisfied.

New Concepts Introduced

MANAGER	INTEGRATED STYLE
TASK ORIENTATION (TO)	DEDICATED STYLE
RELATIONSHIPS ORIENTATION (RO)	RELATED STYLE
BASIC STYLE	SEPARATED STYLE
BASIC-STYLE POINT (BSP)	

Basic Style   The way in which a manager behaves as measured by the amount of Task Orientation and Relationships Orientation he uses. The four basic styles are integrated, dedicated, related, and separated.

Basic-style Point (BSP)   A point score for both Task Orientation and Relationships Orientation each scaled from 0 to 4.

Dedicated Style   A basic style with more than average Task Orientation and less than average Relationships Orientation.

Integrated Style   A basic style with more than average Task Orientation and more than average Relationships Orientation.

Manager   A person, occupying a position in a formal organization, who is responsible for the work of at least one other person and who has formal authority over that person.

Related Style   A basic style with less than average Task Orientation and more than average Relationships Orientation.

Relationships Orientation (RO)   The extent to which a manager has personal job relationships; characterized by listening, trusting, and encouraging. Scaled from 0 to 4.

Separated Style   A basic style with less than average Task Orientation and less than average Relationships Orientation.

Task Orientation (TO)   The extent to which a manager directs his own and his subordinates' efforts; characterized by initiating, organizing, and directing. Scaled from 0 to 4.

*There is a definite style to the high quality of accomplish-
ment that marks the exceptional manager.*

ERWIN SCHELL

*The beginning of administrative wisdom is the awareness
that there is no one optimum type of management system.*

TOM BURNS

All truths begin as blasphemies.

G. B. SHAW

The truth is always strange—stranger than fiction.

BYRON

Chapter Four

IS THERE AN IDEAL STYLE?

Managers who want to become more effective will be concerned with the answers to the following questions. Is one style more effective than others? Can any style be effective in certain situations? Is there one perfect style, or is style flexibility the key?

A great deal of effectiveness research has been conducted by these and other psychologists: L. Coch and J. R. P. French, Jr.; J. R. P. French, Jr., et al.; R. C. Anderson; S. S. Sales; E. A. Fleishman and D. R. Peters; and A. K. Korman. The conclusion that emerges strongly from their research is that no single style is naturally more effective than others. Effectiveness depends on a style's appropriateness to the situation in which it is used.

L. COCH AND J. R. P. FRENCH, JR.

In 1948, L. Coch and J. R. P. French, Jr. (40), published a well-designed and well-executed experiment in the use of the participatory management style. The experiment was conducted in a southern United States pajama factory and involved women on four production lines, whose output was measured before and after a change had been introduced. One of the production lines was allowed to participate fully in matters relating to the proposed change, two other lines participated through a representative group of workers, and one line had no particular involvement or participation in the change at all.

The results were dramatic. On the three lines which participated, output climbed rapidly and became stabilized at around 70 units per hour. On the one line which was not consulted at all, output fell rapidly and became stabilized at around 50 units per hour. In this experiment, up to 40 percent higher production was recorded and was apparently due to the use of a high degree of participation.

As this particular study shows, genuine participation can work. Other studies show that participation has increased production (116), decreased absences (128), led to increased concern with costs (129), decreased turnover (192), produced more inventive solutions in problem-solving situations (125), and increased the accuracy of performance ratings (117). All this is clearly, one might think, an argument for the use of the participative style in industry. There is a sequel to the Coch and French study, however.

J. R. P. FRENCH, JR., ET AL.

In 1960, French and two associates (68) published an experiment designed to "repeat the Coch and French experiment published in 1948 and to . . . discover whether the general results . . . conducted in the United States, will hold in a different culture [Norway]." A key finding determined that, "There was no difference between the [Norwegian] groups in the level of production." So, while in the first experiment the participatory style led to higher productivity, it had no effect in another experiment. These results could be explained, in large part, by the extent to which Norwegian workers accept participation. The effects of participation or of any other style probably depends, to a large degree, on the workers' expectations about how they should be treated and what change in behavior or production they will willingly make for being treated differently. Some would welcome participation but others would not. Such differences can be found to exist in two adjacent factories, two departments in the same firm, or even two immediate subordinates.

Vroom (184) found that those individuals with a high need for independence were more motivated and better satisfied under participative supervision than those individuals rated low in independence needs. He also found that individuals with a high score on "authoritarianism" tended to be less satisfied and less motivated under participation. A similar finding was reported by Tannenbaum (178). He found that dependent subordinates reacted negatively to an increase in participation. It would appear that managers who truly value the individual will recognize individual differences and thus not use a participatory approach on those who do not want it.

R. C. ANDERSON

An important review by R. C. Anderson (4), has thrown light on a central stumbling block in leadership studies. He reviewed forty-nine studies in which authoritarian and democratic leadership have been experimentally compared. As his purpose, he writes, "Experimental studies in which authoritarian leadership has been compared with democratic leadership will be reviewed . . . questions will be asked of this research. . . . Is there sufficient evidence that one of these two styles of leadership is more effective?" As his conclusion, he writes, "The evidence available fails to demonstrate that either authoritarian or democratic leadership is consistently associated with higher productivity." He demonstrates that the old "either-or" leadership approaches suggested by such terms as:

Autocrat versus Democrat
Directive versus Nondirective
Supervisory versus Participatory
Boss-centered versus Employee-centered

are not useful ways of describing leadership behavior and that, in any case, one type of behavior is not generally more effective than the other.

S. S. SALES AND OTHERS

In 1966, S. S. Sales (168) published his independent review of the major investigations in the autocratic-democratic literature. He concluded that: "the hypothesis that democratic supervision will evoke greater effort from employees than will autocratic supervision cannot truly be either supported or rejected."

The fact that high relationships is not always the key is further supported by Dunteman and Bass (51) who found that what they called task-oriented supervisors are rated as more effective supervisors than those who are *interaction-oriented*, which is similar to RO. Patchen (159) reported that close supervision and pressure for efficiency tend to increase group performance when the supervisor has power, as evidenced by being the source of rewards and by "going to bat for them." Patchen believes that close supervision may be seen by subordinates as proof of an interest in their welfare.

However, many formal studies show that Task Orientation almost always seems to need a little leavening with some Relationships Orientation. If not, the high TO manager is seen as being little more than a hard-driving taskmaster. Studies are almost consistent in showing that the threatening-punishing superior will produce either lower productivity and satisfaction or both (146, 9, and 44).

E. A. FLEISHMAN AND D. R. PETERS

E. A. Fleishman and D. R. Peters (58) studied thirty-nine managers between line foreman and plant manager in the continuous-production operation of a soap and detergent process. The managers' effectiveness rating was based on an evaluation by their own superiors. Their management style was measured by a sophisticated test. The major conclusions of the study were that "there is an absence of relationship between leadership attitudes and rated effectiveness. . . . No particular combination of structure and consideration attitudes was predictive of effectiveness ratings."

A. K. KORMAN

The leading study for our purposes is that of A. K. Korman (115). In 1966, he published the most comprehensive review made so far of twenty-five key leadership studies conducted by trained psychologists. He did not go about it casually: "All those journals which would be expected to carry research of this nature were examined . . . and private correspondence was engaged in with those psychologists who are prominently associated with research . . . in order to uncover unpublished studies. . . ."

He looked for those studies which investigated the relationship between a manager's use of initiating structure and consideration and his effectiveness. (Initiating structure and consideration are similar to TO and RO.) The many psychologists involved in the chosen studies used a variety of effectiveness yardsticks such as productivity, salary, and performance under stress.

He concluded that "At the current time we cannot even say whether they [Structure and Consideration] have any predictive significance at all. . . . There is as yet almost no evidence on the predictive efficiency [bearing on effectiveness] . . . of 'Consideration' and 'Initiating Structure.'" This means, simply, that Korman was unable to find any evidence that suggested one style was generally better than another. Naturally enough some individual studies did show relationships, but when all were taken together, as much evidence was found on one side as on the other. It appears, then, that since situations vary, so must management style. Numerous findings and common sense support this position.

There Is No Ideal Style

All this research suggests strongly that the notion of a single ideal style is not sound and, therefore, not useful. There is no consistent evidence that one style is generally more effective than the other. To suggest that there is, is to make what the social scientists call the *normative error,* that is, to suggest that one thing is better than another based only on what one prefers to believe rather than on what the evidence suggests.

Managers must say farewell to the manager who picks up a single behavioral theory at a seminar and spends the next few years chanting, "Let us all become like I became," and who changes no one in the process. The theorist on whose theory the seminar design was based certainly hoped he would not become that rigid. Management is too complex to be encapsulated by a single belief. Over the centuries, a rigid ideology has always been attractive and exciting in the short run, but in the long run, it causes wars. We need fewer of the "true believers" that Eric Hoffer (90) described so well. We need rationality and objectivity instead.

Managerial training must aim at style flexibility rather than at style rigidity—not even at a rigid ideal style. It is true, of course, that ideal styles do have some kind of magic to them, and they provide a convenient flag to rally the faithful around. This, though, appears to be shaky ground on which to base programs of organizational change and of managerial effectiveness.

Some managers have learned that to be effective they must sometimes create an atmosphere which will induce self-motivation among their subordinates and sometimes act in ways that appear either hard or soft. At other times, they must quietly efface themselves for a while and appear to do nothing. It would seem more accurate to say, then, that any basic style may be used more or less effectively, depending on the situation.

Styles are best seen in relation to specific situations. Any style has a situation appropriate to it, and many situations inappropriate to it. The fact that styles are best seen as being embedded in situations can be represented in a way shown in Exhibit 4.1. The added third dimension could be labeled "appropriateness of style to situation." As this appropriateness results in effectiveness, "E" for short, this term is used instead. Thus, the more appropriate style and the more effective style mean the same thing.

Eight Managerial Styles

Any basic style then may be more effective or less effective depending on the particular situation in which it is used. Each basic style has its more effective and less effective counterpart, as demonstrated in Exhibit 4.2. The front of the diagram is the plane of less effectiveness, the middle is the basic-style plane, and the back is the plane of more effectiveness. The eight styles which reflect the effectiveness level are called *managerial styles* to distinguish them from the four basic styles. The two basic dimensions are still TO and RO. The third dimension is managerial effectiveness (E), or the extent to which a manager achieves the output requirements of his position.

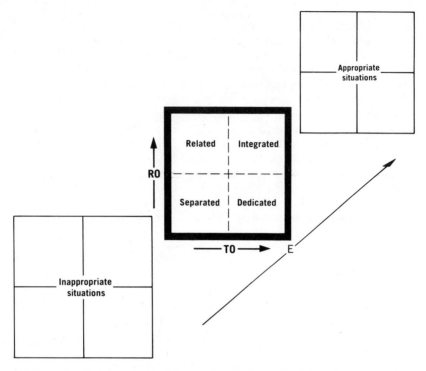

Exhibit 4-1   Styles are embedded in situations. Basic styles are used in situations which are inappropriate or appropriate to them.

The vital distinction between the more effective and less effective styles does not lie in managerial behavior expressed in terms of TO and RO. Any amounts of either or both do not guarantee effectiveness. Effectiveness results from a style's appropriateness to the situation in which it is used. Thus the dedicated basic style, when inappropriately used, is perceived as and called "autocrat," and when appropriately used, it is perceived as and called "benevolent autocrat."

The less effective and more effective versions of the basic styles are shown in the following table:

WHEN USED INAPPROPRIATELY AND THEREFORE LESS EFFECTIVELY	BASIC STYLE	WHEN USED APPROPRIATELY AND THEREFORE MORE EFFECTIVELY
Compromiser ⟵	INTEGRATED ⟶	Executive
Deserter ⟵	SEPARATED ⟶	Bureaucrat
Autocrat ⟵	DEDICATED ⟶	Benevolent autocrat
Missionary ⟵	RELATED ⟶	Developer

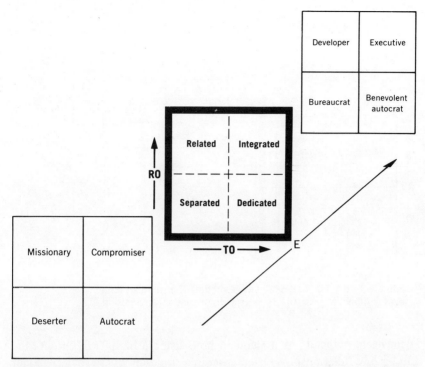

Exhibit 4-2   The 3-D style model. The complete 3-D style model consists of four basic styles, four more effective managerial styles, and four less effective managerial styles.

The eight managerial styles may be represented alone on a 3-D model (Exhibit 4.3). And they are defined in this way:

Executive   A manager who is using a high Task Orientation and a high Relationships Orientation in a situation where such behavior is appropriate and who is, therefore, more effective; perceived as a good motivating force who sets high standards, treats everyone somewhat differently, and prefers team management.

Compromiser   A manager who is using a high Task Orientation and a high Relationships Orientation in a situation that requires a high orientation to only one or neither and who is, therefore, less effective; perceived as being a poor decision maker, as one who allows various pressures in the situation to influence him too much, and as avoiding or minimizing immediate pressures and problems rather than maximizing long-term production.

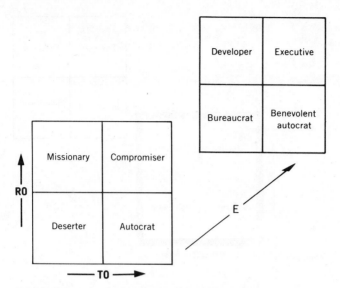

Exhibit 4-3 The 3-D managerial-style model. The middle plane may be omitted once the basic style concept is understood.

Benevolent Autocrat   A manager who is using a high Task Orientation and a low Relationships Orientation in a situation where such behavior is appropriate and who is, therefore, more effective; perceived as knowing what he wants and how to get it without creating resentment.

Autocrat   A manager who is using a high Task Orientation and a low Relationships Orientation in a situation where such behavior is inappropriate and who is, therefore, less effective; perceived as having no confidence in others, as unpleasant, and as interested only in the immediate task.

Developer   A manager who is using a high Relationships Orientation and a low Task Orientation in a situation where such behavior is appropriate and who is, therefore, more effective; perceived as having implicit trust in people and as being primarily concerned with developing them as individuals.

Missionary   A manager who is using a high Relationships Orientation and a low Task Orientation in a situation where such behavior is inappropriate and who is, therefore, less effective; perceived as being primarily interested in harmony.

Bureaucrat   A manager who is using a low Task Orientation and a low Relationships Orientation in a situation where such behavior is appropriate and who is, therefore, more effective; perceived as being primarily interested in rules and procedures for their own sake, as wanting to control the situation by their use, and as conscientious.

Deserter   A manager who is using a low Task Orientation and a low Relationships Orientation in a situation where such behavior is inappropriate and who is, therefore, less effective; perceived as uninvolved and passive or negative.

WHAT'S IN A NAME?   The eight managerial-style labels were deliberately chosen as strong stuff, and each suggests that the style is good or poor. This greatly facilitates the model's use in training. For university teaching, research, and other settings, style valences are used instead. Developer becomes related (+), missionary becomes related (−), autocrat becomes dedicated (−), and so on.

Certain of the eight style labels such as deserter and autocrat will jar some readers. They were selected to do this because their main use is on training courses.

As far as 3-D is concerned these three are equivalent:

Separated (−)
Using the separated style inappropriately
Deserter

For scientific work "separated (−)" tends to be used; in conversation "using the separated style inappropriately" is often used instead; while in training courses "deserter" is the most common. For training purposes the strong labels make the point clearly. Autocrat is the best example. One or two such as Missionary admittedly are open to a variety of interpretations, but not if the concept is fully understood and the definition of it is available. If any reader finds that he has trouble with a style label he is welcome to change it for his purposes. It is the idea not the name that is important.

MANAGERIAL STYLES ARE THREE DIMENSIONAL   Styles themselves represent fairly wide ranges of behavior. Any of the eight managerial styles may represent more or less TO, RO, or E. Exhibit 4.4 shows the compromiser style as it really is: not a point but rather a range of behavior.

How the Third Dimension Works

A manager may move along the third dimension of effectiveness by matching his basic style to the needs of the situation. It is quite possible and reasonable for behavior labeled "deserter" in one situation to be labeled

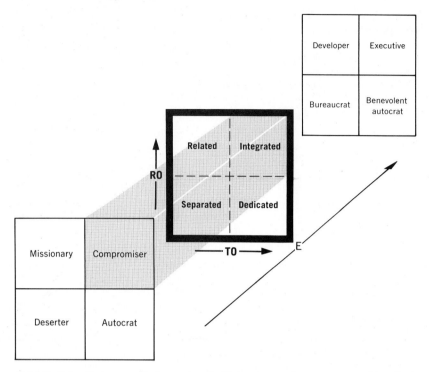

Exhibit 4-4   Styles are 3-dimensional. Styles are not narrow concepts. Each managerial style, such as the compromiser shaded here, includes a wide variety of behavior and range of effectiveness.

"bureaucrat" in another. Managerial style, with its connotations of effectiveness, simply cannot be defined solely with reference to behavior. It always must be defined with reference to the demands of the situation. When an assessment is made of managerial style, two things must be considered. One is the behavior actually being used, expressed in TO and RO, and the other is the demands of the situation in which it is used. If the particular behavior does not meet the demands of the situation, then one of the less effective style labels should be used to describe the situation. If the behavior is appropriate to the situation, one of the more effective style labels is used instead. Managerial-style assessment thus includes what is a frequently unconscious assessment of the needs of the situation as well as the conscious assessment of behavior.

This twofold assessment is captured beautifully by such expressions as "I am firm; you are obstinate; he is pigheaded." The "antics with semantics" quips of Sydney J. Harris which appear in many North American daily newspapers get to the heart of the matter. He continually demonstrates that we judge not behavior alone but its impact on us and our personal feelings about it. For instance: I am "pragmatic"; you are "opportunistic"; he is "Machiavellian." Or, I express "ancient truths"; you express "received wisdom"; he expresses "stable platitudes." Or, I am "impartial"; you are a "fence-sitter"; he is a "straddler."

What some see as resilient, others see as rigid. They all may observe identical behavior yet evaluate it quite differently. The best explanations of these differences is in terms of the perceptions about what the situation demands. If we think that that particular behavior is appropriate to the situation, then we will give it a positive, more effective label, and vice versa.

LABELS ARE JUDGMENTS ABOUT EFFECTIVENESS   This list has positive, more effective labels on the left and negative, less effective ones on the right.

Style or Situation?	
MORE EFFECTIVE	LESS EFFECTIVE
Warm-hearted	Sentimental
Flexible	Weak-minded
Dignified	Pompous
Firm	Rigid
Businesslike	Brusque
Conservative	Reactionary
Progressive	Left-wing
Sensitive	Soft
Dynamic	Overbearing

Both labels on any line could refer to identical behavior. The left-hand label is typically used when the behavior is seen as appropriate; the right-hand label is used when the behavior is seen as inappropriate. This underlines what actually occurs when an evaluation of effectiveness is being made. The behavior and situation are considered together. If they match and the style is seen as appropriate, the more effective label is applied. If they do not, then the less effective label is applied.

As a simple example, a man who yells, "Everybody out," in a burning theater would be labeled "benevolent autocrat." Precisely the same comment used to close an office or restaurant for the night might be labeled "autocratic." Managerial-style labels indicate perceived appropriateness of behavior as well as actual behavior style. This is a key feature of the 3-D Theory which distinguishes it from most other approaches.

To take another case, one might point out that many managerial jobs are purely administrative. They consist, essentially, of taking documents from an in-tray, applying a few decision rules to them, and placing them in an out-tray. Often, the quantity of work coming to the in-tray is not within the control of the administrator, and he has only nominal subordinates, perhaps with similar pieces of paper going from his out-tray to their in-tray. What style is required or even demanded for this work? Obviously, separated behavior is ideal. A manager who could use separated behavior in this job would be labeled "bureaucrat."

Suppose a sales manager or general foreman behaved this way. They might be perceived and described as a "deserter" since separated behavior in most work of their kind is highly inappropriate. Thus identical behavior, as represented by the separated style, is effective in some jobs but not in others. It is clear from all this that a manager must know about, and the 3-D Theory must have a lot to say about, sizing up situations and about increasing style flexibility so that the right style can be used.

Extending the Usefulness of Style Labels

All eight managerial-style labels have been found to be useful in describing managerial behavior. Some additional concepts enable an even more comprehensive description to be made, such as dominant style, supporting style, and overrejected style. Any one of these three concepts can refer to either basic or managerial style. Thus, when assessing a manager on them, only one of either basic- or managerial-style sets of labels should be used.

DOMINANT STYLE

A manager's *dominant style* is the single managerial or basic style he most frequently uses. Any of the eight managerial styles or four basic styles may be a dominant style.

For some managers, the dominant style is very easy to detect as it is used very often. For other managers, it may be only slightly dominant and thus is difficult to identify without close observation and careful analysis over a long period of time. Dominant styles are most clearly displayed when either a manager's TO or RO is very high or very low.

Some managerial situations require a manager to use two dominant styles in different parts of his job. He may, for example, be dealing with salesmen and customers, or scientists and clerical workers.

SUPPORTING STYLE

A manager's *supporting style* is the basic or managerial style next most frequently used after his dominant style. Any style may be a supporting style to any dominant style although some dominant-supporting combinations seem to occur more often than others.

OVERREJECTED STYLES

An *overrejected style* is a single basic or managerial style which a manager uses far less frequently than does the average manager. Overrejection is desirable when the overrejected style is less effective. Some managers, however, overreject such styles as developer or benevolent autocrat. An unwillingness or incapacity to use either of them when the situation requires it would lead to a loss of effectiveness.

MANAGERIAL-STYLE POINT

As with the TO and RO scales, the E scale runs from 0 to 4. Zero is no effectiveness; 4 is maximum effectiveness.

Like the basic-style point, the *managerial-style point* (MSP) provides a numerical assessment of style behavior. Three numbers are used to represent TO, RO, and E. The scale for each number is from 0 to 4. An MSP of 1.0, 1.0, 1.0 would be deserter. An MSP of 1.0, 3.0, 4.0 would be developer.

New Concepts Introduced

EXECUTIVE	MANAGERIAL STYLE
BENEVOLENT AUTOCRAT	MANAGERIAL-STYLE POINT (MSP)
DEVELOPER	DOMINANT STYLE
BUREAUCRAT	SUPPORTING STYLE
COMPROMISER	OVERREJECTED STYLE
AUTOCRAT	
MISSIONARY	
DESERTER	

Autocrat   A manager who is using a high Task Orientation and a low Relationships Orientation in a situation where such behavior is inappropriate and who is, therefore, less effective; perceived as having no confidence in others, as unpleasant, and as interested only in the immediate task.

Benevolent Autocrat   A manager who is using a high Task Orientation and a low Relationships Orientation in a situation where such behavior is appropriate and who is, therefore, more effective; perceived as knowing what he wants and how to get it without creating resentment.

Bureaucrat   A manager who is using a low Task Orientation and a low Relationships Orientation in a situation where such behavior is appropriate and who is, therefore, more effective; perceived as being primarily interested in rules and procedures for their own sake, as wanting to control the situation by their use, and as conscientious.

Compromiser   A manager who is using a high Task Orientation and a high Relationships Orientation in a situation that requires a high orientation to only one or neither and who is, therefore, less effective; perceived as being a poor decision maker, as one who allows various pressures in the situation to influence him too much, and as avoiding or minimizing immediate pressures and problems rather than maximizing long-term production.

Deserter   A manager who is using a low Task Orientation and a low Relationships Orientation in a situation where such behavior is inappropriate and who is, therefore, less effective; perceived as uninvolved and passive or negative.

Developer   A manager who is using a high Relationships Orientation and a low Task Orientation in a situation where such behavior is appropriate and who is, therefore, more effective; perceived as having implicit trust in people and as being primarily concerned with developing them as individuals.

Dominant Style   The basic or managerial style a manager most frequently uses.

Executive   A manager who is using a high Task Orientation and a high Relationships Orientation in a situation where such behavior is appropriate and who is, therefore, more effective; perceived as a good motivating force and manager who sets high standards, treats everyone somewhat differently, and prefers team management.

Managerial Style   An assessment of the appropriateness and, therefore, effectiveness of a particular basic style in a situation.

Managerial-Style Point (MSP)   A point score for Task Orientation, Relationships Orientation, and managerial effectiveness, each scaled from 0 to 4.

Missionary   A manager who is using a high Relationships Orientation and a low Task Orientation in a situation where such behavior is inappropriate and who is, therefore, less effective; perceived as being primarily interested in harmony.

Overrejected Style   A basic or managerial style a manager uses far less frequently than the average manager.

Supporting Style   The basic or managerial style a manager uses next most frequently after the dominant style.

All the world's a stage,
And all the men and women merely players,
They have their exits and their entrances,
And one man in his time plays many parts.

WILLIAM SHAKESPEARE

Chapter 5

WHAT IS STYLE FLEX?

Over the course of their careers, managers are asked to be effective in a variety of situations. During one period of their career, they find themselves closely directed by a hard-driving, production-centered senior manager; during another period, they may be virtually independent and even work alone. At one time, they may find themselves supervising up to ten middle or junior managers and then, later, a small staff unit. At one time they wield a great deal of power; at other times they wield very little. What kind of manager succeeds in all of these situations? Certainly he is not one who reacts to all situations in the same way. He is the "flexible manager" who is currently the focus of much attention (89, 102, 110), as is the parallel personality type, "open-minded" (167), and the roughly equivalent cultural type, "other-directed" (165).

Style Flex—A Key 3-D Concept

Style flex is the 3-D term used to describe the ability to vary one's own basic-style behavior. Some managers use one basic style consistently, whatever the situation: these have *low flex*. Other managers use a variety of basic styles regularly: these have *high flex*.

The low-flex manager has a narrow range of behavior with which to respond to a situation. For this reason he tends to prefer to have things very clear, to have the power in his hands or know where it is, and to be interested in controls.

The high-flex manager has a wide range of behavior with which to respond to a situation. For this reason, he tends to be more willing to accept changes, not unhappy if things are loosely structured, and not too interested in power or controls.

MISTAKEN CURRENT VIEW OF HIGH FLEX   Most of both the psychological and management literature currently suggest that a manager with high flex is likely to be effective in every situation, and a manager with low flex is likely to be less effective in every situation. The term most often used for high-flex behavior is "flexibility," while for low-flex behavior, it is "rigidity." The incorrect suggestion is that one is generally good, and the other is generally bad. This fuzzy thinking about flexibility has led to tests which have low validity when checked against managerial performance. In speaking of two tests designed to measure rigidity, an industrial psychologist reported (192) that "neither the Gough-Sanford Rigidity Scale nor our version of the F-Scale yielded any sort of predictive validity. All the way through we found nonsignificant correlations with criteria. . . . These findings leave us in something of a dilemma." It appears that rigidity as defined by these tests did not generally predict low effectiveness, and flexibility did not generally predict high effectiveness.

The way out of this dilemma seems to be in sharpening the difference between flexibility and rigidity. One is not always good and the other always bad as the names themselves suggest. It is quite possible for a high-flex manager to make a mess of things because he is too willing to change his style. Low-flex is sometimes just what the situation demands. Low-flex behavior and high-flex behavior are not more or less effective in themselves. Their effectiveness depends on the situation in which they are used.

Four Style-flex Concepts

To build this line of thought into the 3-D Theory, four basic concepts are used to describe both the range of a manager's style behavior and whether it is used appropriately.

Style flexibility (appropriate high flex)
Style drift (inappropriate high flex)
Style resilience (appropriate low flex)
Style rigidity (inappropriate low flex)

Style flexibility is a measure of the extent to which a manager changes his style appropriately to a changing situation. *Style drift*, on the other hand, is changing one's style inappropriately, usually to lower pressure on oneself rather than to increase effectiveness in the situation. *Style resilience* suggests the maintenance of an appropriate and therefore more effective basic style under stress. *Style rigidity* suggests the maintenance of an inappropriate and therefore less effective style.

FLEXIBILITY AND DRIFT

If a high-flex manager is in a situation where his wide range of behavior is appropriate, he is seen as having style flexibility. He is perceived as oriented to reality, sensitive, adaptive, and open-minded.

Even with little ongoing change about them, managers sometimes find they need to have high flex in the apparently unchanging job they have. A manager supervising ten men might easily find that two work best when left alone, two need continuous direction, three need to be motivated by objectives, and three others need a supportive climate. So, in the space of a day an effective manager may well use all four basic styles when dealing with such a variety as a dependent subordinate, an aggressive pair of coworkers, a secretary whose work has deteriorated, and his superior who is interested only in the immediate task at hand. Obviously, to try to use a single basic style in these situations would lead to low effectiveness to say the least. To the extent the organization and technology allow individual treatment, a high-flex and sensitive manager could satisfy the demands of all these different situations and so achieve maximum effectiveness.

Many positions demand high flex because they require the manager to deal with several different kinds of people or groups. The head of a voluntary agency could have to deal with a hostile or friendly board, a tough central fund-raising organization, professionals, volunteers, the press, the general public, and his own immediate subordinates. If one viewed this position as a whole at one time the total flex demanded would be very high indeed.

High flex is likely to be demanded even more in the future. In many firms it is becoming commonplace, for younger managers especially, to undergo periodic changes in position [106] with consequent demands for high flex. In addition, an ongoing organizational change can lead directly to departmental and job changes so that even in particular positions the situation changes. Rapidly changing technology and management techniques themselves produce further change. Sometimes the change is dramatic and sometimes gradual. No matter what the cause of the change, the rate of change is increasing and is imposing more strains on managers to learn new behavior patterns and discard the old.

Whenever the topic of high flex is discussed, a manager will usually ask "Is high flex really role playing?" The suggestion is made that role playing is not being oneself or that it is somehow manipulative. The use of high flex is the ability to play a large number of roles, or use several styles, which is the same thing. Such high flex is best seen as using other parts of oneself as appropriate.

If a manager continually changes his style and so uses this same high flex in a situation where wide range of behavior is inappropriate, he will be seen as having style drift. He is perceived as yielding, unpredictable, and perhaps too sensitive.

RESILIENCE AND RIGIDITY   If a low-flex manager is in a situation where his narrow range of behavior is appropriate, he is seen as having style resilience. He is perceived as self-confident, orderly, stable, and consistent. Style resilience is not a popular subject for many management educators. It clearly should be taught, however, and given a positive value. While there is conflicting evidence, some studies do appear to indicate that subordinates are more likely to be satisfied with any particular style as long as they know what it is. They are less satisfied when they perceive no particular consistent style. Predictability, resilience, and subordinate satisfaction often go together. A high-flex manager succeeding a low-flex manager often finds that his attempts to "loosen things up" are not as rapidly successful as he had expected. His subordinates' expectations about how he should behave inhibit his introduction of managing with a higher flex.

Many situations demand qualities associated with resilience. The manager who wants to be flexible about everything he does will not last long. The modern organization is a recent and almost wondrous social institution. Its continuity and effectiveness, in part, are based on stability, predictability, and reliability. Its growth may, however, depend on quite different qualities. Obviously an appropriate mix of qualities associated with resilience and flexibility must be sought.

A low-flex manager may find himself in a situation where a much wider range of behavior is appropriate; he is then seen as having style rigidity. He will be perceived as having a closed mind, as intolerant and unsociable, and as resisting change.

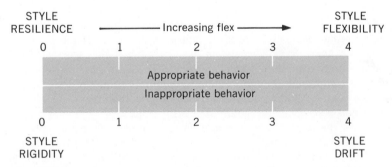

Exhibit 5-1   Style flex scale. The degree of style flex a manager has can be expressed on a scale from 0 to 4.

Style-flex Scale

The *style-flex scale* provides a convenient way for talking about the amount of flex a manager has. Style flex is considered to range from a low of 0 to a high of 4, as shown in Exhibit 5.1.

On the left of the scale both style resilience and rigidity are shown. Each represents low flex. On the right of the scale both style flexibility and style drift appear. Each represents high flex.

A manager with very low flex might be labeled as "resilient" or "rigid" depending on whether his low-flex behavior is appropriate or inappropriate to the situation. A manager with high flex would be labeled as having "flexibility" or "drift" depending on whether his high-flex behavior were appropriate or inappropriate to the situation.

PLOTTING FLEX

A manager's flex may be indicated by drawing a shape on a basic-style chart. For some managers this shape will be large in area, indicating a high flex which could lead to flexibility or drift. For others it will be small

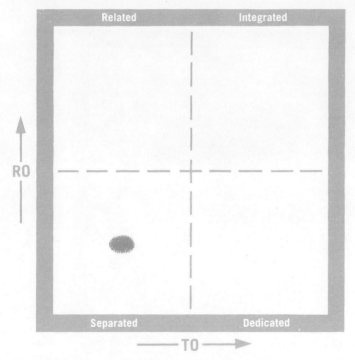

Exhibit 5-2   Flex of zero. This manager has a very narrow range of behavior in the separated basic style. Unless fortunate enough to be in a position demanding that particular narrow range of behavior, his managerial style is deserter.

in area, indicating a low flex which could lead to either rigidity or resilience.

A comparison between the size of the flex area and the total area is used to decide whether the flex should be indicated as 0, 1, 2, 3, or 4. If the flex area is very small, 0 is used to describe it; if it is about 50 percent of the area, 2 is used; and if it is most of the area, 4 is used.

Exhibit 5.2 depicts a manager with a flex of 0 and a separated basic style. Such low flex can occur anywhere on the chart. A manager could have a flex of 0 and be *separated, related, dedicated,* or *integrated.* The low-flex related style, for instance, is well known. He is the manager who will always put the employees' personal needs first, no matter what the actual situation demands him to do in order for him to be effective. He is the rigid missionary.

Exhibit 5.3 shows a flex of about 1 spread over the related and integrated styles. As shown here, the flex area may be sausage-shaped, indicating flex only along a particular dimension—perhaps more or less task, more or less relationships, or a constant ratio between each. This manager is capable of using more than average amounts of RO and within limits can increase or decrease the amount of TO he is using.

Exhibit 5.4 shows a flex of about 2 spread over separated and related and integrated, but the manager is mostly separated.

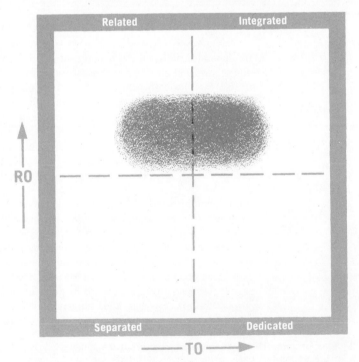

Exhibit 5-3   Flex of one. This manager can use the related and integrated style.

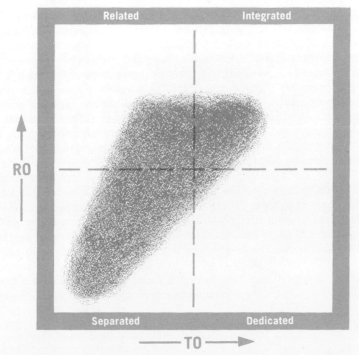

Exhibit 5-4 Flex of two. This manager has a wide range of separated behavior but can also use the related and integrated style.

Exhibit 5.5 shows a very high flex of about 4. This manager has a very wide range of behavior. If he also has a sensitivity to situations and knows when to use each style, he could be effective in many different situations.

USE OF INDICATORS TO PLOT FLEX

An approximate idea of a manager's flex may be obtained by the use of the People and Organization indicators of Chapter 8. When the appropriate indicators are chosen the flex shape can be drawn using the method outlined in Chapter 7. For each indicator ask "Does the manager enjoy doing this and can he do it easily and well?" When managers rate themselves without training they tend to distort and believe they can be all things to all men. Others therefore should make such ratings.

New Concepts Introduced

STYLE DRIFT
STYLE FLEX (FLEX)

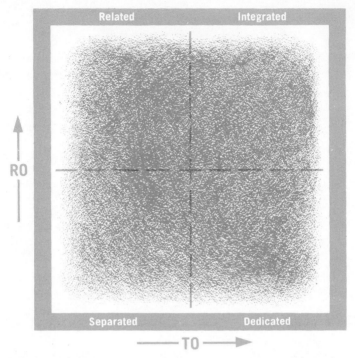

Exhibit 5-5   Flex of four. This manager can use any basic style.

STYLE FLEXIBILITY (SF)
STYLE RESILIENCE
STYLE RIGIDITY

Style Drift   Varying one's basic-style behavior inappropriately so that managerial effectiveness decreases.

Style Flex (Flex)   The ability to vary one's basic-style behavior. Scaled from 0 to 4.

Style Flexibility (SF)   Skill in varying one's basic-style behavior appropriately to a changing situation so that managerial effectiveness increases. Scaled from 0 to 4.

Style Resilience   Maintaining a single appropriate basic style so that managerial effectiveness increases.

Style Rigidity   Maintaining a single inappropriate basic style so that managerial effectiveness decreases.

Part 2

SITUATION

Some suggestive signs exist that the manager of the future will be different. . . . He will be more of a Manager of Situations.

R. BELLOWS, T. Q. GILSON, AND G. S. ODIORNE

Chapter Six

FIVE SITUATIONAL ELEMENTS

The effectiveness of any behavior depends on the situation in which it is used. To know how to be effective then a manager needs to know how to read situations. However as the idea of "situation" is rather broad it is necessary to break it down into smaller elements which can be looked at independently of each other. 3-D breaks the situation into five elements called *Technology, Subordinates, Coworkers, Superior,* and *Organization.* All of these are easily understood and each alone is the basis of schools of thought in management.

Over the past fifty years or so five distinct schools have developed starting with scientific management.

Scientific management to organization theory			
EMPHASIS	INTERFACE	SCHOOL	PERIOD
Technology	Work-worker	Scientific management	1920s
Subordinates	Worker-climate	Human relations	1930s
Coworkers	Manager-group	Group dynamics	1940s
Superior	Manager-subordinate	Management styles	1950s
Organization	Manager-organization	Organization theory	1960s

These are rough categories at best, and other arrangements could easily be made. The time period is primarily an indication of widescale theoretical development and initial management interest as expressed through expenditure on research and training programs. All of the schools are very active today.

SCIENTIFIC MANAGEMENT   One popular view in management is that a key to efficiency is in getting the worker to fit the job. This leads to developing him so that he can perform efficiently in the highest grade of work for which his natural abilities fit him. The best-known name in the field was that of Frederick Winslow Taylor (179), an American engineer who started off as a laborer. The man-job fit which he sought was more physiological than psychological. The method used, in part, was to train workers to move in the best way at an optimum speed. This general approach is termed *scientific management.*

Fayol (52), while concerned more with management than with the worker-job relationship, is associated with Taylor, and together they constitute the *functional school of management.* This school is sometimes referred to as being primarily concerned with organizations without people. The primary emphasis of this approach is on the way work is or can be done, that is, the technology.

HUMAN RELATIONS   Some long-term experiments conducted by Harvard University led to what has been identified as the *human relations school.* The emphasis switched from the worker's physical work to his psychological makeup. Emphasis was placed on the informal organization rather than the formal. The worker and his personal psychological needs were emphasized.

It became clear in the course of many experiments that productivity was affected by the worker's perception of the interest management had in him. It also became obvious that output could easily be, and perhaps normally was, restricted by social pressures to conform to standards set by coworkers.

Elton Mayo (135, 136) has often been called the founder of the human relations movement and of industrial sociology. He was an Australian who spent most of his working life at the Harvard Business School. Immediately prior to his death in 1949 he was consultant on industrial problems to the British government. His most famous research project was an investigation at the Hawthorne Works of the Western Electric Company near Chicago. This and other research demonstrated the importance of groups in affecting the behavior of individuals at work. These Hawthorne studies led to much research into the psychological and sociological forces in industrial organizations. Morale and job satisfaction became of paramount concern. Much of this led to the approach being termed "people without organizations." Fritz Roethlisberger who made a further series of enquiries into the human effect of work and working conditions (166) is another important figure of this school.

Two currently prominent figures in the human relations movement are

Argyris (5 to 8) and Herzberg (85, 86). Both start with the primacy and nature of the individual and show how the expressions of the organizational philosophy or of technology interact with him and inhibit his psychological maturity or motivation to work.

Many believe that some proponents of the human relations approach were and still are a trifle one-sided. It has been shown that production was not necessarily related to morale (34) and that it is not generally realistic to seek favorable attitudes toward management to the exclusion of the organization's objectives (26). The human relations school has been criticized by McNair (142) and Whyte (189). While it is reasonable to say that the school overemphasizes a single point of view, it is clear that an important situational element must be subordinates.

GROUP DYNAMICS   The *group-dynamics school* with its interest in the interaction among people received its initial attention in the 1950s. Emphasis was given to informal organization, to lowering the power differential between superior and subordinate, and to thinking of group rather than individual dynamics.

This school has been involved with group dynamics training, called "sensitivity training," under the auspices of the National Training Laboratories of the United States. This school has many writers who became social scientists soon after World War II. Many of them show their passionate concern for man's inhumanity.

The nature of the approach, in part, appears to have resulted in no single dominant figure emerging. Prominent names include Bradford (27 to 30), Bennis (17 to 19), and Miles (146 to 148). There are many others. Group dynamics as a training device for managers has been most vehemently attacked by Odiorne (156) and strongly defended by Argyris (5). This school carried to its limit suggests that organizations should move to eliminate boss-subordinate roles; they would become coworkers instead. Whether or not managers agree they could go that far, it is clear that coworkers is an important situational element.

MANAGEMENT STYLES   The growing interest in *management styles* began in the late 1950s and is with us today. The idea is that a manager should respond either in a particular way to most situations or in a flexible way depending on the situation. The focus on styles implies that the manager was seen primarily as responding to subordinates or situations rather than changing them. The approach is essentially psychological in that classification schemes of style theorists tend to focus more on personality variables, usually task and relationships, rather than on situational variables, such as technology. Current prominent names include McGregor (140), Blake (23), and Jennings (103).

This primary focus on management styles rather than, say, subordinate styles or technology alerts us to another structural element—that of superior.

ORGANIZATION THEORY   Organization theory views the organization as a single entity with a life or culture of its own. This culture will often be independent of the technology or of the styles of those occupying positions in it. The approach is purely sociological, and personal factors are eliminated from consideration. While there is no doubt that this broad view can provide helpful insights, it is also a fact that people do exist and must be considered if a comprehensive view is to be developed.

Taken as it is, however, the school does alert us to the idea of the culture, philosophy, ethic, or climate of the *organization* as an important situational element.

Each of the five approaches mentioned has a unique point of view and has provided valuable insights and opportunities for improving effectiveness. Each has strong adherents and practitioners today, and each is being taught at management development courses and at universities all over the world. While each has strengths and has been found useful, no impartial observer would seriously claim that any one offers solutions for all management problems. They each tend to deal with different aspects of the total situation a manager is concerned with. Thus, the opportunity that managers should seek is to take the best of all these approaches and not focus unduly on any one. Today managers want to focus on the total situation rather than solely on the technology, subordinates, coworkers, superior, or organization. The growing emphasis on situational theory will help managers to do this.

SITUATIONAL THEORY   *Situational theory* draws on all five of these schools. While only now becoming popular, it is nothing really new. As far back as the 1920s, Mary Parker Follett (65–66) was proposing that managers structure the situation and follow the "Law of the Situation." Follett was a Bostonian who spent her last five years studying and lecturing in England. Her approach started with a question about technology demands, "What do you want people to do?" and then, "How do you scientifically control conduct to accomplish this?" A currently popular term given to situational theory is "leader-follower–situation approach."

Current prominent situationists are Fiedler (53), Likert (119, 120), and Stogdill (175). They all have done a remarkable job of piecing together research to develop a comprehensive situational theory of worker performance. They recognize the complexity of the relationships between production, satisfaction, and morale that some people take to be simple and thus for granted.

The 3-D Situational Elements

The 3-D Theory is a situational theory. It takes into account the core idea of the five approaches developed thus far. It asks a manager to look outward at the situation, not inward toward himself. To look outward he needs to know what to look at. In 3-D terminology he is asked to look at the five *situational elements:* organization, technology, superior, coworkers, and subordinates.

The five elements, shown in Exhibit 6.1, are intended to be all-inclusive. They are capable of being viewed separately with attention being focused on them one at a time. They are as few as possible.

What do each of these five terms mean?

"Organization," which is short for organization philosophy as used in the 3-D Theory, refers to all those factors which influence behavior within a social system that are common to essentially unrelated positions. It is sometimes referred to as "extrinsic job factors," "culture," "climate," "values," or simply "the way we do things around here."

"Technology," as used in the 3-D Theory, refers to the way work may be done to achieve managerial effectiveness. Making widgets, making decisions, and making inspections are forms of work that could be done in different ways from each other; their technology is different.

The concepts "superior," "coworkers," and "subordinates" are used in the generally accepted sense. The subelements "styles" and "expectations" are included for each of these three elements.

Each of these five elements makes demands on the manager's style.

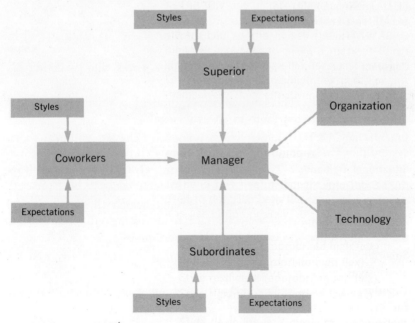

Exhibit 6–1   3-D situational elements. These are the five things in a situation a manager must recognize, respond to, or change.

These demands can be expressed in terms of one or more of the basic styles required to satisfy them. Anything that affects a manager's effectiveness can be said to be expressed through one or more of them. They are, in effect, the sum of all the demands of his position. This means that a manager need only to appraise these five elements accurately in order to make a comprehensive situation diagnosis. Further, if he learns how to change each, he can manage the total situation. The manager is not listed as one of the five elements in the situation, yet he is obviously in it. Why is this? The 3-D Theory sees managers as being active rather than passive, as being flexible rather than adaptable. It is the manager's job to control the situation, and by doing so, he must first control himself. Keeping the situation and the manager separate underlines the fact that situations exist for managers to work in them and to increase their managerial effectiveness.

Managers obviously need to know the nature of the demands of these five elements, and how they can be appraised. We start with technology since many of its principles also apply to one or more of the other four situational elements.

New Concepts Introduced

SITUATIONAL ELEMENTS TECHNOLOGY
SITUATIONAL DEMANDS   SUPERIOR
ELEMENT DEMANDS   COWORKER
ORGANIZATION   SUBORDINATE

Coworker A person with whom a manager works who is neither his superior nor a subordinate.

Element Demands The basic style required by a situational element in order for it to contribute to effectiveness.

Organization All the factors which influence behavior within a social system that are common to essentially unrelated positions.

Situational Demands The basic style required by all dominant situational elements in order for managerial effectiveness to be increased.

Situational Elements Five elements through which all the situational demands on a manager may be said to be expressed: organization, technology, superior, coworkers, and subordinates.

Subordinate A person over whom a manager has authority and for whose work he is responsible.

Superior A person having authority over a manager and responsibility for his work.

Technology The way work may be done to achieve managerial effectiveness.

Effective organization is a function of the work to be done.

WILFRED BROWN

Chapter Seven

TECHNOLOGY INFLUENCES STYLE

Technology is usually a powerful but in some ways invisible influence on management style. There is not complete agreement on this however. While some theorists see *technology* as virtually the central determining feature of the nature of the firm (35) others say it is not (161). One research study in an automobile plant showed that over a three-year period important aspects or organization philosophy and the relationships between superiors, coworkers, and subordinates changed dramatically, while technology remained unchanged (79). Yet a practicing managing director (33) says in discussing the relation of organization to work:

> Effective organization is a function of the work to be done and the resources and techniques available to do it. Thus changes in methods of production bring about changes in the number of work roles, in the distribution of work between roles and in their relationship one to another. Failure to make explicit acknowledgment of this relationship between work and organization gives rise to non-valid assumptions, e.g. that optimum organization is a function of the personalities involved, that it is a matter connected with the personal style and arbitrary decision of the chief executive, that there are choices between centralized or decentralized types of organization, etc. Our observations lead us to accept that optimum organization must be derived from an analysis of the work to be done and the techniques and resources available.

TECHNOLOGY REDESIGN

Work can be divided up in many ways depending on the job to be done, and even particular jobs may be organized in different ways. An expensive car can be assembled by a few workers or by hundreds or even thousands. A teacher may teach by lecture alone or with a team of others or by group methods or by the printed word alone. A worker may be given one operation to perform, perhaps an inspection, or may be given hundreds of sequential operations to perform.

It is clear that:

The work to be done affects to some extent
the organization of the work.
Any work is capable of being organized in
many different ways.

It is this second point which has received great attention. In the past Technology redesign was accomplished after analysis by work study methods. These methods assume that the worker is an intelligent machine. Today job redesign is being accomplished by Herzberg need analysis, sociotechnical system analysis, and 3–D technology analysis. All of these see work as capable of being designed better so that it gives more satisfaction without decreasing productivity, and almost always increasing it.

SOME JOBS ARE EASY TO REDESIGN

Most assembly work may be accomplished by a single person or by many. A radio or TV set may be wired from single components by a single worker at a single work place or by dozens or hundreds working sequentially. If errors are hard to discover and hard to correct and the total job involves many essentially similar operations and components, the work might best be done by an individual.

Some widely known redesigns of assembly technologies in America have been clearly successful but widely misinterpreted. Suppose a firm made high quality, expensive, small, short production run devices, and suppose the firm changed its technology from each operator doing a small part of the job to each operator doing the whole job. Suppose too production shot up and workers earned 50 percent more than before. All this is excellent and clearly should be replicated whenever possible.

The difficulty arises when analysts of these schemes use the wrong concepts to describe what went on and the wrong reasons to explain it. The successful example could be explained in such psychological terms as:

"Integrating the needs of the individual with the needs of the organization"

"Self-actualizing on the job"
"Optimizing self-utilization and self-control"
"Motivation by job enrichment"

What happened can be explained this way but it does not always help much and can sometimes lead to confusion. By focusing on the individual in this way and not the technology, the suggestion is that almost all jobs can be redesigned and that a manager must be backward or autocratic if he does not do it. There is also the suggestion that the organization philosophy of firms in these situations should change over to integrated, but a more accurate philosophy would be related which is highly appropriate for this revised technology. The point being made is, simply, that while many jobs can and have been redesigned and this has led to higher output, the reason for the success is best sought in the nature of the work being done and not the assumed needs of those doing it.

SOME JOBS ARE DIFFICULT TO REDESIGN

Most banks are organized so that workers interact very little. One person may look after savings deposits, another foreign currency, another withdrawals, and another loans. The individuals involved relate all their work to a master ledger or computer which is balanced every day. The operations are essentially unskilled but accuracy, honesty, and judgment are important. Virtually all operations are routine and, with minor changes, are repeated hundreds of times every day. The nature of the service customers want and their expectations concerning it make it difficult to redesign these kinds of jobs. The style always demanded of the bank manager or chief accountant is separated or related. It is related if he trusts the bank's control system and if it is a good one. If not, he becomes the control system and so moves to a separated style.

HOW TO ASSESS TECHNOLOGY DEMANDS

There are many classification schemes for technology (35, 161, 171, 180, 191) which consider such things as difficulty of task, cooperation requirements, size of production run, and specialization and standardization. All these schemes are useful and full of promises for research and ultimately for organizational design. Most of them have looked, quite appropriately, at the demands work makes on worker behavior rather than on managerial behavior. The 3-D Theory looks at the demands the technology makes on managerial behavior. This makes it directly useful to the manager as a guide for his behavior.

A recognition of these demands and of the potential for modifying them is essential to managerial effectiveness. Some technologies demand be-

Related	Integrated
A Subordinate skill	A Subordinate interaction
B Commitment required	B Subordinate interdependence
C Method autonomy	C Manager interaction
D Discretion span	D Solution Multiplicity
E Creative component	E Pace autonomy
A Intellectual component	A Physical component
B System control	B Manager knowledge
C Intrinsic interest	C Unscheduled events
D Subordinate autonomy	D Directions needed
E Task simplicity	E Performance measurability
Separated	Dedicated

VERY Important

RO

——— TO ———→

Exhibit 7—1 Technology demands indicators. These twenty indicators can be used to discover the range of style demanded by any particular technology.

havior that is primarily dedicated or separated, and so on. Like basic styles themselves, not all technologies fit cleanly into one of the four 3-D classifications. Most, in fact, will overlap at least two.

Technology demands can be appraised by the use of twenty *technology demands indicators*, five for each of the basic styles (Exhibit 7.1). Once these are understood, it is a relatively simple matter to determine the behavior the technology is demanding of the manager.

SEPARATED TECHNOLOGY INDICATORS

Intellectual Component The degree to which the subordinates are required to think rather than to act.

System Control The degree to which the subordinates' work and work method follow established procedures.

Intrinsic Interest The degree to which the subordinates' work is in and of itself interesting, motivating, or attractive.

Subordinate Autonomy   The degree to which the subordinates have discretion over their effectiveness standards.

Task Simplicity   The degree to which the subordinates' tasks are simple to perform.

A technology demanding separated behavior by the manager, then, would be one in which subordinates do more thinking than acting, where what subordinates actually do follows established procedures, where the work is very interesting in itself, where subordinates can to a large degree decide their own effectiveness standards, and where the tasks are basically simple.

RELATED TECHNOLOGY INDICATORS

Subordinate Skill   The degree to which the position makes high skill or judgment demands on the subordinates.

Commitment Required   The degree to which the position requires the subordinates to be personally committed if all effectiveness standards are to be fully achieved.

Method Autonomy   The degree to which the subordinates can select the method, tools, or approach they wish to use.

Discretion Span   The degree to which time can elapse before substandard work of the subordinates is detected.

Creative Component   The degree to which the position requires the subordinates to develop new methods and ideas.

A technology demanding related behavior by the manager, then, would be one in which subordinates need a high degree of skill, where their commitment is required, where they can decide their own work method, where their output is difficult to evaluate in the short run, and where subordinates are required to be creative.

DEDICATED TECHNOLOGY INDICATORS

Physical Component   The degree to which the subordinates are required to use physical effort.

Manager Knowledge   The degree to which the subordinates know less about the task than the manager.

Unscheduled Events   The degree to which unplanned and unanticipated events might occur which require corrective action by the manager.

Directions Needed   The degree to which the subordinates need to be given directions frequently, in order for them to complete their task.

Performance Measurability   The degree to which the subordinate's performance is measurable, and the impact of remedial actions taken by the manager can be evaluated.

A technology demanding dedicated behavior by the manager, then, would be one in which physical effort is required of subordinates, where the manager knows more about the task then the subordinates, where unscheduled events requiring intervention by the manager are likely to occur, where directions are frequently required, and where subordinate performance is measurable.

INTEGRATED TECHNOLOGY INDICATORS

Subordinate Interaction   The degree to which the subordinates must talk with each other to complete their task.

Subordinate Interdependence   The degree to which the subordinates must depend on each other in meeting their own effectiveness standards.

Manager Interaction   The degree to which the manager must talk with subordinates as a group for them to complete their tasks.

Solution Multiplicity   The degree to which more than one effective solution is possible, where relative effectiveness of these solutions is difficult to measure, and where the number and evaluation of solutions is improved by interaction.

Pace Autonomy   The degree to which the subordinates may set their own pace, effort, or involvement level.

A technology demanding integrated behavior by the manager would be one in which the subordinates must talk to, and depend on, each other; where the manager has to meet with his subordinates as a group; where more than one solution is possible, although some are more effective than others; and where subordinates can set their own pace.

Here is an illustration of the use of a single indicator "Subordinate Interaction" from the integrated indicators:

In a large trucking company the style demands of two groups of workers were compared: One group was involved in the package and handling operation and the other with truck driving and dispatching. The technology of the package and handling operation required that the men interact frequently. The truck drivers usually worked alone and had little contact with anyone else in completing their task. The only exceptions were the dispatchers from whom they needed accurate information. Since the truck drivers generally worked alone, they were not concerned particularly with relationships but were concerned about the system underlying the job in terms of where and when they were to deliver or pick up. If one ignores the other nineteen indicators this example indicates that the package and handling workers might achieve higher output if managed with an integrated style while the truck drivers could be better managed with a separated style.

PLOTTING TECHNOLOGY FLEX

The flex of a technology may be plotted in much the same way as can the flex of a manager. The twenty technology demand indicators are used. Each set of five indicators is looked at to see how many of them describe the technology being considered; this produces a number between 0 and 5 assigned to each basic style. These numbers from 0 to 5 are grouped into three sets: 0 to 1 (weak), 2 to 3 (medium), and 4 to 5 (strong). Thus for each of the four styles, one of these three sets of numbers or terms will apply. The numbers obtained are used with the plotting guide shown in Exhibit 7.2 to obtain a flex shape. Numbers 0 to 1 are not plotted.

Notice that the flex shapes are drawn with only general boundaries and there is a degree of rounding off and averaging out. This illustrates that at this point of development such behavioral theories as 3–D should not get trapped into the belief that human behavior can be seen as cut and dried. Flex maps help us, but they are only as good as the data they get. Experts sometimes disagree on the data, so flex maps are best seen as approximations and simply as a basis for clearer thinking about situations.

Frequently indicators appear for one style only. If 2–3 indicators appear, a simple circle is drawn as in 7.2(a). If 4–5 indicators appear, a circle at the extreme corner of the style is drawn as in 7.2(b). Why have the same shape with more indicators? The reason is that the more indicators that apply, the more extreme the demands. If five indicators apply for a single style, a very powerful and particular demand is being made, and this is shown by the positioning at the extreme of the basic style.

If indicators of two styles apply, shapes 7.2(c) to 7.2(h) are drawn. If indicators of three styles apply, shapes 7.2(i) to 7.2(n) are drawn.

It is only very rare that situations involving all four styles occur. The two extreme examples are 2–3 for each style 7.2(o) and 4–5 for each style 7.2(p). If combinations of both 2–3 and 4–5 are needed for four styles, the 2–3 flex shape is used as the basic shape and the 4–5 shape added to it for the style that applies.

The technology flex of any managerial position can be plotted in this way. The twenty indicators are powerful and have general applicability.

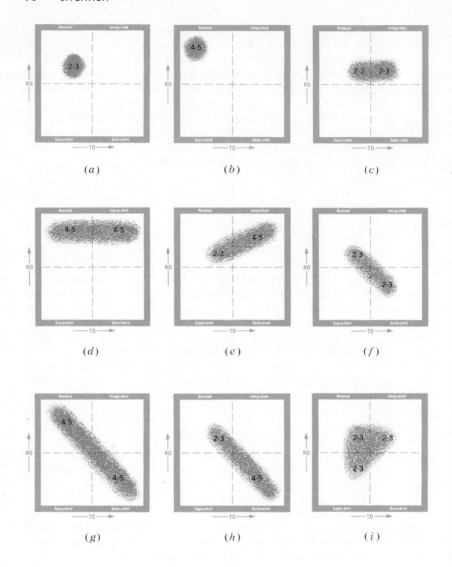

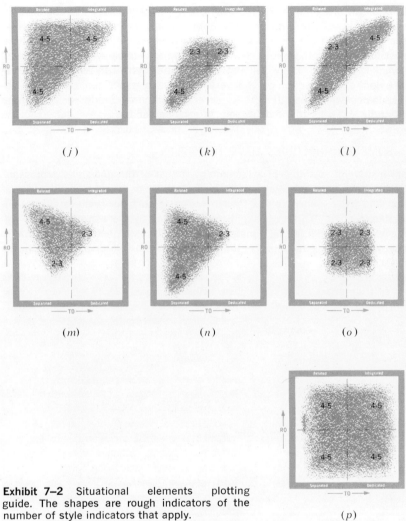

Exhibit 7–2 Situational elements plotting guide. The shapes are rough indicators of the number of style indicators that apply.

The following exhibits, 7.3 to 7.8, show the technology flex of several managerial positions with the indicators that apply also shown. In studying each consider the elements included and omitted. When this is done it is possible to grasp the whole idea of sizing up a technology for the demands it makes on style. There will not be full agreement with all the elements included or omitted since the very brief titles given could represent a technology which could exist in several variations. Study each diagram carefully and refer to the definitions of each demand.

SOME TECHNOLOGIES HAVE HIGH FLEX

An extreme example of a technology is that of the university professor. College teaching technology demands are so weak in any particular direction and have such high flex that it is best to consider them to be no real demands at all. This is brought about in part by the variety of teaching techniques considered legitimate; the low power his department chairman has over teaching technology; the independence of the operation, as there

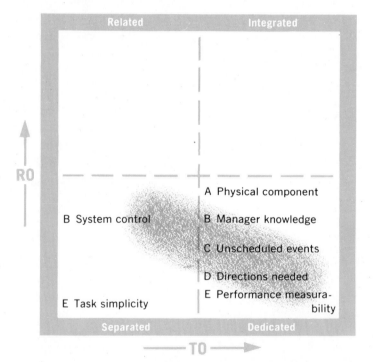

Exhibit 7–3 Managing an assembly line. All dedicated elements apply, and two of the five separated elements apply. Some foremen though may quite appropriately be bureaucrats, not benevolent autocrats.

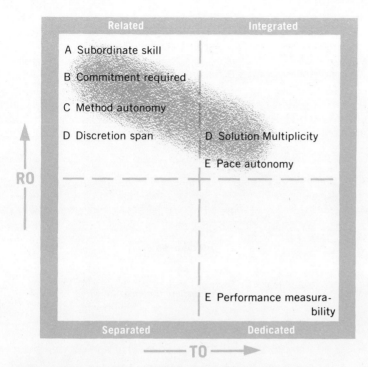

Related   Integrated

A Subordinate skill

B Commitment required

C Method autonomy

D Discretion span   D Solution Multiplicity

                           E Pace autonomy

RO

                           E Performance measura-
                                              bility

Separated   Dedicated

——— TO ——→

Exhibit 7–4 Managing non-interacting division managers. Most related elements apply for these managers but only two of the integrated and one dedicated. Many top managers operate very successfully this way.

are no coworkers; the high power the teacher has over the students, and the virtual invisibility of his performance to any but his students. The college teaching technology flex would follow the perimeter of flex map as in Exhibit 5.5. That is, the flex would be the maximum possible. At the other extreme, the job of a typical foreman of a production line has much lower technology flex.

SHORT- AND LONG-RUN PRODUCTION TECHNOLOGY

A change from small- to large-quantity production can have many effects on technology and ultimately on the behavior demanded of the foremen involved, all of which can be anticipated. While not always true the initial impact of such a change would be something like this:

Duration of a particular production run lengthens.
Speed of operation rises.

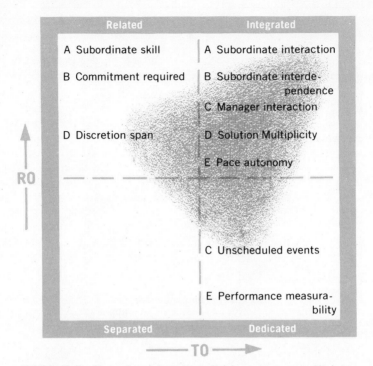

Exhibit 7–5 Managing interacting division managers. All integrated elements apply. They typically do when a manager supervises interacting managers.

Greater emphasis is placed on planning.

Tooling and fixtures men become more important.

Skilled men become mechanics instead.

Unskilled men remain so or become operators.

Discretionary element of operators decreases.

Foreman manages a large number of operators, not a small number of skilled workers.

Foreman works with staff assistants who report elsewhere.

Staff function emerges and moves upward into organization.

All of these changes have their effects on the most appropriate style a

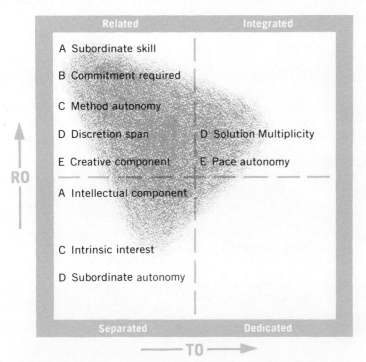

Related   Integrated

A Subordinate skill

B Commitment required

C Method autonomy

D Discretion span   D Solution Multiplicity

E Creative component   E Pace autonomy

A Intellectual component

C Intrinsic interest

D Subordinate autonomy

Separated   Dedicated

RO

TO

Exhibit 7–6 Managing research scientists or managing a university department. Creative professionals need to be handled with kid gloves.

foreman should use. This style may be determined by estimating the effect of each of these changes on the twenty technology indicators.

TIME PRESSURES AFFECT TECHNOLOGY DEMANDS

An open-hearth steel mill foreman, or almost anyone for that matter in an emergency situation, has a different technology from when there is no emergency. Aspects of the technology have changed because time pressures have changed. Some managers are less effective because they see time pressures which do not in fact exist. This usually leads to inappropriate behavior which is seen as autocratic.

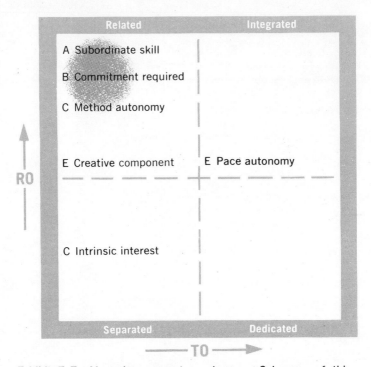

Exhibit 7–7 Managing computer salesmen. Salesmen of this kind, who may need to make only a sale a year, are treated quite differently from encyclopedia salesmen.

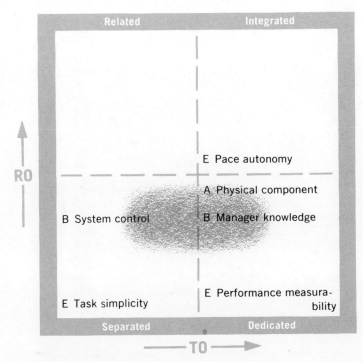

Exhibit 7–8 Managing encyclopedia salesmen. "Get out there and really drive it."

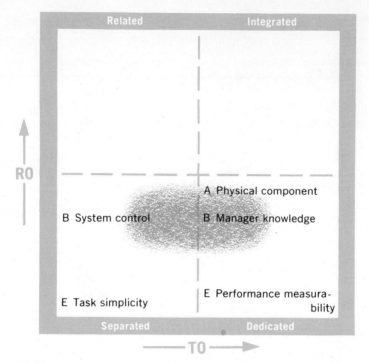

Exhibit 7–9   Toaster making: method A. A simple production-process technology.

TECHNOLOGY, NOT PRODUCT

The nature of the ultimate item produced in a department cannot of itself predict the technology demands. In fact, almost any product may be produced by a variety of technologies. One technology is often better than the other although it may or may not be the one in current use. The application of 3-D at worker level aims at discovering and installing the best one.

As a simple example of the varieties of technology possible with a single product consider these four possible technologies for the production of automatic electric toasters.

METHOD A   The technology could be designed so that each worker contributed a small part to the total construction of the toaster that was delivered to him and taken from him automatically in a predetermined speed. The technology demands would look like that shown in Exhibit 7.9. Notice the dedicated-separated demands made by this technology.

METHOD B   The technology could be designed so that each worker made a whole toaster according to the design he wanted. He could be as creative as he wished in any way he wished, as demonstrated in Exhibit 7.10. This is clearly a heavily related technology.

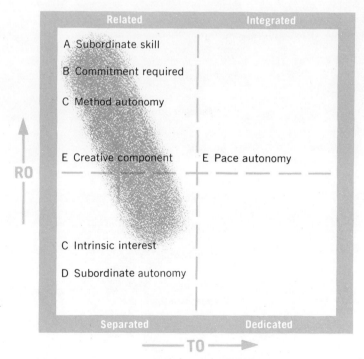

Exhibit 7–10 Toaster making: method B. A heavily related technology that would probably produce fewer but more original toasters.

METHOD C   The technology could be designed so that the manager gave instructions to his subordinates covering the various elements of their work. No one person would do one job continuously, and the manager, himself, would decide who did what, how, and when. In Exhibit 7.11 there is obviously a dedicated technology demanding a dedicated basic style.

METHOD D   While the reasons for doing it would be difficult to imagine, the technology could be designed so that the subordinates and the manager continuously interacted over the ideal way the toaster should be made. This would be an integrated-related technology, and it would look

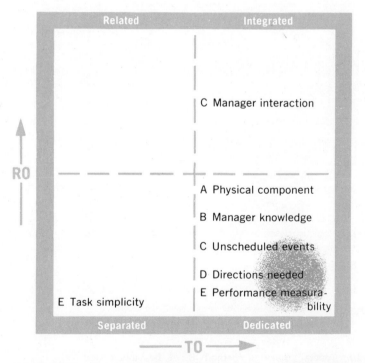

Exhibit 7–11 Toaster making: method C. Toaster making would seldom justify such a dedicated technology.

like the one in Exhibit 7.12. Not too many toasters would be made, although some original designs would probably appear. Integrated-related technology is seldom used for producing simple physical products but is often used for small, complex physical products or for producing ideas or decisions.

THE MANAGER'S OWN TECHNOLOGY

Managers may now wish to plot the technology of a situation they are now in or will soon enter. It is helpful to compare answers with an associate. It would be useful to consider the toaster example and consider to what extent technology could and should be modified.

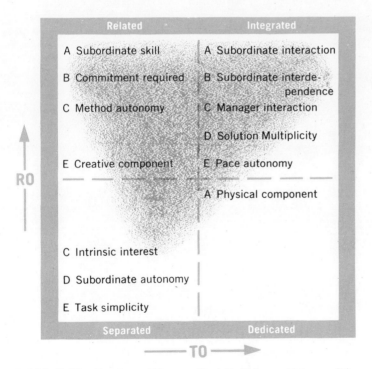

Exhibit 7–12 Toaster making: method D. This would be a wild way to make a toaster but often a good way to make a decision.

The primary task of management is to arrange the situation so that people co-operate readily of their own accord.

MARY PARKER FOLLETT

I will pay more for the ability to deal with people than any other ability under the sun.

JOHN D. ROCKEFELLER

Chapter Eight

ORGANIZATION AND PEOPLE INFLUENCE STYLE

In the same way that technology makes demands on managerial behavior, so do the three human elements—superior, coworkers, subordinates—as well as the remaining element, organization itself. Like technology, the demands on behavior that each of these four make can be assessed and described in terms of the basic style demanded of the manager. The style demanded by the human elements depends in part on the styles of the particular superior, coworker, or subordinate involved and also on the expectations each has of how others should behave toward him. When attempting to predict how others will act or when attempting to influence their behavior, the concept of expectations is much more useful than that of needs. Needs are hidden, varied, and to some extent hypothetical. Yet you can actually ask people about their expectations and within reasonable limits get an accurate answer.

The terms superior, coworkers, and subordinates are used in the generally accepted sense and described briefly while the term organization philosophy is given considerably more explanation.

SUPERIOR

The superior's style is the style a manager's superior uses toward him. This element becomes very powerful at senior levels in management where there is frequent interlevel interaction and where there tend to be fewer subordinates. Superior's expectations are the expectations the superior has about the way the manager should behave. Some superiors are very flexible in their expectations so long as objectives are achieved. Others tend to have strongly held expectations, particularly if the superior previously occupied the manager's position or sometimes if there is a wide age or experience difference between them. For some managers the combination of superior's style and expectations is the dominant element with which they have to deal and which most influences their effectiveness.

COWORKERS

Coworkers' styles are the styles a manager's coworkers use toward him. This element is more important when a manager is to some extent interdependent with his coworkers and interacts frequently with them. Coworkers' expectations are the expectations a manager's coworkers have about the way the manager should behave. This is particularly important when there is frequent interaction and when trading and bargaining for resources, such as budget money or raw materials, is an important element of the technology.

SUBORDINATES

Subordinates' styles are the styles a manager's subordinates use toward him. This element can represent subordinates as a group if there are many subordinates since the manager does not usually deal with them as individuals. It is a strong element when there are few subordinates and when they interact a great deal with their manager. Subordinates' expectations are the expectations a manager's subordinates have about the way the manager should behave. Although not always recognized, this alone has a tremendous influence on a manager's effectiveness and can be a major restraining force in change. It is one of the things that managers may most easily change if they acquire the skill to do it. It is this that so often can explain why a particular style might work in one situation but not in another, why some North American practices will not work in many British firms, and why a manager just returned from a training course has little success with the new hat he tries to wear. It is particularly important for a manager to understand subordinates' expectations when moving into a position previously occupied by another manager. If the prior manager had been liked and had been there for some time, the subordinates may have rather rigid expectations to which the new manager may have to adapt at the beginning.

One study, by Foa (64), has shown that leaders who conformed to the expectations of subordinates were more likely to have satisfied workers than either autocratic or democratic leaders, even when subordinates expected and received autocratic leadership. This is generally supported by the behavior of Norwegian factory workers (68) who did not increase output when treated in a participative manner, perhaps because they did not expect or want participation.

ORGANIZATION

Organization philosophy, shortened to organization, is all those factors which influence behavior in an organization which are common to essentially unrelated positions in the organization. In a nutshell, it describes how companies, taken as a whole, differ from one another in the behavior they expect. Such differences are influenced by and expressed through such things as standard operating procedures, overall organization structure, and other often unwritten but powerful guides to behavior.

There are four basic types of organization philosophy, separated, related, dedicated, and integrated. A manager needs to be sensitive to what is his own organization philosophy as it is difficult to change, dangerous to violate to any degree, and has a powerful impact on subordinate expectations.

The typical organization environment is a complex one. While the organization chart appears clear and the standard operating procedures well established, much of importance is not written down. In all organizations there exist expectations about what is appropriate behavior and there are often some aspects of behavior or dress that are almost sacred while there are others which may be safely ignored. That there are major differences among organizations is clear when one compares the basic philosophy of a defence force, the public service, a university, a life insurance company, and a typical factory. Some organizations have a very clear and powerfully expressed philosophy; the military is a good example. The clearly dominant style of the military, as revealed by the management-style-diagnosis test, is dedicated. Like the military, many types of organizations limit the use of the related style; others encourage it. Hutchins and Fiedler (97) found that effective leaders of military units maintain greater than customary psychological distance between themselves and their subordinates. Many aspects of the military's organization philosophy are dedicated or separated in part due to the emphasis on distance, rules, structure, and hierarchy. On the other hand, large administrative organizations have no observable philosophy and have an essentially flat distribution of style demands, giving rise to one student's remark, "The bland leading the bland."

INFLUENCES ON ORGANIZATION PHILOSOPHY

Organization philosophy is shaped from the top and from the past. The primary influences, not in order of importance, are:

Top-man style   The way in which the top man thinks an organization should be run and the way he acts with his own subordinates. In a large organization this top man may be a regional or divisional manager.

Founder style   The impact of the founder can carry on for years or even forever. This is particularly noticeable in religions but is also clearly present in business firms.

Dominant group   Some company executive committees are staffed primarily by one of the following: marketing types, actuaries, engineers, accountants, alumni of another firm, playboys, or even college dropouts. A concentration of any single kind in positions of power will influence organization philosophy.

Dominant family   Families as well as individual founders can exert a profound influence on philosophy particularly, but not necessarily, if the firm is small.

Technology   To a degree organization philosophy is dependent on technology but to a degree it is independent of it. The degree to which one is dependent on the other can be seen by comparing a group of automobile plants with a group of bank offices. The technology within each group is similar and, to a large extent, so is the organization philosophy. However, suppose we compare the two most different automobile plants with the two most different bank offices. We may find that one of these automobile plants is closer in organization philosophy to one of these banks than to the other automobile plant.

Other important influences on organizational philosophy are:

Size
Ratio of workers to managers
Objectives and corporate strategy
National importance and visibility
Legislative control
Degree of external control
Location—isolation
Physical structure

SENSING ORGANIZATIONAL PHILOSOPHY

Organizational philosophy can be sensed very quickly or deduced from the answers to questions like these:

What kind of manager gets ahead?
What behavior is most likely to be rewarded?
What is considered to be a reward?

What behavior is discouraged?
What is considered to be a punishment?
How wide are status differences between levels?
How are mistakes handled?
How is conflict handled?
How are decisions made?
What is the communication network?
What is an acceptable level of performance?
Do people trust each other?
How easy is it to change things?

In some organizations no one ever gets fired; in others the standing quip is, "I wonder who my boss is today." In some organizations any innovation must be cleared by the top of the organization; in others each level is given wide freedom. In some outstanding performance is rewarded; in others it is ignored. Managers, particularly those who have recently entered the organization from a quite different one, have little difficulty in diagnosing organization demands in terms of being one or a combination of integrated, dedicated, related, or separated.

HOW TO ASSESS HUMAN ELEMENTS AND ORGANIZATION DEMANDS

The demands made by superior, coworkers, subordinates, or organization on a manager's behavior may be assessed by using these twenty human element and organization demands indicators, five for each of the basic styles (Exhibit 8.1). The assessment must consider only the demands as seen from a particular managerial position, since demands can be different in different parts of the organization.

SEPARATED HUMAN ELEMENT AND ORGANIZATION INDICATORS

Examine   The degree to which continual careful systematic, and deliberate examination of material, or documents of any kind is expected.
Measure   The degree to which a considerable amount of objective measurement or evaluation of any kind is expected.
Administer   The degree to which conscious and deliberate administration in accordance with existing principles, rules and procedures is expected.
Control   The degree to which close control is expected to avoid variations in any kind of plan, schedule, budget, or design.
Maintain   The degree to which the primary expectation is the maintenance of records.

Related	Integrated
A To trust	A To participate
B To listen	B To interact
C To accept	C To motivate
D To advise	D To integrate
E To encourage	E To innovate
A To examine	A To organize
B To measure	B To initiate
C To administer	C To direct
D To control	D To complete
E To maintain	E To evaluate
Separated	Dedicated

RO

TO

Exhibit 8–1   Human element and organization demands indicators. These twenty indicators can be used to discover the range of style demanded by any of superior, coworkers, subordinates, or organization.

RELATED HUMAN ELEMENT AND ORGANIZATION INDICATORS

Trust   The degree to which absolute trust and open candid communication across departmental or status and power levels is expected.

Listen   The degree to which attentive sincerely interested listening, sometimes over long periods, is expected.

Accept   The degree to which complete, active, genuine acceptance of other's motives and actions is expected even when sharply different from one's own.

Advise   The degree to which a considerable amount of helpful friendly advice is expected.

Encourage   The degree to which extensive approving and sympathetic encouragement is expected.

DEDICATED HUMAN ELEMENT AND ORGANIZATION INDICATORS

Organize The degree to which extensive planning and regular re-organization of work is expected.

Initiate The degree to which many new tasks are expected to be initiated independently.

Direct The degree to which a considerable amount of active direction of the work of others is expected.

Complete The degree to which it is expected that the primary consideration is to complete the immediate task at hand.

Evaluate The degree to which rigorous evaluation of performance is expected and appropriate action taken.

INTEGRATED HUMAN ELEMENT AND ORGANIZATION INDICATORS

Participate The degree to which it is expected that most decision making will be by fully participative methods.

Interact The degree to which a considerable amount of task oriented interpersonal interaction is expected.

Motivate The degree to which a considerable and approximately equal amount of both relationships orientation and task orientation is expected to be used in the influence process.

Integrate The degree to which individual needs and organizational goals are expected to be suitably balanced and seen as one.

Innovate The degree to which a very high number of original ideas concerning methods of improving both relationships and production is expected.

To use these indicators, select the particular element in question, say organization, and ask "which indicators best describe how the manager should now act as far as the organization as a whole is concerned so that his managerial effectiveness is increased?" It is difficult to be precise, but a reasonable degree of accuracy may be obtained. If all the separated indicators apply and none other, the organization is clearly making separated demands on the manager's behavior. It usually happens that one or another set of basic style indicators is dominant but not exclusively so.

It is important to understand that this appraisal of demands is not the same as an appraisal of style though they are often the same. The organization in the example just given is not being appraised. What is being appraised are the demands this organization makes on the manager him-

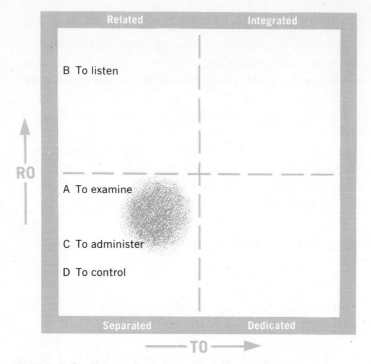

Exhibit 8–2 Organization demands of a public servant in an administrative position.

self, that is, how the manager himself needs to respond to the organization so the manager's effectiveness is increased.

VIEWS OF ORGANIZATION PHILOSOPHY DEMANDS

Here are some examples of how the organization philosophy demands would be seen from each of five different positions. As no particular person or particular organization is being considered, there is room for alternative answers. Use these examples to grasp the general idea.

A public servant in an administrative position would be likely to see

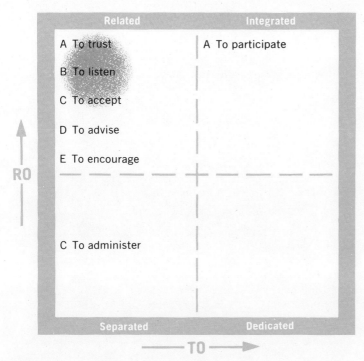

Exhibit 8–3   Organization demands of a university department head.

the organization demands on him as shown in Exhibit 8.2. Notice that most of the demands are in the separated style. At high levels in the public service demands are often sharply different from this. Effective managers in the public service learn about this quickly and so avoid unsuccessful attempts at carrying the wrong style upward.

While universities do vary somewhat in their organization philosophy, and while department heads have different perceptions of what is demanded, the demands as seen from such a position generally look something like Exhibit 8.3. The colleague relationships demanded produce related demands while the examination and to some extent information distribution function can produce more separated demand than are shown here.

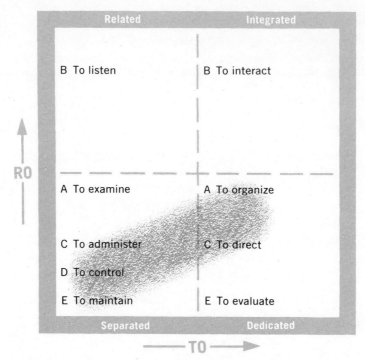

Exhibit 8–4   Organization demands of an army captain in peacetime.

An army captain in peacetime might have a view of the organization demands as shown in Exhibit 8.4. At this level the military is customarily separated-dedicated in peacetime and moves to dedicated in wartime. Outside the unit level, at headquarters, demands tend to have a higher integrated-related component in peacetime, but they also tend to move to dedicated in times of war.

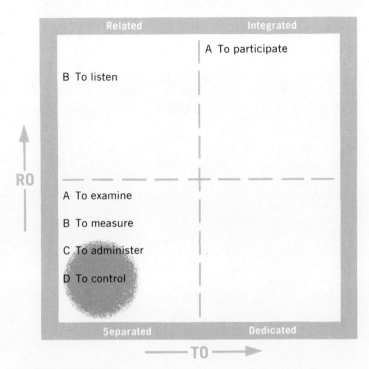

Exhibit 8–5   Organization demands of a personnel manager.

The function of the personnel manager is now changing. Most of the mid-20s to mid-60s type would probably see organization demands as shown in Exhibit 8.5. The position has had essentially bureaucratic organization demands and most personnel managers would prefer to see the demands change. Some have succeeded in moving to what is essentially a role of internal behavioral consultant.

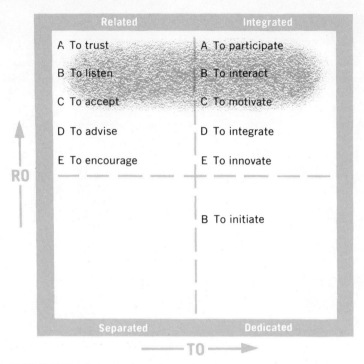

Exhibit 8–6 Organization demands of an internal behavioral consultant.

An internal behavioral consultant was asked to describe how he saw his organization demands which he thought of as shown in Exhibit 8.6. His position was essentially "internal change agent," and this was generally understood and accepted by the organization. He saw his job as "getting the organization to where it wants to go" with no real direction from him.

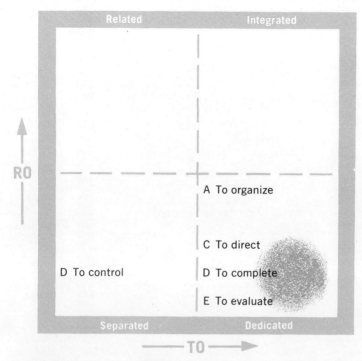

Exhibit 8–7   Superior's demands of a foreman in a heavy machinery plant by his superior, the general foreman.

VIEWS OF SUPERIOR'S DEMANDS

The foreman in a heavy machinery plant might see the demands being made of him by his superior, the general foreman, as shown in Exhibit 8.7. The dedicated style, while appropriate here, would be most inappropriate on a marketing team.

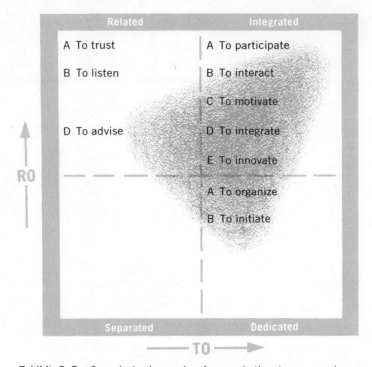

Exhibit 8–8 Superior's demands of a marketing team member by his superior, the vice-president of marketing.

A marketing team member might see the demands shown in Exhibit 8.8 as being made on him by his superior, the vice president of marketing. True teamwork usually requires the integrated style. Not all teams work in this way.

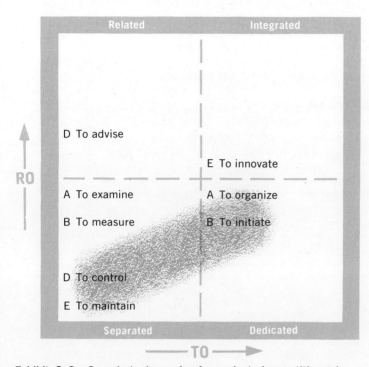

Exhibit 8–9   Superior's demands of a work study practitioner by his superior, the production manager.

A work study practitioner might see the demands shown in Exhibit 8.9 as being made on him by his superior, the production manager. If the practitioner had a major implementation responsibility, some additional related and dedicated demands would appear.

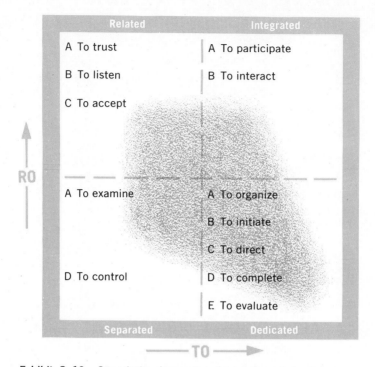

Exhibit 8–10 Superior's demands of an army brigade commander by his superior, the divisional commander, in wartime.

An army brigade commander, in wartime, might see the demands shown in Exhibit 8.10 as being made on him by his superior, the divisional commander.

In times of peace, these demands would most probably make a shift over to integrated-related. However, the personal style of the army brigade commander's superior, the divisional commander, could in fact cause a shift in the demands anywhere.

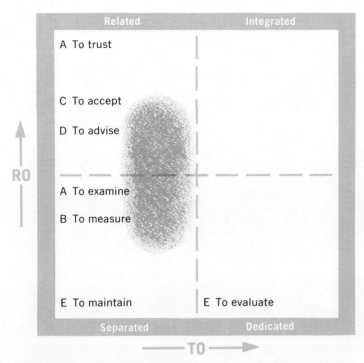

Exhibit 8–11   Coworker's demands of a head of design from his coworker, the head of engineering.

VIEWS OF COWORKERS' DEMANDS

Coworkers' demands may very sharply, but technology is a major factor in shaping them which can often predict fairly well what they would be.

A design head might see the demands of Exhibit 8.11 as being made by his coworker, the head engineer. This is a rough approximation—much will depend on how each man sees his job and responsibilities.

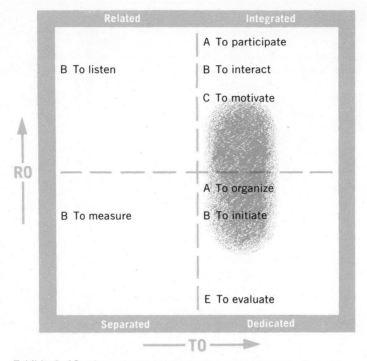

Exhibit 8–12   Coworker's demands of a sales manager from his coworker, the advertising manager.

A sales manager might see the demands shown in Exhibit 8.12 as being made on him by his coworker, the advertising manager.

As in the previous example, the demands could be quite different from this. It depends on the individuals involved and to some extent on the style of their superior, the marketing manager.

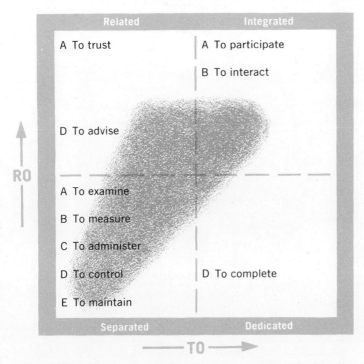

Exhibit 8–13   Coworker's demands of an accounting team making an audit.

An accounting team making an audit might see the demands shown in Exhibit 8.13 as being made by each other.

The high degree of joint responsibility for accuracy produces these separated demands. The professional relationship produces the related-integrated demands.

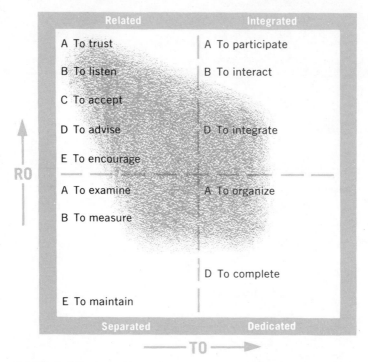

Exhibit 8–14 Coworker's demands of collaborating physical science researchers.

Collaborating physical science researchers might see the demands shown in Exhibit 8.14 as being made on each other.

Scientific researchers have often been considered difficult to manage, and this together with their profit potential has led to the fact that much is being written about how to manage them. The flex of the demands here gives some clue to the high degree of job enrichment which is inherent in their position. Failure by a superior to recognize this would have a tendency to contribute to low effectiveness.

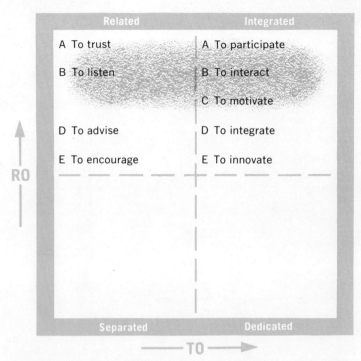

Exhibit 8–15 Subordinate demands of a president from his general manager in a one-over-one relationship.

VIEW OF SUBORDINATE'S DEMANDS

While very powerful, subordinate demands are often easy to modify, and so these examples, again, should be considered as indications and not absolutes.

A president might see the demands of Exhibit 8.15 as being made by his subordinate, the general manager, in a one-over-one relationship. Like many such senior relationships over policy, demands are integrated-related.

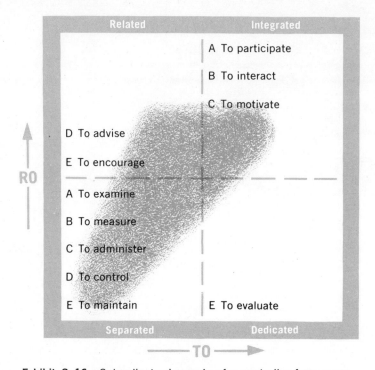

Exhibit 8–16 Subordinate demands of a controller from a professional accountant reporting to him.

A controller might see the demands shown in Exhibit 8.16 as being made on him by one of his subordinates, an accountant.

The nature of the responsibility produces the separated demands. The nature of the professional relationship produces the integrated-related demands.

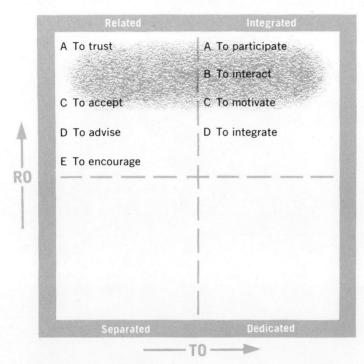

Exhibit 8–17   Subordinate demands of a middle manager from a newly minted active M.B.A.

A middle manager might see the demands shown in Exhibit 8.17 as being made on him by a newly minted active graduate with a master's degree in business administration.

The new man may wish to be treated, as is shown here, as a senior associate from the start.

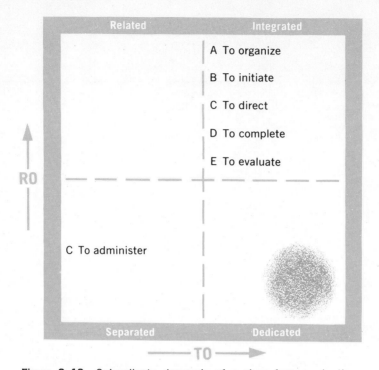

Figure 8–18 Subordinate demands of a shop foreman in the United States from a recently arrived immigrant from northern Europe.

A shop foreman in the United States might see the demands shown in Exhibit 8.18 as being made on him from a recently arrived immigrant from northern Europe.

Cultures vary in what is seen as the ideal superior-subordinate relationship. Northern Europeans general expect and receive dedicated behavior.

My intention being to write something of use to those who understand, it appears to me more proper to go to the real truth of the matter than to its imagination; and many have imagined republics and principalities which have never been seen or known to exist in reality; for how we live is so far removed from how we ought to live, that he who abandons what is done for what ought to be done will rather learn to bring about his own ruin than his preservation.

MACHIAVELLI

Chapter Nine

COMMON SITUATIONAL PROBLEMS

Up to now each situational element has been looked at individually. All the observations can be brought together however so that an appraisal of the total situation is made. This appraisal can be depicted on a *situational flex map*. This and the next chapter teach how to draw and use them.

In addition to their use in situational appraisal, these maps are excellent devices as an aid in counseling. They are usable with counselees having no prior acquaintance with 3-D. Their primary use however is to enable a manager to obtain formal practice in sizing up situations so that after such training he can decide on more appropriate courses of action that he could before it.

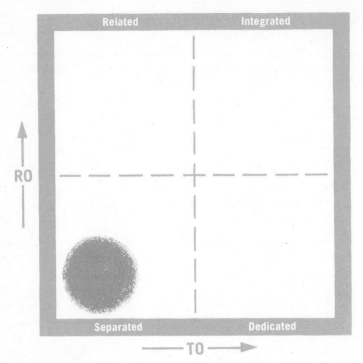

Exhibit 9–1 A manager may be capable of using only the separated style.

The flex map is based on the same simple two-dimensional chart used to depict basic style and flex. As explained in Chapter 5, a manager's basic style and flex may be represented as shown in Exhibit 9.1. The shaded area depicts the flex of a manager who is basically separated. On situational flex maps, as shown here, the manager's flex is always shaded to distinguish it from that of the five situational elements.

One or more of the situational elements can be depicted on the same map. Their position and shape indicate the demands they make on the manager's basic style.

Suppose this separated manager were in a situation dealing with one

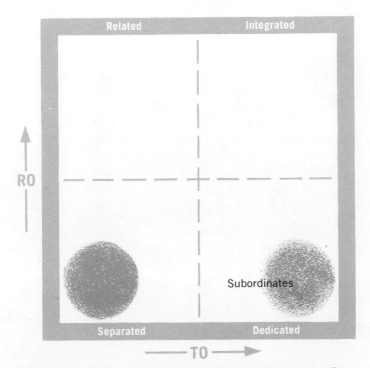

Related   Integrated

RO

Subordinates

Separated   Dedicated

TO ➝

Exhibit 9–2   Stand off. A separated manager will not be effective if he should use the dedicated style with his subordinates but cannot.

or more subordinates who expected him to be highly task-oriented. In other words, the particular situational element involving subordinates demanded a dedicated style in order for it to contribute to effectiveness. This situation could be depicted as shown in Exhibit 9.2. Clearly it is a problem situation, as effectiveness cannot occur. The manager does not have the flex to deal with the demands of the subordinates. It is called "stand off" to indicate that neither the manager nor his subordinates will flex to accommodate the other. Faced with a situation like this, a manager has the alternatives of changing his style, increasing his flex, or changing the demands the subordinates are making.

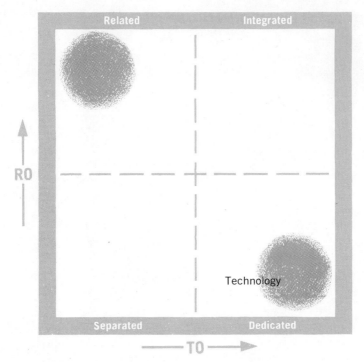

Exhibit 9–3   Mismatch. A related manager may be pleasant but cannot be effective if the technology is dedicated.

Another situation familiar to most managers is "mismatch," which represents a manager in the wrong job. In the situation depicted in Exhibit 9.3, the manager is highly related yet the technology demands dedicated behavior. This kind of mismatch can occur in a variety of ways. The principle, however, is that the manager cannot meet the style demands of the technology. A successful military commander, when posted to a capital city staff job where he cannot fire his secretary, sometimes experiences mismatch, just as the scientist promoted to manager might. The possibility of mismatch is lessened if the manager or the technology has high flex. Introducing technology flex is also called "job enrichment." This can

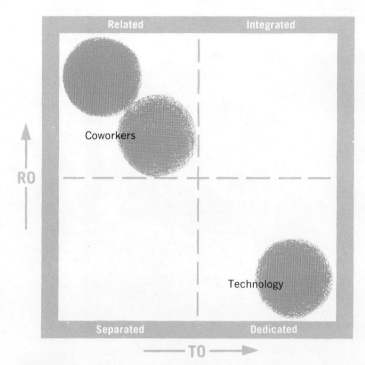

Exhibit 9–4   "Let's not fight." A manager and others with whom he works decide not to behave in a task-oriented manner even though the technology demands it.

mean designing jobs with sufficient flex so that, within limits, the job can suit the man. This idea is easier to apply if combined with flexible job trading; then other managers pick up the unwanted part of the job.

This mismatch may be compounded if, in addition to the manager, the superior or subordinates or coworkers are also related while the technology remains dedicated. This produces the "let's not fight," situation shown in Exhibit 9.4. This warm, highly related situation is essentially a missionary one. If the department has no real job to do, interacts little with other departments, and has no established effectiveness standards, the situation could continue unchecked.

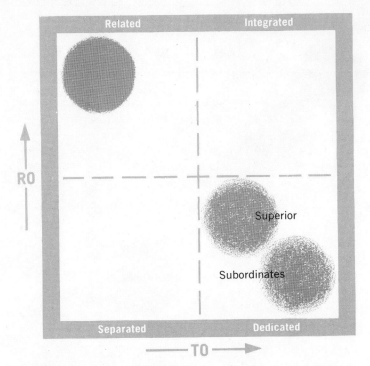

Exhibit 9–5 "Let me help." A manager who is related when dedicated behavior toward superior and subordinates is needed if the manager is to be effective.

Another situation, "let me help," arises when a manager is related but all the *situational elements* demand something else (Exhibit 9.5). The manager wants to help when the situation demands that he direct. The manager may be liked but he will not be effective. Thus he will be seen as a friendly missionary.

An opposite situation occurs when subordinates, because of the technology, have strong expectations that the manager should behave in a related way, yet the manager does not share these expectations. The sub-

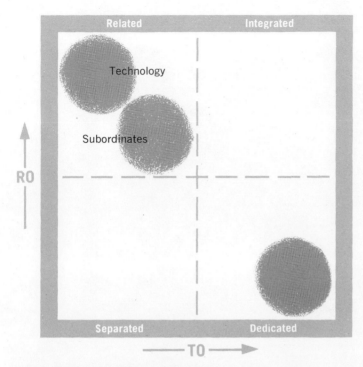

Exhibit 9–6 "He doesn't understand us." A new manager may want to sweep clean when things have been cosy before.

ordinates may expect their manager to take a personal interest in them, have long conversations with them, and go to bat for them even when they may be at fault. The manager, on the other hand, may believe he should act in a dedicated way, push for production, keep a tight check on output and timings, and generally take an interest in output rather than subordinates. This leads to a "he doesn't understand us" situation where the manager is using dedicated behavior inappropriately (Exhibit 9.6). He is then seen as an autocrat.

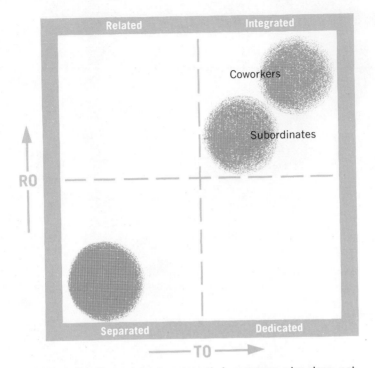

Exhibit 9–7 "I want to be alone." A manager who does not want to get involved might as well not be there.

Some managers are basically separated, and nothing will change them. They may remain passive and uninvolved in a situation where the integrated style, or some other, is demanded (Exhibit 9.7). A manager in a situation like this who suggests "I want to be alone," will be labeled a "deserter."

The "tightrope" situation (Exhibit 9.8) occurs when a manager is faced with two situational elements with conflicting demands. The subordinates

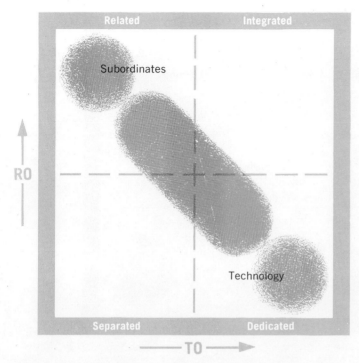

Exhibit 9–8   Tightrope. A manager sometimes does a balancing act between antagonistic situational demands.

may wish to be treated in a separated way and the technology may demand the dedicated style. Instead of matching the two demands, the manager may attempt to satisfy both independently. He in effect uses himself as a link. He might for instance continue to treat subordinates warmly and not push them and in effect do himself what they should be doing about the technology.

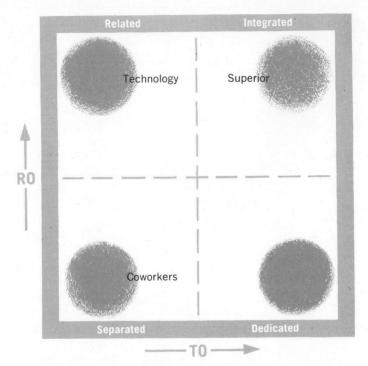

Exhibit 9–9 "How did we get into this mess?" "If you can keep your head when all about you are losing theirs, maybe you just don't understand the situation."

Sometimes everything goes wrong and the situation might be depicted as in Exhibit 9.9 and described as, "How did we get into this mess?" At some time in every manager's career, he sees the situation somewhat this way, but fortunately something almost always changes to bring about effectiveness.

This chapter has explained the basic concept of the situational flex map. The next chapter pins down things more tightly.

The task of administration is so to design the environment that the individual will approach as close as practicable to rationality (judged in terms of the organization's goals) in his decision.

HERBERT A. SIMON

Structural relationships are not once and for all prescriptions but are "rules of the game" which are adaptable to changing situations and the changing desires of the participants.

OGDEN H. HALL

Chapter Ten

SITUATIONAL DYNAMICS

This chapter shows how to put flex maps to practical use. It explains how to use them to determine whether managerial effectiveness is occurring or is likely to occur, and, if not, which things to change so that it does.

SPECIFYING THE SITUATION

The total situation a manager is in is composed of many different specific situations, each of which can be represented on a different flex map. One situation may be primarily with his superior, which together with organization and technology may compose three dominant elements. Another situation may be with his subordinates, in which technology demands will often be a dominant element. While not common, it is possible that several situations with quite different style and flex characteristics occur with the superior alone. It may be that quite different style demands spring from superior and long-run policy, and say superior and union relationships. Clearly the situation being described on a flex map must be plainly specified, first by the name of the manager involved and next by some other more specific descriptive label which might be "before change occurred" or "involvement with unions" or something else. After the situation is specified, the dominant elements are identified.

DOMINANT ELEMENTS   Not all five elements make demands in all situations, and those present are not usually of equal strength. In some situations technology is of most importance with perhaps organization and coworkers being of no importance at all. Therefore it is rarely, if ever, necessary to depict all five elements on a single flex map. Apart from the problem of visual complexity, the elements are seldom all sufficiently powerful to warrant inclusion. Two or three *dominant elements* are usually selected and drawn.

ELEMENT STRENGTH   Even the dominant elements will normally vary in relative strength. This is indicated by distributing 10 points over the dominant elements to indicate strength. If there are two elements, and they are of equal strength, for instance, then each has 5 points allocated to it.

When allocating strength to the various elements, it is useful to think of them as five things impinging on a situation a manager is in. In the hypothetical example found in Exhibit 10.1 organization is weighted 2, technology is weighted 3, and superior is weighted 5.

In Exhibit 10.2 the same points allocated to strength may be indicated on a flex map by a number at the boundary of the flex line. The more dominant elements with higher numbers may also be indicated by a thicker boundary on the flex lines, so that in this example, superior, weighted 5, would be drawn with a thicker boundary than organization, weighted 2. The only reason for doing this would be to make the flex map easier to read. Allocating strength to the elements is a skill not easily taught by a book. The question the manager must ask and answer is: "What is really important in this situation which most influences my behavior?" The

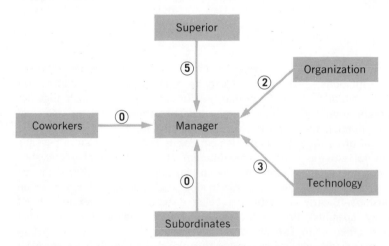

Exhibit 10–1   Element strength. Total element strength always adds up to ten and usually the strength of one or more of the five elements is zero.

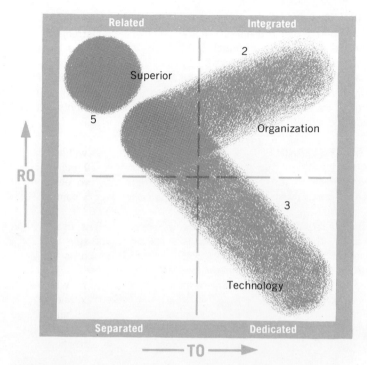

Exhibit 10–2   Element strength on flex map. Element strength is shown on a flex map by a number cut into the flex shape. The size or position of the flex shape has nothing to do with element strength.

strength of both organization and technology tend to be underrated, and the strength of superior overrated. Organization and technology are less visible, but can be just as powerful as the other three elements.

AREA OF EFFECTIVENESS

A situational flex map usually has the flex of at least one element represented on it, together with the flex of the manager himself. A flex map with the single element, technology, and the manager drawn on it could look like that in Exhibit 10.3. This map shows a basically integrated manager whose flex is roughly an equal mixture of TO and RO. It also shows technology demands that are basically related-integrated. The area where the technology flex intersects with the manager's flex is shaded heavily. This is the *area of effectiveness.*

The area of effectiveness is the area on a flex map where the flex of all the dominant situational elements intersect with the manager's style flex. It represents, then, the type of behavior the manager can and must use if the demands of all the situational elements are to be satisfied.

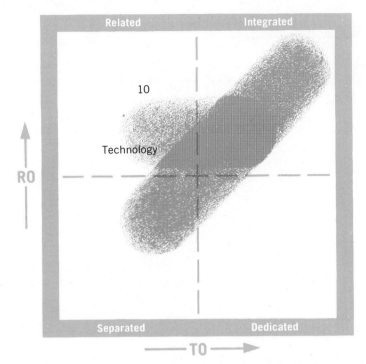

Exhibit 10–3 Area of effectiveness. The area of effectiveness occurs where the manager's flex intersects with the flex of all the elements drawn.

It is clear that a manager's skill in situational sensitivity, style flexibility, and situational management will increase the possibility of effectiveness occurring at all. An important part of any manager's job is to sense, modify, integrate, and then satisfy the demands of the situational elements. This is the same as asking him to create or to enlarge his area of effectiveness.

Managerial effectiveness does not increase as the size of the area of effectiveness increases. As long as the area occurs at all, in any size, the manager has a point at which he personally is capable of operating and, at the same time, satisfying the style demands of all the dominant elements. A large area simply guarantees that the area has stability over time. It is less likely to disappear owing to minor changes in the demands or flex of the elements.

AREA OF POSSIBLE EFFECTIVENESS   It can happen that while the situational elements make some common demands on style, the manager's flex does not intersect with that of the situational elements.

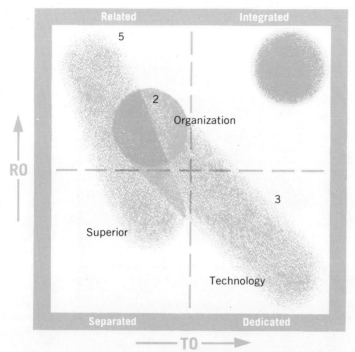

Exhibit 10–4   Area of possible effectiveness. Sometimes the flex of the elements intersect but the manager is not "where it's at."

Exhibit 10.4 shows three elements, organization, technology, and superior, whose flex intersect. The intersection of the flex of the situational elements is called the *area of possible effectiveness* and is always shaded as is the manager's flex. In the situation, the manager is shown as integrated, and his flex does not intersect with the area of possible effectiveness. He will have to change his own style or the style demands of all three elements in order to achieve managerial effectiveness. It is obvious what he should attempt first.

SITUATIONAL FLEX FORM

Prior to actually drawing a flex map, it is useful to make a note of the name of the manager, the situation being considered, his basic style and flex, and the strength and degree of demands of the elements. It takes the form shown in Exhibit 10.5.

The data on this flex form represent the flex map of Exhibit 10.3 showing the area of effectiveness. The manager is basically integrated-separated

Manager	Situation	Basic	Flex
S. Keith	Ongoing	I-S	1

Elements	Strength	Style demands			
		S	R	D	I
Organization	0	0	0	0	0
Technology	10	0	2-3	0	2-3
Superior	0	0	0	0	0
Coworkers	0	0	0	0	0
Subordinates	0	0	0	0	0

II
10

Exhibit 10–5 Situational-flex form: area of effectiveness. This is Exhibit 10–3 stated another way.

and this is shown by an I-S while his flex is estimated as 1. Only one element, technology, is shown on the map, and so it has a strength of 10. The element has related-integrated demands of 2-3.

The flex form shown in Exhibit 10.6 represents the flex map of Exhibit 10.4 showing the area of possible effectiveness.

USES OF FLEX MAPS

Flex maps do not provide answers but do allow a manager to see his alternatives. Flex maps are essentially a method of disciplined enquiry into a situation. Managers find that drawing them leads to the identification of problems and opportunities for exercising situational management they had not earlier considered. They are only as sound as the manager's situational sensitivity. As with computers, "gigo" (garbage in, garbage out) applies. They are only as useful as his skills in style flexibility and situational management.

Flex maps point up sharply that no one style is necessarily best and that situational management and style flexibility are key managerial skills. They reveal the variety of strategies available for improving managerial effectiveness. To increase his effectiveness, a manager may not need to change himself at all. Instead he could improve his selection of subordinates for particular jobs, modify subordinates' expectations, increase technology flex, or many other things.

Manager	Situation	Basic	Flex
D. Walling	On joining department	I	0-1

Elements	Strength	Style demands			
		S	R	D	I
Organization	2	0	2-3	0	0
Technology	3	0	2-3	4-5	0
Superior	5	2-3	4-5	0	0
Coworkers	0	0	0	0	0
Subordinates	0	0	0	0	0

II

10

Exhibit 10–6 Situational-flex form: area of possible effectiveness. This is Exhibit 10–4 stated another way.

Also, flex maps are very useful in counseling. They provide a dramatic and clear picture of the situation under discussion. When the counselee has drawn the flex map, it usually becomes quite clear to him what his options are and what action he should take.

Flex maps are used primarily to depict a single situation at one point in time. Usually, the demands of the elements are sufficiently constant over time that a map may be considered to represent a continuing situation.

ADDING OTHER ELEMENTS

The five situational elements provide a way of making sense out of a confusing situation. They break the total situation into smaller pieces which can be viewed separately. The elements are intended to be inclusive, that is, from among them, all parts of a situation can be described. Some things, such as unions, economic fluctuations, and domestic arguments, which at first appear to have little relationship to the elements, can be built into flex maps. For a first-line manager the impact of a militant union is typically expressed through subordinates' expectations, while at higher levels of management it is expressed through the organization philosophy. In effect, the subordinates' expectations of the way they should be treated are the expression of union militancy while the organization philosophy is the response. The subordinates' expectations generally move toward related demands while organization philosophy is moved toward dedicated demands. The impact of a recession is typically expressed through subordinates' and superior's expectations at every level. Generally, both subordinates and a superior tend to move their expectations to dedicated.

A domestic argument is not expressed in terms of the situational elements. The impact of such an argument is on the manager himself, not directly on the situation he is in. Such an event might result in a lower RO with little change in TO. While this is an oversimplification, the point it shows is that anything affecting the manager himself affects his own TO and RO, not one of the five situational elements.

While the five situational elements can be considered inclusive, they are not sacred. These five apply to all management positions and in most cases are all that is needed. However, if desired, such additional elements as "unions" or "customers" or others may be added. As indicated, however, these can often be included as a component of one of the other elements. Customers may be considered as an aspect of technology or as coworkers.

EASE OF CHANGING ELEMENT AND DEMANDS

The situational elements vary in the ease with which their demands can be changed in this order: technology, subordinates, coworkers, superior, and organization. That is, technology is usually most easily changed, subordinates next, coworkers are harder to change, and superior and organization philosophy are usually the most difficult to change. The element that varies most in its change susceptibility is technology. Some managers can change their technology with relative ease. Other managers may have virtually no control over the nature and demands of their technology.

MANAGING SITUATIONS

A manager should not simply respond to situations but also should manage them. A manager should see all situations as opportunities for situational management, that is, opportunities to so arrange the situation that all elements work with, rather than against, each other. Career success is not best explained as a result of luck but as a result of skill used day after day—skill in reading a situation, adapting to it if appropriate, and changing it if necessary and possible.

It is hardly necessary to look at formal research studies to make this point. We have all witnessed cases like this:

> As with many ambitious young managers, Joe Grimes had ideas about his new job. As the newly appointed marketing manager in a firm that was not marketing-oriented, he knew change would be resisted. He first

made a thorough analysis of the situation and then formulated a plan. He carefully considered the restraining forces he had to deal with. A major one was the controller, who made it clear he was interested solely in budgetary controls and who saw advertising as an expense rather than as an investment. Grimes considered the expectations his superior, the manager of production, had about the way he would behave the first few months on the job and to what extent he could modify these expectations. As he analyzed the situational elements, he made a shrewd appraisal of those which he had to adapt to and those which he could change in the long or short run. He also thought about the president's values and managerial philosophy. He then worked within the constraints of the system in order to change it. He did not frontally attack the controller and ask for a doubled budget. He started, rather, by satisfying the controller's desire for tight control. He then worked with the controller on a measuring system for the marketing department's work. Next, he sold this idea to his superior for use in all his superior's departments. He treated each man differently and waited, when waiting was necessary. He saw the firm as an integrated system that he had to study and understand, not simply as pockets of resistance to his ideas. He then considered how to free the marketing function from the production function. He discovered what advantages his superior, the manager of production, saw in the existing system and what reservations he had about its being moved. He particularly considered his superior's future plans and in what way the marketing department helped or hindered them. He not only considered the total system of which he was a part but also each manager individually.

What did Grimes have? We could call it simply good judgment for it was obviously that. A clearer description of Grimes' qualifications would see him as having situational sensitivity, style flexibility, and situational management skill.

THREE MANAGERIAL SKILLS

From the central principle of the 3-D Theory that managerial effectiveness results from a match of style to situation, the three key skills of an effective manager may be logically described as situational sensitivity skill, style flexibility skill, and situational management skill. A manager needs situational sensitivity to diagnose a situation and either style flexibility to match his style to it or situational management skill to change the situation itself. The acquisition of situational sensitivity, style flexibility, and situational management skill is usually called experience. Together they bring to mind a prayer of St. Francis of Assisi, demonstrating that social science can draw on the old as well as the new:

THE SITUATIONIST'S PRAYER	3-D THEORY
O Lord—	
Give me the serenity to accept what cannot be changed,	Style flexibility
The courage to change what should be changed,	Situational management skill
And the wisdom to distinguish one from the other	Situational sensitivity

It is these three qualities, then, that a manager acquires through his working life, and that can lead directly to increased managerial effectiveness. Future chapters will look at each of these key skills.

New Concepts Introduced

AREA OF EFFECTIVENESS	DOMINANT ELEMENTS
AREA OF POSSIBLE EFFECTIVENESS	ELEMENT STRENGTH
SITUATIONAL FLEX MAP (FLEX MAP)	MANAGERIAL SKILLS

Area of Effectiveness   The area on a situational flex map where the flex of all the dominant elements intersect with the manager's style flex.

Area of Possible Effectiveness   The area on a situational flex map where the flex of all the dominant situational elements intersect.

Dominant Elements   Those elements, in a particular situation, which make the strongest demands on a manager's basic style.

Element Strength   The relative strength of a dominant element in a particular situation expressed as some part of a total of 10 points.

Managerial Skills   Three skills required for managerial effectiveness: situational management, situational sensitivity, style flexibility.

Situational Flex Map (Flex Map)   A chart depicting the element flex of the dominant situational elements and the basic style of the manager.

To be great, to be a person of stature, a man must have character, judgment, high intelligence, a special aptitude for seeing his problems whole and true—for seeing things as they are, without exaggeration or emotion.

FIELD MARSHAL MONTGOMERY

Chapter Eleven

SITUATIONAL SENSITIVITY

A key managerial skill is the ability to size up a situation. A manager with the sensitivity to read a situation for what it actually contains, and the sensitivity to know what behavior would actually constitute effectiveness in it, is more likely to be effective (46). *Situational sensitivity is the ability to read situations correctly for what they really contain.* In 3-D language, it is the ability to appraise the five situational elements in terms of their task and relationships demands, their flex, and their relative strength.

Age and experience do tend to improve situational sensitivity as this skill is a component of experience. However young managers just out of college sometimes show a brilliant understanding of situations and of what must be done to produce effectiveness. They know when to push hard, when not to, whom to see, and the appropriate timing. The sensitive manager will know what resistances stand in the way of being effective and what he can overcome and must overcome to be effective. Although situational sensitivity is seldom perfect, the manager can learn ways to improve it.

Sensitivity requires intellectual alertness and curiosity. The sensitive manager fits scraps of information and hunches together. Like any social scientist, he looks at details to construct the whole. From a firebed and an arrowhead, an anthropologist constructs a civilization. From the way in which a policy is received by different divisions, a sensitive manager can construct the reality of power politics in an organization.

Situational sensitivity is a particularly useful skill when dealing with other departments. As often occurs in such situations, the manager has no real power. He must elicit cooperation based on mutual understanding. He is more likely to be effective if he pays some attention to the realities and the fantasies of how each department operates, who the key people are, where the power really lies. While useful, sensitivity is not such a crucial skill in stable or highly structured environments. When a manager is trained for years for a particular kind of situation which is unchanging, his need for sensitivity decreases. In some such situations it may even be a hindrance because the manager may be acutely aware of what is needed yet be unable to do anything about it.

For the new man in any position, situational sensitivity is crucial. He simply must know the answer to the question, "What does it take to be effective here?"

DO NOT TRUST TO LUCK   Many highly sensitive managers, politicians, or, for that matter, entrepreneurs are often described as lucky. The term "luck," like magic, is really simply a device to explain what is to some an otherwise inexplicable outcome. Luck seldom explains managerial effectiveness. The manager in the right place at the right time with the appropriate resources did not come there solely by chance, although it may appear that way. He very often understood the existing or potential situation and was prepared for the opportunities as they came.

Managers with low sensitivity tend to have more difficulty than others in learning 3-D. The 3-D Theory was designed to be reasonably free of bias and of any particular ideology save managerial effectiveness. Unlike many theories it does not suggest that flexibility, resilience, or relationships are always good. It operates this way, in part, through the use of tight definitions and a situational approach. Some managers have difficulty in learning 3-D because they cannot see the difference between one situation and another. Without some skill at this level, it is impossible to understand the usefulness of 3-D, let alone have the skill to use it.

SITUATIONAL-SENSITIVITY SCALE   Like style flex and situational management skill, a manager's degree of situational sensitivity is expressed on a five-point scale:

0 Very low
1 Low
2 Moderate
3 High
4 Very high

Although skill in situational sensitivity varies widely from manager to manager, it can be improved by experience and training and by an understanding of the reasons which lead all of us to distort the real world.

Situational Insensitivity

For a variety of reasons we sometimes are unconsciously not interested in making a sound situational diagnosis. It may be that if we made a realistic diagnosis, we would discover things we do not like, or things we simply do not want to know, or things we do not know how to handle. The main, unconscious mental protective devices we use are known as defense mechanisms originally proposed by Sigmund Freud. The main defense mechanisms managers should be aware of in themselves and others are *rationalization* (inventing reasons) and *projection* (it's you, not me).

Defense mechanisms are not necessarily psychologically unhealthy. All healthy personalities need temporary protection from time to time. The problem occurs when the temporary protection turns into a permanent drop in situational sensitivity, to a distortion of reality.

The defense mechanisms operate entirely outside a manager's awareness. They operate in the unconscious. They serve to hide or to shield him from what is unacceptable, threatening, or repugnant in the situation so that these things become unrecognized or unacknowledged. In layman's language, defense mechanisms give us blind spots we unconsciously think we need.

In addition to the two mechanisms of rationalization and projection, the following five factors also lead to low sensitivity: *negative adaptation* (accepting things as they are), *symptoms for causes* (mistaking appearance for cause), *lack of conceptual language* (not talking the same language), *limiting value system* (having one test for everything), and *high levels of anxiety* (being a worrier).

RATIONALIZATION (INVENTING REASONS)

Rationalization involves inventing and accepting interpretations which an impartial analysis would not substantiate. It is kidding ourselves about what the world is really like. Rationalization serves to conceal motives and impulses that are unacceptable. It also serves to construct our view of the situation in such a way that the problem is in the situation, not in ourselves. The justification of such interpretation usually involves giving socially acceptable reasons for behavior or apparently logical reasons for the view of the situation. In business life, what is rationalized in this way is usually believed by the manager but is often not believed or understood by the listener.

All managers are familiar with rationalization. They see it in the manager passed over for promotion who decided he did not want it anyway. This is called "sour grapes" (after the fable about the fox who could not get at some grapes and who then decided they were sour). Managers who continually "sour grape" may turn into one.

A manager transferred against his wishes may later find that he likes his new job. This is called "sweet lemon" to suggest that we invest an unpleasant object or event with positive references when it is forced on us. It is clear that rationalization at times is an excellent adaptive mechanism which enables us to meet negative circumstances. The change in opinion, of course, might be real and based on objective reality. In this case this is not rationalization but a factual reappraisal.

A manager who is consistently late with his reports finds many ways to rationalize his behavior. He may blame subordinates, overwork, or unanticipated problems. For none of these delays, he feels, can he be held responsible. The real reasons may be fear of being evaluated by the report, unconsciously wanting to inconvenience report recipients, or simply incompetence. These real reasons are not known to him. If he knows them and still puts excuses forward, he is not rationalizing. He is lying.

Rationalization is not rare. Whereas some managers use it so much it incapacitates them, most use it to some extent: "The job was not completed because other things came up," "The promotion was missed because the superior was biased," "The subordinate was fired because he was incompetent."

Ordinary levels of rationalization cannot be regarded as serious, but overuse can assume exaggerated proportions. An incompetent manager, with a high need for achievement and an excessive fear of failure, might easily develop almost pathological rationalizations, perhaps leading to delusions of persecution. He might believe that his superior "has it in for him." This rationalization may protect him from facing the real reasons for failure and lack of promotion. The overuse of rationalization may so remove a manager from his real problems that he may end up with a crisis that cannot be solved. If we "save face" too much, we may simply end up without a true identity.

Rationalization is sometimes excusable on the grounds that it eases the shock of an unpleasant situation. It softens our misgivings about ourselves, eases our conscience, and enables us to restructure reality slowly so that it does not affront our view of ourselves. Some would say if we did not rationalize, we would go crazy. There is truth in this for less effective managers. For the effective manager, however, there is no substitute for reading a situation clearly, facing it squarely, and dealing with it realistically.

The problem with rationalization is not so much that we fool ourselves but that it provides no guidelines for appropriate action. The essential ingredient of rationalization is distortion to protect ourselves. This distorted perception leads to the identification of the wrong elements to change. Typically a manager who is rationalizing may want to change others or perhaps the technology, when he really should change himself.

College students who do not participate enough in case-study classes usually have a set of rationalizations to explain their behavior. These include: "Too many talk with nothing to say," "Still water runs deep," "We should have a public speaking course," and even, "I was quiet when a child."

The best tip-off to rationalization in ourselves or others is the too perfect, too logical, or too consistent explanation. Life is fairly complex, and somewhat tentative explanations are what we usually must use. The rationalization, however, is usually a logical masterpiece. All the bits fit together to make a perfect cover-up story. Another tip-off is the insistence with which the rationalization is offered as an explanation. Shakespeare illuminated this with "The lady doth protest too much, methinks." Winston Churchill was said to have sometimes written in the margin of his speeches, "weak point—shout."

PROJECTION (IT'S YOU, NOT ME)

Projection is seeing in others what we do not want to see and cannot see in ourselves. It operates primarily in those with low-style awareness— those who do not know how they, in fact, behave.

The mechanism is most clearly seen in delusions of persecution. A new manager may be in the process of making changes in his department. Not all will like the changes, and each will react somewhat differently. A subordinate might feel aggressive toward this new manager but, because of his social training, may not express it or even be aware of it in himself. By the mechanism of projection, he then may suspect his manager of having these feelings toward him and, as an extreme, believe he is a victim of a conspiracy.

Such statements as these may reveal projection at work: "The production department is not to be trusted," "They are wolves in sheep's clothing," and "Every man has his price."

Projection may be combined with rationalization with undesirable results. A manager who cannot accept and does not see the hostility in himself may project this onto others and see them as mean and aggressive. He then may have to rationalize why they act this way toward him. He may develop a belief that they want his job or are trying to get him fired.

Typical examples of projection are the slacker who sees others as lazy, the selfish person who complains that others do not share, the manager with low Relationships Orientation who is concerned that no one seems to take an interest in him. University students often project their unconscious feeling about the instructor onto the instructor himself. They say the instructor does not like them and is being personal when the opposite—but unacceptable to them—condition is true. A managerial example:

> A manager making changes in his department was mystified at the behavior of two subordinates who resisted him at every step, even to the extent of an unsuccessful attempt to get him fired. The two subordinates claimed that the manager was simply changing the department to suit his own ends. The manager was convinced he was not, and an objective external appraisal showed the changes were long overdue. The sub-

ordinates were almost certainly projecting their own feelings onto the manager. They wanted the old way as it suited their needs. But as this was unacceptable to admit to themselves, they convinced themselves it was the manager who was serving his.

Projection is costly to managerial effectiveness because it can only be maintained at the cost of continually misperceiving social reality. Although such distortion is designed unconsciously to protect the manager, the effect, in the long run, may be the opposite.

NEGATIVE ADAPTATION (ACCEPTING THINGS AS THEY ARE)

One of the most important characteristics of human beings is their ability to make a psychological adaptation to an essentially unpleasant situation. Defense mechanisms help them do this. On the detrimental side, many managers adapt to negative conditions in such a way that they lose their sense of perspective about what an ideal situation might be. They believe that they, their department, or the company, are operating reasonably well or even perfectly. An objective view would not confirm this "fact." One particular advantage of a competent outside consultant is that he can see the true situation. He has had no opportunity to make a negative adaptation to the situation.

Negative adaptation is likely to be less common with those managers who have frequent contact outside the organization, with those with much prior experience elsewhere, or with those newly arrived. It can be reduced by a variety of training techniques designed to improve situational sensitivity and also by sharper measures of managerial effectiveness.

SYMPTOMS FOR CAUSES (MISTAKING APPEARANCE FOR CAUSE)

We are all "natural-born" psychologists and this leads us into many difficulties when diagnosing organizational events. Most managers, in fact, customarily make a psychological interpretation of events rather than a sociological one, even when the sociological one is correct. The "personality-clash" diagnosis, for instance, in most cases is incorrect. The clash is often only a symptom and should not be diagnosed as a cause. To diagnose it correctly, it must be demonstrable that the managers involved will fight on the golf course or over a drink. If they are reasonably affable in these circumstances, it cannot be their personalities which clash. A more accurate diagnosis of the underlying cause might be "role conflict." That is, their respective jobs are so designed that clashes are inevitable.

As an example, suppose one manager was responsible for decreasing marketing costs and another for increasing sales; they did not report to the same manager and so had an ambiguous power relationship to each other. These managers, if committed to their jobs, would almost certainly fight. Is this best explained as personality conflict or role conflict? Clearly role conflict is the better explanation. The danger in calling it personality conflict is that both managers might be asked to take a human relations course and to be nicer to each other. Certainly this action would not get to the root of the problem, whereas a role-alignment meeting might.

Other such diagnoses which may be symptoms rather than causes are "communication problem," "empire building," and "apathy." Like "personality clash," these are not always best explained by saying "People are like that."

LACK OF CONCEPTUAL LANGUAGE (NOT TALKING THE SAME LANGUAGE)

Managers who talk and work together need a common set of concepts which they share and agree on. Without such a set, intelligent discussion is hindered. Disraeli spoke for many when he said, "If you want to converse with me, define your terms."

One of the cornerstones of knowledge is the concept. A concept is simply a bundle of related ideas. To make talk more precise and economic we all use concepts. For example, we do not say that the car moved over a length 60 times 1,760 times 36 inches every sixty minutes. We, instead, make an equivalent but shorter statement and say that the car's speed was 60 miles per hour. Without concepts—in this example, speed, miles, and hours—language would be clumsy.

So it is with management. Concepts make discussion more precise and often much briefer. Arguments are not, then, over definitions but over the realities of the situation itself. Without the concept of style resilience, it is difficult to quickly make the point that style rigidity has its good side. Without the concept of personal effectiveness, it is difficult to explain how a man can be more effective and yet less effective at the same time.

The 3-D terms provide a conceptual language to make discussion and analysis more precise. The concepts are the fewest possible needed to consider styles, situations, and effectiveness. They are usable to improve *situational sensitivity* because they force a focus on elements, activities, or outcomes that might otherwise be ignored or misinterpreted.

LIMITING VALUE SYSTEM (HAVING ONE TEST FOR EVERYTHING)

Some managers have what amounts to an intellectual rigidity by espousing a single value or point of view which colors and sometimes covers reality. They may believe that all problems are human ones, that all work must always be satisfying, or that bigness destroys initiative. Whatever the view, when deeply held, the manager is compelled to distort reality so that it fits his established point of view. This produces very simple explanations, since everything is explained in the same way.

With a similar kind of simplified approach, some attribute the same motive to whomever it is they disagree with. An example of a motive might be "power need." But managers are not psychologists, and even psychologists do not agree upon which motives might be operating for a particular person in a particular situation. It is far safer and more accurate to observe and interpret behavior, not motives, especially if we have a favorite motive we like to project onto others.

HIGH LEVELS OF ANXIETY (BEING A WORRIER)

Some stage fright is usually a good thing. Moderate levels of anxiety tend to improve performance. Terror, on the other hand, usually does not. The relationship between anxiety and performance goes something like that shown in Exhibit 11.1. This relationship starts in one direction and then changes to another. As anxiety increases through low levels, performance also increases. There comes a point A of stage fright level, after which further increases in anxiety lead only to decreases in performance.

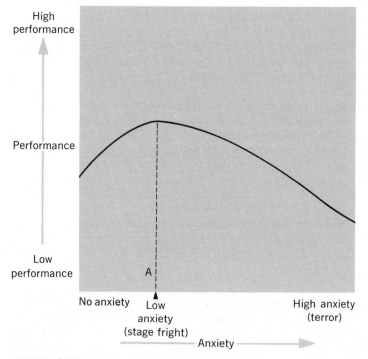

Exhibit 11–1   Anxiety and performance. Performance moves upward through stage-fright levels of anxiety, but at higher levels of anxiety, it drops.

Some persons are permanently anxious whatever the situation. They usually build up deep psychological defenses to protect themselves from reality. The additional anxiety induced by a new superior, perhaps, or any other change, puts them in effect past point A. Physical habits, or strong ideological positions about what is right, are less likely to become distorted as a result of high levels of anxiety. Perception, interpretation of motives, and feeling about others are likely to become distorted however.

Situational sensitivity in particular can be sharply reduced as anxiety increases. But this is precisely the time when it is needed most. Managers at these times are wise to turn to less anxious associates in order to read the situation; and this is what they usually do.

Style Awareness

A first step toward improving our situational sensitivity is to improve our *style awareness*. Style awareness is the degree to which a manager can appraise his own style correctly. It is knowledge of our impact on others, not of our impact on ourselves. The prime usefulness of this self-knowledge is to enable a manager to make a more effective impact on the situation, not so that he can marvel at his own psychic interior.

An effective manager must know the impact he is having on others. Without this knowledge, he cannot assess the situation he is in and cannot predict the results of his own behavior. Many types of group-dynamic management training courses attempt to, and usually can, improve style awareness—as can a wife or even children.

FOUR PARTS OF SELF

Everything known and not known about ourselves can be put under one of four headings:

1. What we know and others know (style awareness). (This is everyone's business.)
2. What others know and we do not know (style unawareness). (We must make this our business.)
3. What we know and others do not know (personal history). (This is only our business.)
4. What we and others do not know (unconscious). (This is no one's business.)

These can be arranged as demonstrated in Exhibit 11.2. The idea on which this diagram is based (only terminology is changed) was developed by two psychologists, Joe Luft and Harry Ingham. They call it the *Johari Window*.

This diagram sharpens the importance of decreasing our degree of style unawareness. The style-unawareness area is that part of our behavior which others are well aware of but we are not. In simple terms, we may be acting

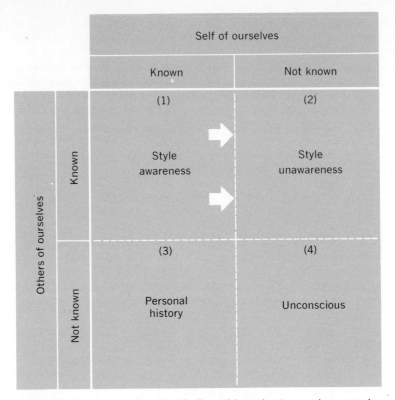

Exhibit 11–2   Four parts of self. Everything about ourselves can be put in one of these four boxes. To improve his effectiveness, a manager needs to make box (1) bigger and box (2) smaller.

in ways toward others, perhaps rejecting them, of which we are essentially unaware. Clearly to be effective with others, we must know just what kind of impact we are making. To become more effective, then, a manager needs to make window (2) smaller by increasing the size of window (1).

Without a reasonable degree of style awareness, it is difficult to use 3-D concepts. Without knowing our own basic style, it is all too easy to distort the style of another or the basic-style demands of a situation itself.

As a result of training, managers often experience a marked style-awareness shift. They see their style behavior in a markedly different way. As part of prework to the Managerial Effectiveness Seminar, managers complete three different managerial inventories which reveal how they see different aspects of their style. A total of 240 points is distributed over the eight managerial styles or 80 on each inventory. On the last day of the seminar, the inventories are again completed according to how the managers now see their typical style behavior as it existed before the seminar. A record is made of the amount [of shift points] from one style to another.

The maximum shift is 480 points. A shift of 0 points would indicate no basic change in style awareness. On almost every seminar, some managers shift over 250 or even 300 points indicating a marked change in style awareness. The average shift is about 140 points.

An Australian staff specialist who participated in a Managerial Effectiveness Seminar in Sydney, Australia, appraised his style before the seminar as shown on column A of Exhibit 11.3, and after the seminar as shown in column B. While he did the two appraisals before and after the seminar, he was asked each time to appraise his preseminar style. Column C shows his style-awareness shift. His total style-awareness shift of 304 points was very high. The main changes in his perception of himself was a shift from executive (−75) and developer (−70) toward compromiser (+82), benevolent autocrat (+42), and autocrat (+24). As a result of the seminar he came to see that his preseminar style was not as effective as he though it was. This gave him a clear idea of what changes he had to make to become effective.

Exhibit 11-3

Style awareness shift of staff specialist			
	PRESEMINAR A	POSTSEMINAR B	SHIFT C
Executive	118	43	− 75
Benevolent autocrat	24	66	+ 42
Developer	89	19	− 70
Bureaucrat	3	0	− 3
Compromiser	0	82	+ 82
Autocrat	0	24	+ 24
Missionary	6	2	− 4
Deserter	0	4	+ 4
	240	240	304

NO SINGLE DIRECTION

At the same time that the style-awareness shift for an individual is often very markedly toward one style and away from another, the style-awareness shift for a group of managers does not have any single direction. The shifts of individual managers taken together tend to average out.

A recent study (100) analyzed the style-awareness shift of the 104 senior managers of a single firm in eastern Canada. A single inventory was used for analysis so that the total points assigned to all styles would be 80. Exhibit 11.4, column A, shows how managers saw their preseminar styles at the beginning of a Managerial Effectiveness Seminar. On the average, 26.3 points were assigned to executive, 15.5 points to benevolent autocrat, and so on. Column B shows how managers, on the average, saw their preseminar styles at the end of the seminar. Column C is the difference between B and A.

Exhibit 11-4

Style awareness shift of 104 managers			
	PRESEMINAR A	POSTSEMINAR B	SHIFT C
Executive	26.3	26.4	+ .1
Benevolent autocrat	15.5	16.8	+ 1.3
Developer	19.3	19.0	(−) .3
Bureaucrat	9.5	5.4	(−) 4.1
Compromiser	3.2	5.5	+ 2.3
Autocrat	2.1	2.9	+ .8
Missionary	3.9	3.5	(−) .4
Deserter	.2	.5	+ .3
	80	80	0

As these 104 managers had an average, and normal, individual shift on this inventory of 47.9 points, the important information in column C is that the shifts around each style is very small. There is no general shift, for instance, either to or from executive. What this indicates, and it is important, is that the Managerial Effectiveness Seminar does not alert or sensitize participants to one style more than another. In some seminars with such pre-post measurement, there is a marked shift either toward or away from a particular style, need, or approach that was being induced by the seminar. Like the 3–D Theory itself, then, the Managerial Effectiveness Seminar is designed not to heighten preference of one particular style over another.

SOME QUESTIONS FOR THE MANAGER TO ASK HIMSELF

Style awareness is difficult to improve by simply thinking about it, but some assistance may be obtained by answering each of the following questions honestly:

1. If someone said of you, "He sometimes acts like a kid," what behavior would he be thinking of?
2. What do you do that gets you into trouble?

3. Are there any major themes in your life which seem to repeat themselves, perhaps in different contexts?
4. Do you care more about yourself than others?
5. If you obtained a livable pension today, would you still like to keep your job?
6. What did you do when your father was angry at you? Mother angry at you? Friends angry at you?
7. What does your wife think of you? What do your children think of you?
8. What do you do when your superior is angry with you? Subordinates angry with you? Coworkers angry with you?
9. What do you typically do when under attack or faced with conflict?
10. What are your major disappointments in life?
11. What are your major disappointments at work?
12. Who is responsible for your major disappointments?
13. What made you proudest as a boy? As a man?
14. What is your favorite daydream? Do you see anything in it that might be making you a more or less effective manager?
15. What is your single major accomplishment?

Most of these questions tap the manager's underlying personality dynamics. They are questions which we seldom think about. The answers to them differentiate ourselves sharply from others.

THE FATAL FLAW

All of us have flaws; a few of us have fatal flaws which we seem condemned to keep repeating in different contexts. The flaw is best identified by looking at the situations which most often lead to more trouble than they should. The situation may involve a superior—that is, when the manager is in a low-power situation—and it may involve a coworker or a subordinate. It may involve planning, organizing, or controlling. It may be confronting disagreement, making a difficult decision—usually its postponement—trying to satisfy everyone, overreacting to criticism, being vague about poor performance, or any one of many more.

Fatal flaws often come disguised. The same basic flaw may have occurred in a dozen different ways. Only if a flaw is recognized, can it be managed. It can only be managed by the person whose flaw it is.

STYLE DISTORTION

Style distortion arises in part from low style awareness. It is the perception of more or fewer occurrences of a particular style than actually exist. If we distort our basic style, it is easy to misinterpret that of others. As style awareness improves, style distortion decreases. Some managers see far more autocrats or missionaries than may actually exist. This kind of distortion leads directly to inappropriate responses to the situational demands.

Style distortion may be easily measured. In the Managerial Effectiveness Seminar, participants are shown a film which shows managers in action. They are asked to privately appraise the *dominant* and *supporting* style of each manager. In all, ten appraisals are made. These evaluations are then compared to the best possible ones based on the thousands of answers of participants of prior seminars. Typical distortions might be seeing twice as many of the executive style as actually exist, seeing too few effective styles, too many autocrats and benevolent autocrats, or other combinations. All this information is fed back to them. As a manager discovers his typical distortions, he can begin to correct them.

TOO MANY AUTOCRATS

Another method of obtaining an accurate picture of the degree, nature, and direction of style distortion is with the Style Quotation Test. This test consists of eighty statements which managers are asked to appraise as being representative of one or the other of the eight managerial styles. Most managers tend to see more or less of certain styles than actually exist. Seeing two or three more or less of any particular style than actually exist is normal, but anything outside this range represents distortion.

On the Managerial Effectiveness Seminar, where the test is used, one managing director obtained these results:

STYLE	NUMBER OF TIMES STYLE WAS SEEN MORE (+) OR LESS (−) THAN ACTUALLY EXISTED
Deserter	+1
Missionary	−2
Autocrat	+7
Compromiser	−1
Bureaucrat	−2
Developer	−4
Benevolent Autocrat	−6
Executive	+7
	0

That is, he saw seven more autocrats, four too few developers, six too few benevolent autocrats, and seven more executives than actually existed. Analysis revealed that this arose because he tended to appraise developers as executives and benevolent autocrats as autocrats. His own basic style was related, and he thus tended to see related behavior as more effective. This led to his appraising developers as executives. Also he saw dedicated behavior as less effective, and this led to his appraisal of benevolent autocrats as autocrats. By knowing his distortions, he was able to correct them and so improve his situational sensitivity.

Situation-feedback Loops

To increase their sensitivity, managers should attempt to build situations which have immediate feedback loops incorporated into them. The loop may be simply a candid subordinate who tells the manager quickly when things are not to his liking. The loop might also be the measurement of a production process that needs involvement and teamwork to keep it going. Effective managers cultivate short-term feedback loops so that they can get quick readings on the effect of their actions. Psychologists have shown in a variety of experiments, that performance improves when the results of performance are known. To put it more directly, without feedback there is little learning. To improve our style, we must have feedback on its effects.

Feedback loops are built into many types of technical systems. They are designed to provide corrections to the planned course. Such loops keep guided missiles on target or radio receivers on frequency. When the actual events vary from those planned, they provide a means of correcting the deviations.

Grapevines and rumor are forms of feedback. While both tend to be quick, they also tend to distort reality.

TYPES OF FEEDBACK

Feedback may be classified by its timing, evaluative content, validity, and direction.

TIMING	Immediate Delayed
EVALUATIVE CONTENT	Nonevaluative Positive Negative
VALIDITY	Valid Invalid
DIRECTION	Upfeed Downfeed Crossfeed

It is better for feedback to be immediate than delayed. The computer has already, and will even further, shorten the customary delay between managerial actions and their effects. Consider a situation where we could discover the effectiveness of our actions within minutes. The learning potential would be enormous, not to mention the early corrections to poor decisions. Clearly managers should consider the timing of their existing feedback loops. How long does it take to know how a situation has changed, what it has become, or what the level of effectiveness is in it?

The best feedback is nonevaluative—that which simply "tells it like it is." Feedback, on which action must be taken, is less effective if feelings, positive or negative, are transmitted along with the information. For example, a subordinate is much more likely to respond to "You did not meet your objectives," than the same statement with the often unspoken override of ". . . and I do not like you because of it." The first is nonevaluative feedback; the second is negative feedback. The terms "negative" and "positive," then, refer not to the content of the feedback but to the feelings that go with it. Unless specially designed to be otherwise, mechanical feedback devices or computer printouts are completely nonevaluative. Although difficult to accomplish, managers find that the closer they come to such feedback, the easier it is for others to really hear it and take action on it.

Feedback is either valid or not. Valid feedback may be negative, positive, or nonevaluative, but it is always accurate.

Feedback may come from any direction in an organization. To indicate its direction, it is called upfeed, downfeed, or crossfeed. Downfeed almost always occurs plentifully; crossfeed and particularly upfeed have to be planned.

THE FEEDBACK-LEARNING CYCLE

Learning from feedback can be seen as a cycle continuously repeating itself. So long as the cycle is maintained, learning can continue. The two key elements in the cycle are making a sound situational diagnosis and obtaining feedback on the results of the actions.

The situational-sensitivity cycle of Exhibit 11.5 has six steps. The sixth step leads into a repetition of the cycle.

1. A situational diagnosis is made.
2. The manager decides to adapt to the situation or to change it.
3. He takes action.
4. He obtains feedback on the results of his actions. Without this step, the feedback-learning cycle cannot continue. It is its weakest link since it depends on the climate the manager has created and his skill in listening and observing.
5. He evaluates the effectiveness of his action. He decides whether it led to more or less effectiveness and how much more effectiveness is possible.
6. The action taken is continued or discarded.

Learning is a continuous process. It is difficult to suggest where it starts or ends. An effective manager is constantly making a diagnosis of the situation, using style flexibility or situational management, and assessing the effectiveness of his actions so that he can improve on the nature of his interventions.

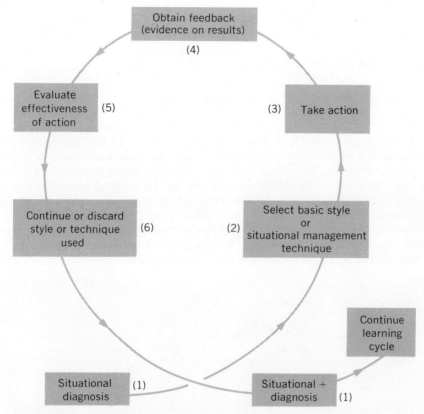

Exhibit 11–5 Situational-sensitivity cycle. Learning, like music, goes around and around.

APPRAISING SITUATIONAL SENSITIVITY

If a manager makes a series of interventions in situations which prove effective, then it is highly probable that he has a high sensitivity to situations. If not, he would have made the wrong moves. If, however, a manager does nothing, this alone does not indicate whether or not he has a high or low sensitivity. He may know what is wrong but not know how to do anything about it.

Situational sensitivity is a diagnostic not an action skill. This simply means that a manager may score high on the situational sensitivity scale, and yet do nothing with the skill he has. The well-trained psychologist, sociologist, or anthropologist may have the highest-possible situational sensitivity yet the lowest-possible effectiveness as a manager. To be effective, the sensitivity must be matched with one but preferably both of either *style flexibility* or *situational management skill.*

Management training exercises are available which measure situational sensitivity with great precision. They consist of depicting a situation by a film or written case study and then asking the manager to make a series of observations concerning it.

SITUATIONAL SENSITIVITY ALONE

Situational sensitivity alone is of little value to the practicing manager. If a manager cannot use what he knows, he might as well not know it. Those who go through life as hostile or only as friendly observers of the scene are serving some need to appear intellectual rather than to be useful and, therefore, effective. No one likes to feel he is being analyzed, and this is what situational sensitivity alone can lead to.

Sensitivity must be related to an action program of either managerial flexibility or situational management. Some managers have high sensitivity but low flex. They usually tend to change situations rather than change themselves. They use situational management.

New Concepts Introduced

SITUATIONAL SENSITIVITY (SS)
STYLE APPRAISAL SKILL
STYLE AWARENESS
STYLE DISTORTION

Situational Sensitivity (SS)   Skill in appraising situational elements in terms of Task-Orientation and Relationships-Orientation demands, flex, and strength. Scaled from 0 to 4.

Style Appraisal Skill   Ability to appraise another's style correctly.

Style Awareness   Degree to which a manager can appraise his own style correctly.

Style Distortion   Perceiving more or fewer occurrences of a particular style than actually exist.

In 1789 Ben Franklin wrote to a friend, "But in this world nothing is certain but death and taxes." He neglected to mention a third certainty . . . change.

A. JUDSON

How can we avoid the two extremes; too great bossism in giving orders, and practically no orders given? . . . My solution is to depersonalize the giving of orders, to unite all concerned in a study of the situation, to discover the law of the situation and obey that.

MARY PARKER FOLLETT

Chapter Twelve

SITUATIONAL MANAGEMENT SKILL

The professional manager is a manager of total situations. *Situational management skill* is nothing more than changing the demands of situational elements so that managerial effectiveness is increased. As this always involves change, a central skill in management is the smooth introduction of change, or put another way, overcoming resistance to change.

A manager's situational sensitivity can help him determine the existing conditions in the social system he manages. It will also lead him to decide what problems require solutions and what the solution, or ideal state, should be. All this requires intellectual skill. To apply this knowledge to reality he must devise an action program to increase acceptance for the change and then see that the change is implemented. The change to be made may be reassigning duties, modifying a work process, gaining acceptance for a new or different type of manager, changing the role of a staff unit, or perhaps changing an organization structure that has not been touched in years.

Professional managers have no need to passively adapt to situations in which they find themselves. At times, of course, they must, but usually some form of situational management is desirable. Managers should, in fact, seek opportunities to change the demands of one or more situational elements. They should change them only with a view to increasing their own managerial effectiveness. It may be that subordinates' expectations are unrealistic in the face of the job to be done. They may expect to be treated in a related fashion, yet the work system may virtually demand they be treated in a dedicated fashion. Obviously these are in conflict, and one or both must be changed if *managerial effectiveness* is to be maximized.

The objective of situational management is to so arrange a situation that those in it cooperate of their own accord. It produces motivation to work and effectiveness. Motivation is not best seen as being produced by what a manager does to someone. Instead it is best seen as arising from a matching of all the demands of the situation. Situational management has nothing to do with speeches on the year A.D. 2000 or sermons on the virtues of accepting change. It is, instead, concerned with a planned, tested, rational, logical approach that considers as its central issue how change can be effectively implemented.

IS CHANGE LEGITIMATE?

In some particular companies and in some parts of the world, the word "change" itself produces negative emotional reactions. Terms such as "change program" or "change agent" are particularly threatening. So much change has led to upheaval and has been associated with rebels or incompetents that it is difficult for some to see it as a prime management function. Instead of "change," such terms as "education," "training," "development," improvement," "support," "counseling," or "guidance" are used.

Although there is nothing intrinsically wrong with any of these words, it is still best for managers to use "change." It is simple; it is honest; it is direct. It "tells it like it is." In any case, disguises will eventually be uncovered.

Change is healthy and positive, it tends to stabilize rather than upset things. A function of change is to allow the organization to meet reality. This reality may be a changed environment or a new opportunity in it. Change also corrects deviations from an ideal course. The organization may have strayed over the years from a sound plan. The organization chart may have had awkward bits added to it over the years so that a change is needed simply to restore its design integrity. Change, in essence, can be used to maintain an optimum design for a system. It makes things work together as they should.

ADMINISTRATION—MANAGEMENT—LEADERSHIP

The terms "administration," "management," and "leadership" each suggest differences in the degree to which situational management is exercised.

Administration suggests maintaining a going concern with little actual change in key elements such as organization philosophy or technology.

Many managers are in essentially administrative jobs, and in these positions, it is best to use the *bureaucratic* style.

Management is best seen as being descriptive of the skill required in a situation where some of the situational elements are under long-run, and even short-run, control. Some elements can be changed, and new men can be appointed. It is in this kind of situation that *management style* and *situational management* theories are most useful.

Leadership is best seen as the power to modify all or most situational elements in the short run. This occurs most often at the top of organizations, in battle, in politics, and in a variety of critical, unstable, dangerous, or emergency situations. This view of leadership explains why an analysis of management style of men at the top usually leads to no consistent result. The explanation is that these men, having most situational elements under their control, can change the situation to suit whatever style they care to use. Anyone familiar with presidents of companies in the same industry, or for that matter of army generals, deputy ministers, ministers, or undersecretaries is struck by the differences in style among them. Clearly, there is no one best style if you have complete control of the situation.

SITUATIONAL MANIPULATION   Some managers use great skill in managing situations to suit their own ends. They employ change techniques not to improve their managerial effectiveness but simply to improve their personal effectiveness. They may simply be attempting to obtain more power or status, or promotion when these may not lead to improved managerial effectiveness. This is best called *situational manipulation*, not situational management.

THE RELATIONSHIP SIDE OF THINGS

The greatest single factor in any change is human. Important are such things as personal value systems, informal relations, personal ambitions, preferred career routes, and intellectual and emotional capacity. Some of these may be seen as emotional or even irrational factors to consider, but they are as real and as important as any other.

Some managers deride the human factor in change. They fear they might be seen as soft or that human considerations might interfere with those of managerial effectiveness. This is an inappropriate point of view as any change inevitably has human consequences which if ignored can lead to disaster.

Lack of recognition on the human side of change can waste money, time, and people. A manager moved to desertion through mismanaged change is as much to be pitied as blamed. The money cost of his withdrawn involvement can sometimes be estimated, and it is high. The personal cost to him in anxiety and then in loss of personal satisfaction in work is incalculable. The negative influence he has on his subordinates must also be considered as a major cost.

Production organizations are basically social institutions. Technological change almost inevitably leads to social change. Social resistance almost inevitably leads to lower productivity than planned. Managers need to see their job in sociotechnical terms. They must see work and relationships as inextricably bound together. To change one, we must understand and manage both.

"How Will This Affect Me?"

One of the early but often unstated questions in any change is "How will this affect me?" An understanding of how a change might be seen as affecting those concerned is clearly essential to sound situational management.

Any experienced manager can recall many examples of resistance to change directly from his own experience. The resistance may have led to a drop in accuracy, productivity, profits, or morale. To some extent the resistance was anticipated, but it often becomes more extreme and persistent than was expected.

Sometimes resistance to a particular change is clear to all concerned in such a statement as "Sure his style changed. He used to be an autocrat; now he is a hypocrite." Or, a farmer, in reply to advice from an agricultural expert, "I ain't farming now as well as I know how." Or, "That's the best method I have seen but it is not my way."

More often it is covert and takes these forms:

"This is a step backward."
"This is being done too quickly."
"This is not necessary."
"This has not been thought out."
"They have something against us."
"It is being shoved down our throats."
"No one asked my opinion."

Although some of the points in a particular situation may have validity, they still reflect resistance to change.

Deserter behavior (see chapter 15) is a clear, general example of resistance to change. In the deserter's case, the resistance is so profound that it has become generalized as the standard approach to all problems.

Resistance to change occurs at all levels in an organization. Except perhaps in firms with very militant unions, it is just as likely to occur at the top as the bottom.

REACTION TO CHANGE

The following questions summarize the majority of the ways in which change may be seen as affecting an individual. They are useful in getting a sharper focus on one or several underlying causes of the resistance. Use this list by considering each question in turn for an individual or group facing a proposed change. Check each question that seems important in increasing either resistance to or acceptance of, the change. Then put a (+), (−), or (?) against each of those checked to indicate whether that particular factor is likely to increase acceptance, increase resistance, or whether the direction of influence is in doubt. If done well, this analysis provides an assessment of the situation as seen by those affected by the change. It can give leads to the existing restraining forces to be overcome or the main perceived benefits that might be enhanced further.

Change-reaction checklist

SELF

(S-1)   How will my advancement possibilties change?
(S-2)   How will my salary change?
(S-3)   How will my future with this company change?
(S-4)   How will my view of myself change?
(S-5)   How will my formal authority change?
(S-6)   How will my informal influence change?
(S-7)   How will my view of my prior values change?
(S-8)   How will my ability to predict the future change?
(S-9)   How will my status change?

WORK

(W-1)   How will the amount of work I do change?
(W-2)   How will my interest in the work change?
(W-3)   How will the importance of my work change?
(W-4)   How will the challenge of the work change?
(W-5)   How will the work pressures change?
(W-6)   How will the skill demands on me change?
(W-7)   How will my physical surroundings change?
(W-8)   How will my hours of work change?

OTHERS

(O-1)   How will my relationships with my coworkers change?
(O-2)   How will my relationships with my superior change?
(O-3)   How will my relationships with my subordinates change?
(O-4)   How will what my family thinks of me change?

Change-reaction Diagram

The *change-reaction diagram* is used to record the information from the change-reaction checklist. The basic idea of this diagram was proposed by the distinguished psychologist Kurt Lewin. It is useful as a guide for selecting a situational management strategy.

There are two basic strategies which may be used to facilitate change: An attempt to increase the acceptance of change or an attempt to decrease the resistance to change. These two sets of forces are depicted in Exhibit 12.1. The ten arrows pointing downward represent each of the resistance forces, and the ten arrows pointing upward represent the acceptance forces. The number of arrows assigned to each force signifies the strength of the force. The total strength is always ten. The length of an arrow can represent how easily the force may be modified by situational management; so, the longer the arrow, the easier the underlying force is to grasp and modify.

The information obtained from the change-reaction checklist can be put onto the diagram by drawing in arrows and labeling them appropriately (Exhibit 12.2). In this example, three resistance forces are identified with the weights indicated:

NUMBER	RESISTANCE FORCE	WEIGHT
(S-5)	Less-formal authority	5
(O-2)	New superior	3
(W-6)	Higher-skill demands	2
		10

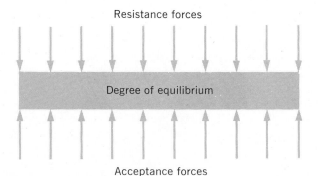

Resistance forces

Degree of equilibrium

Acceptance forces

Exhibit 12–1 Change-reaction diagram. This approach, based on Lewin's force-field diagram, shows how a manager can plot and then think about the resistance forces he must overcome.

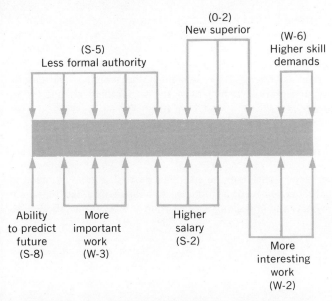

Exhibit 12–2   Example of a resistance analysis. The manager can strengthen any of the acceptance forces or add new ones; he can weaken or eliminate the resistance forces in order to produce change.

The (0-2), new superior, force is drawn with longer arrows since many techniques can be used to decrease the feelings that usually surround the introduction of a new superior. Among the techniques are provision of background information on him, his early request for ideas to improve departmental effectiveness, a transitional period of a few days where old and new superiors work together, and many others.

The acceptance forces are:

NUMBER	ACCEPTANCE FORCES	WEIGHT
(S-8)	Ability to predict future increased	1
(W-3)	More important work	3
(S-2)	Higher salary	3
(W-2)	More interesting work	3
		10

The (W-2), more interesting work, force is drawn longer because many techniques can be used to increase the interest of work. These are primarily of the job-enrichment type.

This kind of analysis is useful because it takes a rigorous approach to what is so often done very casually. It is always best to make such an analysis with at least one other person in order to increase the accuracy of the diagnosis.

As situations may be changed by weakening the resistance forces or strengthening the acceptance forces, each force identified should be so considered in this light.

Change-acceptance Scale

The change-acceptance scale can be used as part of a change-reaction analysis to indicate the degree of acceptance to change. The acceptance of change can be seen as moving along a scale from 0 to 8, from sabotage to commitment:

0 Sabotage
1 Slowdowns
2 Protests
3 Apathy
4 Indifference
5 Acceptance
6 Support
7 Cooperation
8 Commitment

The scale is useful in considering likely reactions under a variety of methods of implementation to set change-reaction targets and to evaluate the actual effects of a method used to introduce change. It has proved to be very simple to use. Managers, having considered all the resistance and acceptance forces, will usually agree on the single scale point representing the degree of acceptance. Obviously a manager's prime job in change introduction is to create conditions where most of the reaction to the change is at the high end of the scale.

Personal reaction to change varies widely from individual to individual. Some men can react only at the extremes of the scale, and they are typically the low-flex "true believers." They are likely to come storming in the office at point 2, try to engage in a shouting match, work off their resistance, and move to point 6 or 7. Others can move gradually along the scale in one direction or another as their perception of the situation changes.

At any one point in time, the two sets of forces find their equilibrium point which may be measured on the change-reaction scale. If the resistance forces far outweigh the acceptance forces, the equilibrium may be at 2. If the reverse condition holds and the acceptance forces are greater than the resistance forces, the equilibrium may be at 7. Two of these scale points are indicated on the force-field analysis. The first indicates the current degree of acceptance; the second indicates the planned degree of acceptance after situational management has been exercised.

New Concepts Introduced

SITUATIONAL MANAGEMENT (SM)
SITUATIONAL MANIPULATION

Situational Management (SM)   Skill in changing the style demands of one or more situational elements so that managerial effectiveness increases. Scaled from 0 to 4.

Situational Manipulation   Changing the style demands of one or more situational elements so that personal effectiveness increases.

- *Those who make things happen.*
- *Those to whom things happen.*
- *Those who watch things happen.*
- *Those who don't even know that things are happening.*

L. APPLEY

There is nothing more difficult to take in hand, more perilous to conduct, or more uncertain in its success, than to take the lead in the introduction of a new order of things.

MACHIAVELLI

Chapter Thirteen

SITUATIONAL MANAGEMENT TECHNIQUES

To apply *situational management,* resistance to change must be over-come. There are seven techniques by which this may be accomplished. They are easy to learn and just as easy to use. Most of them amount to common sense, and all of them are well tested. Through a well-designed organizational development program, all managers should get "hands on" experience with each of the following techniques:

Diagnosis
Mutual objective setting
Group emphasis
Maximum information
Discussion of implementation
Use of ceremony—ritual
Resistance interpretation

The first three of these techniques are specifically designed to give those affected by the change an opportunity to have some influence on the direction, nature, rate, and method of introduction of the change. Giving those affected by it some control over the change enables them to become involved with it, to express their ideas more directly, and to be in a better position to propose useful modifications in the proposed change if it should appear necessary to them.

DIAGNOSIS

Resistance to change may be reduced if a diagnosis of the situation is first made by those affected by the change. The process of making the diagnosis leads to an increased awareness of what is wrong, and this awareness, in turn, can lead naturally to steps to change the situation. The diagnosis may be in the form of a work team discussing the question, "What are the major problems we could solve if we worked together to solve them?" This kind of question has been used repeatedly with success at all levels of management. It is not only the ultimate diagnosis that the question produces that is important. The actual process of making the diagnosis, itself, leads to a profound unfreezing of the men by bringing them together to discuss certain things about their department that they have never discussed before. In such discussions men often gain new perspectives on old problems. They sometimes come to see that they themselves are the prime cause.

The diagnostic, or scientific, problem-solving approach allows for mental double-declutching. It does not require a direct switch from one point of view to another. It provides a period "in neutral" where there is an openness to facts and, therefore, a willingness to consider an alternate view.

> In America during World War II, a company psychologist wanted to persuade his management to engage women workers over thirty. Top management was opposed to this proposed policy change. They believed that older women had a higher rate of absenteeism, lower rate of work, and took a longer time to train. The psychologist involved top management in a research project to test their beliefs. Management established the criteria to be used and the method of collecting the data. Management's finding that older women were far better than they had thought led directly to a policy change and also to a campaign to change the policies of other firms (132).

This is a good example of the effect of a diagnosis engaged to change a stereotype. We do not know, but it is possible that the same facts collected another way, by consultants perhaps, would not have led to the change. They almost certainly would not have led to the management's campaign to get policies changed there and elsewhere.

MUTUAL OBJECTIVE SETTING

Resistance to change is reduced with the use of objective setting by those instituting the change and by those directly affected. Much resistance is simply based on a misunderstanding about, or disagreement about, ends. Once ends have been set and agreed upon, there is usually a straight road to their achievement.

Objectives set by those directly affected are usually more ambitious than those set by persons not so involved.

> In one application of objective setting, a group of girls asked for and were allowed to set their own speed on machine-paced work. Prior to this the girls had failed to meet the required pace. By using a specially installed dial, the girls established their own speed which they varied by the time of day. Their average output was between 30 and 50 percent higher than expected, and the girls reported that their work was easier (190).

Bargaining is a lower, but often necessary, form of mutual objective setting. It is a frank exchange based on: "We will do this if you do that." It is particularly useful and may be the only method to use with union militancy or in situations where hostility has led to poor communication. Bargaining is not necessarily a display of weakness; it may be an acceptance of reality.

Bargaining usually leads to compromise. At its worst, bargaining leads to obstinacy on both sides and a consequent win-lose approach to the final decision. But conditions can at times be created where it leads to a better decision than either side previously considered.

GROUP EMPHASIS

Management training is now moving more and more to a group or team emphasis. It is becoming clear that the individual group member, in isolation, can have little influence without the wholehearted cooperation of the others. The best way to obtain this cooperation is to train the managers as a team so that all ideas are team ideas which the team is committed to as a unit. Some managers say that the first thing to do with an idea is to separate it from the manager who first thought of it—make it group property.

Resistance to change is reduced if the group is made the focus of change rather than the individual. Group decision making has a powerful control over the deviant member, who is holding up the others, because groups develop powerful standards for conformity and the means of enforcing them. In the same way that a group can set up work norms to inhibit change, it can set up norms which facilitate it.

As with any technique, there are times when group decision making is appropriate and times when it is not. For example, it should never be used when management has, or should have already, made up its mind. In fact, it can only be used when both sides have something to gain. Also, it can only operate when a group or potential group actually exists.

These first three techniques of diagnosis, mutual objective setting, and group emphasis all involve participation in different aspects of the change.

The word "participation," itself, has not been used as there is so much misunderstanding about, and disagreement over, what it means. In the three techniques discussed, no promise can be made that management will accept all the ideas suggested, and there is no need for such agreement. The techniques can be used quite successfully when management says, in effect, "This much is decided. What are your thoughts on the rest? We will consider all your proposals but cannot guarantee to accept them."

The success of such methods as these depends on the extent to which they are seen as legitimate, honest, and likely to be successful. Although it can be done, it is difficult for a company to start too suddenly to use these techniques in situations where they have never been used before. A certain degree of trust is important; a certain degree of skill in implementation is crucial; some form of unfreezing, such as the Managerial Effectiveness Seminar, is useful. Needless to say, a manager cannot use these techniques if he has already finally settled on a course of action. To do so is both dishonest and folly. "You can fool some of the people . . ." and it only takes one to tell the rest. Psuedoparticipation is time wasted for everyone, and clearly inappropriate if a degree of meaningful participation could have been used instead.

MAXIMUM INFORMATION

When involved in any change, management goes through four distinct steps:

1. Recognizes change needed
2. Decides on ideal state
3. Designs method of implementation
4. Implements change

These should each in turn lead to four appropriate announcements:

1. That a change will be made
2. What the decision is and why made
3. How decision will be implemented
4. How decision implementation is progressing

Each announcement can produce a particular resistance:

1. To thought of any change
2. To decision itself
3. To method of implementation
4. To changed state itself

When analyzing a change in process or when planning a change, these twelve elements should each be considered in turn. In particular, management should consider how well it is conveying the four separate elements of information required. There is a tremendous fear of incomplete information and people usually believe the worst.

The first piece of appropriate information—that a change will be made —is often omitted or left to rumor; the second—what the decision is and why made—is often made too tersely; the third—how decision will be implemented—is often omitted, and not enough thought, let alone communication, given to it; the fourth—how decision implementation is progressing—is seldom communicated particularly when there is little that is good to communicate.

Maximum information is usually a sound policy after a change has been announced and sometimes, but not always, before it. Testing the wind with hints about forthcoming changes can sometimes provide useful pointers on the state of resistance or acceptance to the change. On the other hand, it can simply raise the level of anxiety and lead to wild rumors. Prior announcements should be crystal clear as far as they go, but they do not have to be complete.

A vague sort of prior announcement or rumor is harmful: "Some organization changes are coming." Rather, a precise prior announcement is helpful: "A reorganization of the top two levels of our A division will be announced on September 1 by the executive committee. The changes will be carried out during the following two months. The basic function of the division will remain unchanged."

Once a change has been announced, the maximum possible information should be distributed about it. Resistance to change is almost always lower if the objectives, nature, methods, benefits, and drawbacks of the change are made clear to all concerned.

Face-to-face announcements are better than the printed word. Not only do they personalize what may be seen as a depersonalized action, but they also allow anxieties to be expressed clearly and perhaps dealt with on the spot.

DISCUSSION OF IMPLEMENTATION

Discussion of implementation is a component of giving the fullest possible information. It calls for distinct treatment, however, as it is a most important step often overlooked.

Resistance to change is reduced if there can be agreement on the rate and method of implementation. It is as effective to have discussions on the way a change is to be introduced as it is to discuss the nature of the change itself. Such discussions will cover what the first steps should be, what the rate of change should be, what the appropriate sequence of changes should be, and who should be involved in what elements of the implementation. When this method is used successfully, it sometimes happens that the unit undergoing the change says to management, "Leave us alone. Come back in two weeks or two months and the changes will be in." A wise manager accepts that kind of offer.

USE OF CEREMONY—RITUAL

Breaking a saucer can eliminate in-law trouble. In some Indian wedding ceremonies a saucer is broken by the bride's father. This act dramatically symbolizes that he no longer considers the bride part of his household. She is now essentially a daughter of the groom's mother. With crowded living conditions, it is important to know who is boss in the kitchen. The saucer clarifies the daughter's new role to everyone and especially to her. She is still a daughter but in a different family.

One of the characteristics of our time, particularly in North America, is the prolongation of adolescence. Children are taking a longer time, and using many devices, to avoid stepping into an adult role. This is not true in all societies. In some, still, you get your first tiger and you get to be a man. Such events or ceremonies of "rites of passage" facilitate the acceptance of a new role. Western society has no such rite.

To put it in primitive form, the "golden handshake" or gold-watch presentation of Western business society is a method of marking a change of status from employed to retired. One problem with the ceremony is that it is essentially one of departure. Only those whom the retired person is leaving are present. This hardly facilitates entry into the community of the retired.

Life consists of a series of periods spent in different statuses. Most of us follow a similar pattern. We are first infants, then school children, then lovers, then adults, then marriage partners, then parents. At school, at work, or in some fraternal orders, similar progressions occur. Some degee of ritual surrounds the passage from one status to another. The more important the status distinction, the more elaborate the ritual: witness the marriage ceremony.

When there are clearly established progressions from one status to another, change becomes much easier to accept. One knows that many people also have done it before. One knows the progressions, is prepared for the future, and knows what behavioral demands the next status will make. One knows the conditions for entering the status and for remaining there, and knows the meaning and use of the various status symbols which might be a wedding ring or a big desk and a fitted carpet.

Some of the particular uses of ceremony and ritual for managers are:

Pass on status, competence, power
Prepare individual or group for change
Provide a clear end and a new beginning
Provide for orderly change
Make change legitimate
Emphasize individual responsibility to organization

A few of the many occasions when one or more of these are accomplished and where ceremony and ritual are therefore useful are:

Retirement
Promotion
New coworker
New superior
New subordinate
New job
Start of new system
Reorganization

Ceremonies well used by a manager can serve to focus the importance of the ongoing institution and to underline the importance of individual loyalty to the institution and to the positions in it.

Clearly managers need to learn how to use ceremony and ritual. Both can facilitate adaptation to what otherwise might be a painful adjustment.

RESISTANCE INTERPRETATION

When people understand why they have been resisting a change, the resistance usually decreases or, at least, becomes more rational. Interpreting resistance with those who are resisting is a key step in psychoanalysis and in organizational-change agentry.

Resistance has been seen as a symptom of something else, perhaps fear of the future or an unwillingness to give something up. The form the resistance takes is often an indicator of what the actual resistance might be. Seldom is the real reason given openly. Uncovering these reasons and discussing them can get at the true cause of the problem.

Such interpretation of resistance is preceded or followed by some manner of blowing off steam. This may be in the form of a private or public "beef" session.

Most Common Errors

Most of the possible errors in *situational management* have been discussed or inferred already. Some, however, occur much more frequently, and are more serious, than others. They are:

Human aspects only
Technical aspects only
No information about change
No planning of introduction
No benefits
Seen as personal

A sole emphasis on the human aspects of change may lead to the changes being distorted from the original plan or may lead to no change at all. Overemphasis on the human side is sometimes induced by human relations training courses. Managers then become either overparticipative or guilty about the methods they have to use.

At the other extreme is a sole emphasis on the technical aspects of change. Engineers and systems department managers are among those who have been most guilty of this in the past. This kind of emphasis can lead to the most extreme personal resistance of all. This resistance leads either to still more impersonal pressure, to compromise, or to an abandonment of the project.

When a firm has a history of resistance to change, it sometimes resorts to the strategy which might be called "no information," "no warning," or "earthquake." It can get away with these strategies, to some extent, in a heavily technical system, or in a situation where payment can be made for compliance and where direct coercion is possible. The negative effects of such an approach are varied but are often intense. They include grapevines, anxiety, and suppressed or overt hostility. Eventually the pool duplicator turns out résumés for those seeking work elsewhere.

A widespread error, and one capable of a simple solution, is lack of planning of the method of introduction. This planning has nothing to do with the actual change itself but solely with the way it is introduced. A new method might have cost several million dollars to design and purchase, yet not even a single man-year, nor even a month, is spent on ensuring smooth implementation. How much time should be spent? What is an appropriate situational-management design-budget percentage? In most firms it is zero. They think that a plan on paper is a short step from a plan implemented. It is not.

All change has associated benefits for the worker, manager, or organization as a whole. In the long run those working in the organization will gain if the organization gains. The benefits of some change may simply be survival, but benefits, in some form, are always present. Even though they may not be individual benefits, they should be stressed rather than ignored.

Sometimes change is resisted simply because it is seen as a result of a personal whim. This kind of objection is unlikely to be raised about the manager at a top of a profit center. It is very likely to be raised about staff men who are seen as empire builders or of very ambitious managers who appear more interested in personal than managerial effectiveness.

The Suppression of Resistance

No normal manager prefers to use coercive means to suppress resistance, yet most managers have and know they will again. There is no argument for suppression unless all else has failed. If absolute time limits are near and if others may suffer because of increased danger or the possibility of adverse economic consequences, then the method may be condoned.

Suppression methods are familiar to all and include threats of punishment, offers of bribes, threatened termination, and the threat of cancellation of concessions already offered. These methods are not recommended unless others have failed or unless special conditions prevail because they can easily lead to increased resistance. If handled properly when they must be used, they can lead to increased respect.

SELDOM MEET FORCE WITH FORCE

It is unwise to interpret deep resistance as an attack on the manager or on the changes he wants to implement. The resistance may simply be an instinctive or learned reaction to something strange. If so, it is unwise to meet force with force because it may turn what was simply an initial objection to a lasting resentment.

Rate of Change, not Introduction of Change

Very few social systems remain unchanged over long periods. Changes may be small and may be introduced slowly, but they do take place. The discussion of change, therefore, should not be solely concerned with the introduction of change itself but also with the rate of change.

In deciding whether to introduce change rapidly, the following factors should be considered:

Is time important?
What will be gained by speed?
What is past custom?
Will speed increase resistance?
Can acceptance be sacrificed for speed?
How would speed be interpreted?
Are other changes still being assimilated?
Must other changes be integrated?

There are some general arguments for both slow and rapid change. The arguments for slow change are:

Usually produces less resistance
Allows for gradual acceptance
Will be seen as evolutionary
Allows for greater understanding
Allows for skill acquisition
Changes can blend with others
Changes and modifications in the proposed change, itself, will be easier
Changes and adjustments to the method used will be easier

The arguments for rapid change are:

Less time taken to reach ideal changed state
Shorter adjustment period
Only one basic adjustment required
Less basic plan modification likely
Adds impression of resilience

The speed of change is an important part of any complete plan for reducing resistance. It should be considered carefully along with the methods to be used.

There is nothing so practical as a good theory.

K. LEWIN

Unapplied knowledge is knowledge shorn of its meaning.

A. N. WHITEHEAD

One of the great differences between the amateur and the professional is that the latter has the capacity to progress.

W. SOMERSET MAUGHAM

Chapter Fourteen

SITUATIONAL THEORY

While on the one hand, 3-D is a practical tool for managers, it is, on the other, a management theory. Most managers are, naturally enough, interested only in its practical aspects. Some, however, will wish to know more about how it differs from other theories and what its most distinctive theoretical characteristics are. This chapter is for those interested in the theories. Training managers and students especially should read it.

What Characterizes 3-D?

What characterizes 3-D? How is it similar to, and different from, other theories, and what is new about it? This can be explored by considering these topics:

Behavioral similarities
Effectiveness as central value
Practicality
Situational management base
Comprehensive conceptual framework
Reality and rationality as focus
Positive alternatives raised

BEHAVIORAL SIMILARITIES   The 3-D concept is essentially a behavioral theory of management. It is not concerned with charts, files, and controls but is concerned with people, social systems, and effectiveness. Other behavioral theorists use many similar concepts to 3-D. For instance, most of the thirty or so managerial-style theories developed so far have an autocrat or equivalent among their styles. At least a dozen use something like Task Orientation and Relationships Orientation as underlying measures of styles. Many, as with 3-D, go to some lengths to describe the styles in detail.

EFFECTIVENESS AS CENTRAL VALUE   The 3-D Theory differentiates itself sharply from most other behavioral theories in the centrality it gives to managerial effectiveness. Obviously many general management books are concerned with this issue, but it is not so true of most behavioral approaches. These approaches tend to place major value on such things as subordinate self-actualization (86), integrating needs of individuals with the needs of the organization (7), or of a particular ideal style (23). These may or may not lead to improved managerial effectiveness. There are research results on both sides (115).

The 3-D Theory suggests the prime purpose of any managerial action is to improve managerial effectiveness. It is in the name of this endeavor that one decides on, initiates, and pursues one particular course of action over another. For profit-making concerns this amounts to the principle of profit maximization at the managerial level. There are those who ask about social values and ask what role managers should have in preserving these. The answer is, of course, that a sound way to protect a culture against outside cultural influence is through the individual firm's economic success due to the effectiveness of its individual managers.

PRACTICALITY   It is a fairly simple matter to develop a theory with little practical application. It is most difficult to develop one which, while comprehensive, can still be used directly by a manager. The 3-D Theory is practical and can be used to improve things. A quick reading of this book may not lead to overnight improvements, of course, but a close study of it could. The most practical part of the theory is the guides provided on reading a situation and adapting to it or changing it.

The 3-D concept is designed to be directly useful as a basis for management development and organizational change. Although this book is concerned primarily with managerial application, the concepts are also useful for viewing team or organizationwide behavior. Managerial effectiveness, flexibility, and resilience, for instance, have a direct and obvious organizational analogy.

SITUATIONAL MANAGEMENT BASE   The idea of situational management is certainly not new, but the stress put on it by 3-D is. The total situation approach has been developed primarily by the leader-follower—situation concepts developed by scientists at the University of Michigan and the Tavistock Institute in Britain.

Self-management as suggested by the purely management-style approach is important, but situational management is more effective. A manager should see himself not simply as a superior, as suggested by the styles approach, but as a manager of a social system, as suggested by the situational approach. The 3-D Theory asks managers to look at the total situation they are in, in particular at technology and at expectations. Whereas a manager needs situational sensitivity to understand such important situation elements as these, he also needs situational management skills in changing them when appropriate.

COMPREHENSIVE CONCEPTUAL FRAMEWORK   The 3-D Theory is sharply different from most behavioral management theories in the number of definitions and concepts which it has. It, in fact, emphasizes concepts and their relationships rather than their description. Other current approaches to management theory that include an extensive set of concepts include Brown (33) and Allen (2).

An important feature of any theory is to provide a common terminology so that the same words and definitions are used by everyone. The common terminology is integrated by a systematic framework which aids both learning and unlearning. Unlearning is of particular importance in the social science area. Many managers are made less effective not through what they do not know but through what they know "ain't so." Concepts help them discover what otherwise cannot be understood.

How do concepts get developed? To take an example, up to now it has been common to perceive flexibility as good and rigidity as bad. These two concepts are seen as opposite poles of a spectrum along which we might move and thus be more or less flexible or rigid. The drawback with this view is that managers know very well that flexibility can be used as a means of avoiding a difficult decision or of lowering the pressure on ourselves. What is this to be called? The 3-D concept for this behavior is "style drift." Similarly, rigidity has its good side and is called "style resilience." The four concepts are put together on the flex scale. Style flex means a change in behavior without any connotation of effectiveness.

The two concepts of flexibility and rigidity have now been expanded to five by adding drift, resilience, and flex. Once understood, the five concepts together add clarity to the subject of style change; they do not confuse it. Concepts that are tied together this way have great usefulness.

As another example, consider again the Coch and French (40). They published an account of an experiment they had conducted concerning *participative management*. The experiment demonstrated that the participative style led to increased productivity. Considering this single experiment, we have two concepts, participation and productivity, with a relationship suggesting that more participation leads to more productivity. Here, then, are two concepts with a demonstrated relationship. Fitting many such relationships together could lead to a theory.

But a problem arose here. In 1960 French and Israel (68) published an account of an attempt to duplicate the experiment in Norway. Participation did not lead to increased productivity. An easy way to deal with this finding would be to say that participation sometimes leads to productivity and sometimes does not. Although this may be correct, it does not get us very far and can hardly form the basis for a useful theory. Suppose an attempt were made to explain why participation produced different results. One hypothetical but probable explanation would be that the effects of participation depend on the expectations workers have about the way they should be treated and what behavior change they would trade for being treated differently. Here a third concept, in this case an intervening variable, subordinates' expectations, has been introduced to explain the data. At this point a theorist might inquire into the possibility of other strong intervening variables and of the chances a manager has of modifying them. Patiently piecing together the various findings and believing in an underlying orderliness in nature, a set of variables and relationships could be established to make sense out of these management-style research results. A good theory must explain all, or at least most, of the data.

It is by the method and in the spirit just described that the 3-D Theory was developed. For managers, the 3-D Theory is essentially a category system. It consists of sets of slots to put things into. This enables them to make sense out of and to explain otherwise what may be a confusing situation. Starting with an adequate perception of the situation, the theory then suggests several strategies to employ to improve effectiveness.

Concepts are sometimes called "jargon." Jargon is often used to describe another's concepts that we do not understand or agree with. If, in fact, another's concepts are unsound or inapplicable to our problems, there is no need to learn them. They may, however, present a new and useful way of looking at our present situation. If so, we have no option but to learn and understand them, or to remain less effective.

To become professional, managers must become much more knowledgeable about concept formation and theory in the social sciences. They will then be less likely to be confused by theories that do not make sense. They must know what constitutes scientific proof and be able to recognize when it has been obtained. There is probably no one tougher in his demands for truth than the scientist. Managerial decision making, alongside the truly scientific approach, appears weak-willed, easily influenced, and beset with past precedent and ideology rather than facts. The scientist is demanding. He insists on knowing what the words used mean, he demands closely defined concepts, and he demands experiments and proof. He uses the scientific approach and has a body of hard facts, concepts, and theories upon which to draw.

REALITY AND RATIONALITY AS FOCUS   Management styles are best seen as rational acts rather than as emotional responses. This is opposite to one approach of teaching management which suggests that facts are facts but feelings are the truth. This is a useful point of view so long as one considers the individual in isolation and ignores other people. It is not so useful for managers of social systems who need to focus on things as they are and need to act as they must. Reality and rationality must influence them, not emotion.

POSITIVE ALTERNATIVES RAISED   The 3-D Theory does not ask managers to change their styles for that is an unreasonable request. What 3-D does do is ask managers to improve their situational sensitivity and to read a situation for what it contains. Then they are asked to increase their range of style flex in order to respond to the situation appropriately and to increase their skill in situational management as a means of changing a situation needing change.

Problem Areas in Behavioral Theory

The absence of a generally accepted theory of managerial effectiveness and of management styles confronts us with a major problem in formal management training which is still unresolved today. Principles are taught that everyone knows are consistently violated. All too often training reflects the thinking of a small nonmanagerial training group who identify with subordinates rather than with managers. Some training officers pass through a stage which might be called *behavioral dilettantism.* They run management courses in which up to a dozen behavioral theories may be discussed. Although the course is labeled "management," a more accurate title would be "a survey of problem areas in socal science." There has been and still is much confusion and uncertainty in the management training area, a fact which is hidden, sometimes, by its becoming a "true believer" of the latest idea. So-called "exciting experiments" are conducted almost continually by some firms. Although not always true, this usually means they are not sure what they are doing or why they are doing it.

In spite of the fact that behavioral theories can help managers, there are some real problems hindering their development. For example, there is the difficulty of measuring some highly abstract but key concepts such as "autocrat" or "power." Physiologists can agree on the precise definition of an organ such as the heart which can be observed, described, and measured, but psychologists define love much less precisely and so far have been able to put forward only a generally acceptable definition of it. This typifies the gap between the soft sciences, like psychology and sociology, and the hard sciences, like chemistry and physics. Some would claim that the soft sciences will remain soft; many, in fact, would prefer that they did on the grounds that hard science and humanism do not mix. Whatever the position we have as individuals, it is clear that real problems exist.

To possess any practical value whatsoever, the various theories of managerial effectiveness must avoid the following six approaches as all can lead to dead ends:

Either-or approach
Types approach
Psychological approach
Ideal-style approach
Normative approach
Is man a beast? approach

THE EITHER-OR APPROACH

The either-or approach to management styles teaches that there are two basic management styles and two only. One is generally good, and the other is generally bad. For example:

BAD		GOOD
Authoritarian	versus	Democratic
Employer-centered	versus	Employee-centered
Teacher-centered	versus	Learner-centered
Autocratic	versus	Permissive
Supervisory	versus	Participatory
Directive	versus	Nondirective

A careful examination of the literature on this polarized approach (4) indicates rather strongly that the either-or approach is truly popular but that it oversimplifies far too much. Certainly it is no help in giving guides to effectiveness. This simple view tends to produce inadequate answers to complex questions. It also leads to the belief that the main consideration is simply the style used rather than the style which is appropriate to a particular situation.

THE TYPES APPROACH

Typology is a technical term meaning a collection of types. "Our team" and "their team" is a two-type typology. The types approach can have some use in management development, as the types provided can be used as convenient reference points. Several approaches, including those of

McGregor (140), Zaleznik and Moment (194), Brown (32), Blake and Mouton (23), and Jennings (103) are worthy of attention.

Typologies are usually clear classifications with extensive descriptions. They do not, however, usually provide tools for changing or optimizing individual and organizational behavior. By themselves they do not deepen our understanding about the managerial process or offer anything new about management. As descriptive labels, however, they have some use.

The current popularity of typologies and the absence of a widely accepted theory indicate that there are not as yet any simple, precise, and practical formulations in management theory that could compare to our knowledge of, say, atomic weights or even of the temperature scale, both of which express precisely a set of relationships among well-defined variables.

Things are improving, however, and will continue to do so as the valuable raw material that now exists is properly digested by theoreticians. This material includes executive biographies (41, 130, 26); top-man autobiographies (36, 172, 67); studies of managers in Russia (75), Europe (76), the United Kingdom (139), France (34), and the United States (189); long-term case studies following individual careers (46); summaries of serious psychological leadership research (177); and the steadily growing collection of Harvard case studies (98). All this material will be brought into focus more and more as management theorists develop stronger and more powerful tools of analysis. The types approach will give way to theory.

THE PSYCHOLOGICAL APPROACH

Many managers and some management theorists believe that psychological explanations are the best ones. They explain organizational problems by pointing to individual needs and styles. No real attention is paid to the impact of technology or even the impact of expectations. Managers are offered a personality theory with managerial labels and asked to use it as a conceptual framework. This kind of framework is far too limiting. A manager must think of the situation as well as the person. He must think sociologically as well as psychologically. He must become a situationist.

On the matter of needs, it is not particularly helpful to try and train managers to attempt to deduce the personal motives of other managers. It is certainly of no value at all for them to consider how a manager happened to acquire the style he now uses, and even psychologists might not agree. Why should a manager try, and what could he do with the information anyway that he could not do equally well without it?

THE IDEAL-STYLE APPROACH

Many, if not most, popular management theorists have based their theory on the idea of a single ideal style and on one or more poorer styles often labeled "autocrat" or "laissez-faire." It is implied or explicitly stated that managers might study and even copy the ideal style.

The ideal-style approach does have real advantages. It provides an image of potential, a standard to aim at, and a convenient collecting point for all behavior seen as "good." It is a useful device to present to managers as a model which they might copy. It makes short, simple development courses feasible because the basic function of the course is to teach a single style and the behavior associated with it. Some could even argue that it is not necessary for an ideal style to be correct because its real function is to highlight the less effective styles.

In spite of the fact that all this is, to some extent, true, the ideal-style approach still has these difficulties:

It is frequently difficult or impossible to apply in practice.

It can establish an impossible target leading to ultimate disappointment.

It may induce guilt and anxiety in managers who cannot use it.

It leads to senior managers being seen as preaching one thing and practicing another.

It can greatly increase subordinate-manager dissatisfaction with existing conditions which perhaps should not and could not be changed.

It can misdirect training efforts.

A combination of the psychological approach and an ideal-style approach takes management theory backward to *trait theory*. The trait theorists suggested that a combination of certain qualities such as judgment, integrity, and perseverance would generally lead to effectiveness in any management job. This is essentially what the ideal-style theory believes except that general behavior descriptions are substituted for traits.

THE NORMATIVE APPROACH

The "normative error," as scientists call it, is the unjustified assertion that one thing is better than another. The ideal-style approach is an obvious example of it, but it can go deeper so that the normative position is not stated at all or is even disguised.

What has happened in the human relations movement that sprung up in the United States in the 1930s is also a good example. As the initial research findings were more and more misinterpreted, the idea that the individual should always be placed ahead of the organization became popular. As recently as the early 1960s, several textbooks used in American colleges clearly had this approach. Much of this was supported by those who thought that the relatively permissive approach of academic life should be transferred to the factory floor. As a value, many, if not most, would hold that this is desirable if possible. As a feasible scientific proposition, however, it is another matter.

The managerial theory cannot be normative. It cannot be a thinly veiled justification for the way the theorist would like to see the world. As persons within the human relations movement, their motives are understandable and even laudable; as scientists, their approach is unacceptable.

THE "IS MAN A BEAST?" APPROACH

Is man a beast? This must seem an unusual question to raise in a book on managerial effectiveness, yet it is an underlying, often unstated, issue in many current behavioral theories based on needs. By understanding the issue, it is possible to see the reasons for fundamental differences in approach.

Some theorists suggest to managers that many problems would be solved if managers only would agree on the nature of man and then treat him in the way the theorists suggest. This approach is unlikely to be successful as the "nature of man" is a philosophical question, one that has interested scholars through the ages, but one with no possible single answer. Attempts to establish yes-no answers will lead simply to rigidity rather than to effectiveness.

The two basic approaches to this question can be summarized in this way:

Is man a beast?

THEORY X	THEORY Y
Man is a beast	Man is a self-actualizing being
Evil is man's inherent nature	Good is man's inherent nature
Biology drives man	Humanism drives man
Force motivates man	Voluntary cooperation motivates man
Competition is man's basic mode of interaction	Cooperation is man's basic mode of interaction
Individual is man's social unit of importance	Group is man's social unit of importance
Pessimistic best describes man's view of man	Optimistic best describes man's view of man

Taking a position one way or the other on this kind of issue is good for an argument. Since neither position is to any extent provable, the argument is based on what each side would like to believe. A much more useful approach for a manager would be Theory Z. It carefully avoids the ideological traps of either X or Y. It sees man as a situationist and as one open to both "good" and "evil."

THEORY Z
   Man has a will
   He is open to good and evil
   Situation drives man
   Reason motivates him
   Interdependence is man's basic mode of interaction
   Interaction is man's social unit of importance
   Objective best describes man's view of man

Each of these three views of man has its supporters in the past and present. Although some may disagree with the exact placement of the "nature-of-man" theorists on this list, it is meant to indicate generally the basic orientation of the writer concerned.

Nature-of-man theorists		
X	Z	Y
Hobbes (88)	Locke (122)	McGregor (140)
Machiavelli (123)	Fromm (70)	Likert (119)
Freud (69)	Sullivan (177)	Argyris (7)
Taylor (179)	Kelly (112)	Maslow (133)
Weber (188)	Drucker (48)	Herzberg (87)

The 3-D Theory is based on Theory Z, the rational situationist view of man.

The 3-D and Other Behavorial Theories

There are many behavioral theories popular today. Many of them are in clear disagreement with each other, not only in terms of what dimensions they suggest are important but also in terms of what they suggest an ideal state should be.

As many of these behavioral theories are taught in management development courses, some form of integration is useful and what follows are some notes on them. The theories are not explained in detail, but enough is given for the general reader and the specialist who wants to know the most important ways in which each may be related to 3-D.

Those discussed are:

Maslow's Needs
McGregor's X-Y
Leader—Followers—Situation

Katz' Administrator Skills
Blake's Grid
McClelland's Need for Achievement
Likert's Management Systems
Herzberg's Motivation Hygiene Theory
Fiedler's Leadership Contingency Model

3-D AND MASLOW'S NEEDS

Maslow (133) suggests that people are dominated by their unsatisfied needs. The unsatisfied needs shape behavior. Although there is an overlap, needs must be satisfied in this order: physiological, safety, belongingness and love, esteem, and finally self-actualization. As one need is satisfied, the next emerges. The need for which Maslow is best known, and which is, in fact, the foundation of his theory, is self-actualization. This is called a "growth" need; the other four are "deficiency" needs.

Maslow says that we are born with these needs, and within limits, we all have them but to varying degrees. He also says that, for most people, the lower-order needs must all be satisfied before the higher-order needs can emerge to be satisfied in turn.

There are many difficulties with the theory including lack of evidence to support it, the meaning of self-actualization, and its strong humanistic bias.

The primary difference between 3-D and Maslow is that Maslow gives primary attention to man's inner needs rather than to the situation he is in. Maslow deals essentially with the origins of subordinate expectations. The theory is useful to managers as it is a straightforward approach to subordinate psychology which can help explain why subordinates have the expectations they do and why money is not always the best motivating force.

3-D AND McGREGOR'S X-Y

McGregor (140) sees a basic conflict between the needs of the worker and the needs of the organization. He believes that neither can achieve all it wishes but that moving toward this state should be an objective for managers. McGregor bases some of his key ideas on Maslow's need theory. McGregor, like Maslow, suggests that man today has to a large extent satisfied his security needs. This being so, management must focus on worker's higher-order needs. In brief, autonomy and esteem, not cash. Workers motivated by higher-order needs will tend toward self-control and tend to be responsive to Theory Y leadership.

McGregor's X-Y Theory is essentially a set of two types of assumptions managers have about people.

THEORY X	THEORY Y
1. Work is inherently distasteful to most people.	1. Work is as natural as play, if the conditions are favorable.
2. Most people are not ambitious, have little desire for responsibility, and prefer to be directed.	2. Self-control is often indispensable in achieving organizational goals.
3. Most people have little capacity for creativity in solving organizational problems.	3. The capacity for creativity in solving organizational problems is widely distributed in the population.
4. Motivation occurs only at the physiological and security levels.	4. Motivation occurs at the affiliation, esteem, and self-actualization levels, as well as physiological and security levels.
5. Most people must be closely controlled and often coerced to achieve organizational objectives.	5. People can be self-directed and creative at work if properly motivated.

McGregor's description of Theory X assumptions shows it to be essentially one that man is a beast. Years before, Mayo had the same idea with his description of the "rabble hypothesis." This X assumption leads, McGregor claims, to centralized decision making, tight control procedures, and marked status and power differences. This assumption leads also to the belief that people are motivated either by material gain or punishment.

These two assumptions lead to two leadership styles. His X type is close to autocrat and Y type is close to executive or developer. McGregor depicted these two types as extremes to make his argument clear. His very strong position on integrating organizational and individual needs make his model fall into the ideal-type class. Essentially he proposes that one style of management is better than another. His ideal state on a flex map would be overlapping shapes in the integrated basic style.

In a sensitive essay entitled "Management of Disappointment," Professor Abraham Zaleznik of the Harvard Business School writes about Theory Y (195):

> Its appeal lies in its humanness and in the subtle way it addresses itself to the underlying guilt which plagues men who exercise power. . . . Unfortunately, McGregor's theories avoid the inner conflicts . . . in their almost singular dedication to creating an ideal organization climate. . . . McGregor missed the point in the study of leadership because . . . he failed in a basic sense to identify with [managers]. His identification was largely with subordinates . . . but to love and be loved is not enough. . . . McGregor's problem I would suspect, developed out of his noble purposes.

Theory Y has deservedly attracted much attention, both positive and negative. There is even a list and discussion of thirty-six reasons why Theory Y may be unrealistic (134). This Theory is useful to study in conjunction with 3-D as it gives a good account of the dedicated and integrated management style and organization philosophy.

3-D AND LEADER-FOLLOWERS—SITUATION

The approach which sees leadership as a function of the leader, the followers, and the situation is close in principle to 3-D and may be written this way:

Leadership = function (leader, followers, situation)
$$L = f (l, f, s)$$

This may be improved by sharpening 'situation' to coworkers, superior, organization, and technology, so:

Leadership = function (leader, followers, coworkers,
superiors, organization, technology)
$$L = f (l, f, c, s, o, t)$$

and still further improved by realizing that it is effectiveness not leadership that is really important and style rather than leadership in any case:

Effectiveness = function (style, followers, coworkers,
superiors, organization technology)
$$E = f (st, f, c, s, o, t)$$

There is no real difference between 3-D and the leader-followers-situation approach. The 3-D Theory has simply emphasized effectiveness not leadership and has specified completely all the elements in the situation.

3-D AND KATZ' ADMINISTRATOR SKILLS

Katz (109) proposes that "Effective administration rests on three basic developable skills—which we will call technical, human, and conceptual." Technical skill is "An understanding of, and proficiency in, a specific kind of activity," particularly one involving methods, processes, procedures, or techniques." In 3-D terms this technical skill is a component of task orientation and a sensitivity to technology.

Human skill is the "Ability to work effectively as a group member." In 3-D terms this is a high relationship orientation and a sensitivity to superior, coworkers, and subordinates.

Conceptual skill is "The ability to see the enterprise as a whole." In 3-D terms this is sensitivity to organization.

The three skills proposed by 3-D of course are:

Situational sensitivity
Style flexibility
Situational management skill

Katz' three skills clearly emphasize situational sensitivity as the most important, and understandably so, as the other two skills proposed by 3-D cannot be used without it.

3-D AND BLAKE'S GRID

Blake's (23) five-style grid theory, like McGregor's theory, is a managerial-style model with an ideal style. Blake uses numbers as a notational device rather than names. His 9.9 is his ideal style. Like McGregor, he recognizes the importance of the situation but he does not emphasize technological demands to any extent. The model is essentially a psychological ideal-style model, not a situational model. Having an ideal style, he does not argue for flexibility as a key managerial quality. Blake later introduced his own third dimension of which he says (24):

> The third dimension of the Managerial Grid represented is the thickness or depth of a given style. . . . It deals with how long a managerial style is maintained in any given situation of interaction, particularly under pressure from tension, frustration or conflict.

Thus Blake's third dimension is similar to the 3-D style resilience.

Blake uses his five styles as collecting points for the research of others. In situational terms, 1.1 is any behavior seen as too weak; 1.9 is any behavior seen as too soft; 9.1 is any behavior seen as too hard; 9.9 is most behavior seen as ideal. The 5.5 style is not so much a style as a statistical device for collecting any behavior not falling into the other four categories. Although managers tend to view the two scales as continuous, that is, moving from 0 to 10, they in fact are not. Blake points out that the 9s in 9.9 are not the same 9s as in 1.9 and 9.1. This means, in effect, that the grid does not exist.

In spite of this, the Blake model is still a very useful training device. A large part of its attractiveness stems from the positive approach to managing suggested by 9.9, from the cross-cultural advantages of using numbers instead of names, and from the ease with which the basic idea can be grasped. Its usefulness in conjunction with 3-D is the very extensive description of five of the eight 3-D managerial styles provided in his book (23). On a 3-D diagram, the Blake five-style model is shown in Exhibit 14.1.

3-D AND McCLELLAND'S NEED FOR ACHIEVEMENT

McClelland of Harvard University has spent a large part of his life investigating the need for achievement, abbreviated to N-ACH. He has

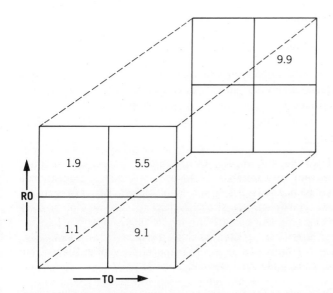

Exhibit 14–1   Grid on 3-D. The managerial grid has four less effective styles similar to those of 3-D but only one more effective style.

worked also on two other needs, affiliation and power, but N-ACH has been by far the most useful and widely investigated. His research methods have been novel and have shown remarkable results (137, 138).

The person with high N-ACH is more concerned with knowing he has done well than with the rewards that success brings. He gets his rewards from his accomplishment rather than from money or praise. This does not mean that the high N-ACH rejects money. It can in fact motivate him if he sees it as a realistic measure of his performance. Such N-ACH people are not gamblers. They set themselves realistic but achievable goals with some "stretch" built in. They prefer situations which they themselves can influence rather than those in which chance has a large influence on the outcome.

N-ACH types can help organizations or can be seen as ambitious or even maverick. To put it simply, high N-ACH managers succeed in high N-ACH organizations; in low N-ACH organizations they would have to find outlets for high N-ACH off the job or they would leave. The high N-ACH is a producer. This is demanded on the boundary of some organizations such as in sales, in some production positions, and sometimes at the top, particularly in small organizations.

N-ACH is not a rough equivalent to the 3-D concept of managerial effectiveness. N-ACH is a need; managerial effectiveness is a condition that arises when an appropriate style to a situation is used. There is a relationship however. The high N-ACH type would be very interested in both personal and managerial effectiveness particularly in a dedicated situation. The high N-ACH type would in fact be most likely to succeed in a dedicated situation. This situation gives reward for effort and usually provides task-related feedback, both of which the high N-ACH person prefers to have.

The high N-ACH is most effective only when the situation allows him to get ahead by his own efforts. He may not be effective otherwise. Thus if a high N-ACH type with a low need for affiliation is in a related situation, he would either have to change the situation or himself or have to leave. If he stayed and the situation did not change, he would probably be less effective.

The concept of N-ACH is remarkably close to that of North American drive. It may be that N-ACH is a useful concept, but it may also be that it parallels a bit too closely the North American ideal type. This may or may not be a suitable ideal for firms in other cultures or for all positions in a single firm in the United States.

3-D AND LIKERT'S MANAGEMENT SYSTEMS

Likert has had such a variety of strong influences on management and the behavioral sciences that it is difficult to select a single point of view which best describes his approach. His most recent contribution, however, was in his model of four organizational styles he calls systems 1 through 4. These are essentially four organizational philosophies which in 3-D terms are (120).

System 1 (Autocrat)
System 2 (Compromiser)
System 3 (Developer)
System 4 (Executive-developer)

A shortened version of his description is:

System 1   Management having no confidence or trust in subordinates. The bulk of the decisions and the goal setting of the organization are made at the top. Subordinates are forced to work with fear, threats, punishment, and occasional rewards. The little superior-subordinate interaction which takes place is usually with fear and mistrust. The control process is highly concentrated in top management, and informal organization generally develops which opposes the goals of the formal organization.

System 2   Management has condescending confidence and trust in subordinates such as in the master and servant relationship. The bulk of the decisions and goal setting of the organization are made at the top, though many decisions are made within a prescribed framework at lower levels. Rewards and some actual or potential punishment are used to motivate workers. The control process is still concentrated in top management, but some is delegated to middle levels.

System 3   Management has substantial but not complete confidence and trust in subordinates. Subordinates are permitted to make minor decisions at lower levels. Communication flows both up and down the hierarchy. Rewards, occasional punishment, and some involvement are used to motivate. There is a moderate amount of superior-subordinate interaction, often with a fair amount of confidence and trust. Significant aspects of the control process are delegated downward with a feeling of responsibility at both higher and lower levels. An informal organization may develop, but it may either support or partially resist goals of the organization.

System 4   Management is seen as having complete confidence and trust in subordinates. Decision making is widely dispersed throughout the organization. Communication flows not only up and down the hierarchy but among peers. Workers are motivated by participation and involvement in developing economic rewards, setting goals, improving methods, and appraising progress toward goals. There is extensive, friendly superior-subordinate interaction with a high degree of confidence and trust. The informal and formal organizations are often one and the same. Thus, all social forces support efforts to achieve stated organizational goals.

Again we have the proposal of a single ideal style and a harsh view of the other three. Most of the work out of Michigan, where Likert is, suggests that a related-integrated style is usually best, while that which comes from Ohio State suggests that any style can be equally effective. Likert pays little attention to technology, and his theories suggest that organizations are really best seen as collections of interacting people without a job to do. This psychological rather than sociological view has encouraged his humanistic bias.

Likert asked managers which style of organization they would prefer. Most said system 4; this is to be expected and does not require discussion. Who would not? But more important, Likert asked managers to rate productivity and the system used in departments known to them and they found the system 4 departments were rated most productive. The 3-D Theory would deny such a correlation could exist. How can it be explained?

When a social system is working well, everyone knows it. The philosophy of the top man fits well with the styles of his followers, and these to subordinate expectations, and these to technology. Like a well-tuned car the system is in running order. The top man may have 100 percent control, or none of it. The top man may make detailed plans or spend all his day chatting. What style he uses is not relevant. What is relevant is how well this style fits with all the other important elements of organizational life. If it fits, members of the organization will give high marks to trust, communication, decision making, etc., because they are satisfied with the way things are. A sound firm in Germany or Japan working under completely dedicated management, which Likert would call system 1 or autocrat, would score itself high on system 4. The point is that on self-report questionnaires that Likert favors, system 4 is not a fact but a statement of how well we like things as they are. Naturally high producing units rate themselves as system 4. The development of better organizational thermometers should lead to better measurement and better theories. Another explanation is that Likert's four systems, like the Blake five styles, are caricatures, not scientific statements. Built into the description of system 1 is the strong inference that things are going badly, and the opposite is true of system 4. To ask which system works best is begging the question. There is the story of the system 4 manager who had only one prayer: "Move over."

3-D AND HERZBERG'S MOTIVATION HYGIENE THEORY

Herzberg has developed a theory of work motivation which has highly practical applications. Herzberg believes that industrial man has two groups of needs which are independent of one another and which affect behavior in different ways. He says that dissatisfaction is most likely to arise from elements in the job environment while satisfaction is most likely to arise from elements in the job itself (85–87).

The environmental or hygiene factors are:

Policies and administration
Supervision
Working conditions
Interpersonal relations
Money, status, security

Changes in these will lower dissatisfaction but not increase satisfaction. Hygiene factors then generally include such things as money, status, security, policies, procedures, administration, supervision, and working conditions. These are extrinsic to the job or technology, not intrinsic to it.

The motivators or job factors are:

Achievement
Recognition for accomplishment
Challenging work
Increased responsibility
Growth and development

Changes in these can motivate people to higher performance. They produce satisfactions and feelings of achievement, growth, and recognition. Changes in these factors can lead directly to improved motivation, performance, and ultimately ability. Herzberg's strategy in organizational development is to induce management to bring about these kinds of changes.

The essence of the Herzberg approach to change is technological re-design. In very general terms he attempts to change work so as to get more of the "3-D People and Organization Demand Indicators" to apply. He calls this job enrichment. It amounts to increasing the flex of situations to match the capacity of the people in them.

The only real restraining factor which might limit his approach is the difficulty of redesign caused by technological factors and cultural differences. As simple examples how can a police patrolman's job be changed or that of a steam plant superintendent? They could both be changed of course but not without major changes in the total organization design.

Herzberg gives little weight to style as a motivator, and in fact he classifies it only as a hygiene factor. Those who have seen two identical technologies, say bomber squadrons with quite different levels of effectiveness owing to the top man's style, might question this. Again, if job enrichment alone is such a key, why do we find many who have enriched jobs although unmotivated? Perhaps it is the style with which they are being managed.

While Herzberg has made a tremendous contribution, 3-D would still see the main issue as an integration of style with technological and other demands rather than simply a change, even if profound, in the technology of the situation. The 3-D Theory matches management style with technology and subordinates; Herzberg matches subordinate needs with technology.

3-D AND FIEDLER'S LEADERSHIP CONTINGENCY MODEL

Of all behavioral theories that of Fred E. Fiedler (53) is closest to that of 3-D. He too has a situational model and is primarily interested in leadership effectiveness. Like most situationists, he sees leadership effectiveness as a function of the extent to which style matches the situation. The key situational elements or dimensions in his approach are power of leader, degree of structure of task, and leader-member relations. In the same way that 3-D uses the three managerial-style dimensions, Fiedler uses his three situational dimensions to produce an eight-type model of situations.

As far as Fiedler is concerned, the most favorable situation in which a leader can influence his group is where these conditions exist:

High position power
High task structure
High leader-member relations

A hard-driving popular senior manager might be an example. The worst situation, Fiedler says, is where the situation is low on all three, a disliked leader of a voluntary organization. In a very rough translation to 3-D,

Fiedler suggests that the integrated situation is good and the separated situation is poor.

The Fiedler dimension of a leader's position power is an aspect of what in 3-D is called "organization." This dimension is the degree to which the organization endows the position, itself, with power to enable the superior to get subordinates to comply with him. It is in essence the potential power the organization provides. To a large extent it is dependent on the design of the organization systems and policies concerned with rewards and punishments, appraisal, status, and hiring-firing. It may be measured by these and, also, by the extent to which the leader's compliments are valued, his opinion is respected, his job knowledge is superior, and by the information or orders he gives.

The Fiedler dimension of task structure is an aspect of technology. He describes the task as the reason for which the group was established. The task structure is based on the extent to which the leader is able to control and supervise his group members by virtue of a structured or programmed task. His control tends to increase with the degree to which the task is structured, the accuracy of decisions are verifiable, the goal is clear, and the routes to the goal and number of possible solutions are limited. The more structured the task, the more enforceable the control.

The Fiedler dimension of leader-member relationships is closer to the 3-D concept of managerial effectiveness than to any other 3-D concept. Fiedler defines leader-member relations as the degree to which leader-member relations are good. The indicators of this are that when questioned, subordinates state that they would choose the leader as a leader in similar tasks as a preferred coworker, and they state he is most influential. The leader in turn states that he feels accepted and relaxed. Fiedler sees this as one of three basic underlying dimensions of interacting groups.

The 3-D Theory on the other hand sees leader-member relations, as measured by Fiedler, as an output rather than an underlying input dimension in a situation. The 3-D Theory would propose that if subordinates want the leader as a leader in a similar task, etc., it would indicate that the leader was probably satisfying the demands of the technology and subordinates. From this, one would expect high correlations between this dimension and an overall measure of group effectiveness.

What leader-member relations would seem to indicate is that both the manager and subordinates believe things are proceeding satisfactorily, with the manager in control of the situation. If the members of a social system believe this, it appears likely that the system is achieving its goals and that *managerial effectiveness* is being achieved.

In an admittedly very rough way, this is how Fiedler's three dimensions and those of 3-D may be related.

FIEDLER	3-D
Position power	Organization
Task structure	Technology
Leader-member relations	Managerial effectiveness

By combining his three dimensions, Fiedler produces eight types of situations. The 3-D Theory, on the other hand, proposes four basic types of situations which when combined with one of four basic styles result in one of eight styles.

Part 3

STYLES

To place and power all public spirit tends;
In place and power all public spirit ends.

THOMAS MOORE

He who is firmly seated in authority soon learns to think
of security, and not progress, the highest lesson of states-
craft.

LOWELL

Chapter Fifteen

SEPARATED—DESERTER—BUREAUCRAT

This chapter and the three that follow describe the behavior associated with the four basic styles and the eight managerial styles. The description is intended to breathe life into the styles so that the styles may be easily recognized and understood.

Each of the four chapters is organized in the same way. The chapters start with a description of the behavior of a single basic style. This is followed by a description of how the impact of that behavior is perceived when used inappropriately and then when used appropriately.

The Separated Manager

SEPARATED INDICATORS

> Cautious—careful—conservative—orderly
> Prefers paper work—procedures—facts
> Looks for established principles
> Accurate—precise—correct—perfectionist
> Steady—deliberate—patient
> Calm—modest—discreet

The separated manager has an orientation to procedures, methods, and systems. Many highly intelligent and effective managers have a separated

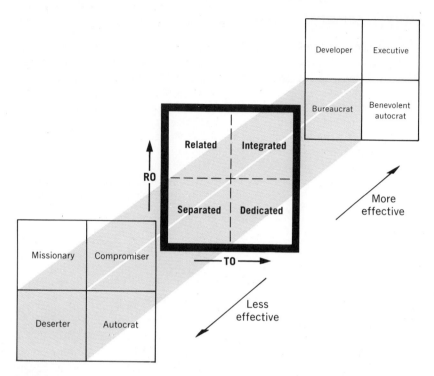

Exhibit 15–1   The separated styles. All have a low Task Orientation and a low Relationships Orientation.

basic style. They are often found in finance, accounting, staff, electronic data processing, research and development, government, and in the control departments of head offices. The separated style may be induced by the relatively lengthy training programs people in these positions often undergo, of which accountancy is the best example. The values induced in such training parallel the qualities of the separated style. There is the emphasis on accuracy, conservatism, prudence, and noninvolvement.

The separated manager often appears not too secure as a person. Instead of interacting with his environment, he takes refuge in the rules. He believes that if he follows the rules really well, he will not encounter too many difficulties. When confronted with decision making the separated manager wants a clearly defined principle to follow. First, he looks at the written rules, for he goes by the book. Then he will look at the customary ways of solving things in the past. Clearly this approach is useful, or even essential, for some positions in some companies at some times. On the other hand, it may at times be quite inappropriate.

IMPERSONALITY

The separated manager is impersonal. This may at times be seen as arrogance and negativism, but it may also be seen as complete fairness and objectivity about people. Not only does he want to be seen as impersonal but he would also be very quick to complain about the slightest show of personal interest between his subordinates and their subordinates. He suspects any helpfulness as favoritism. The separated manager will seldom be guilty of a tyranny of personal whim though the tyranny of rigid rule application can be one of his major faults.

The separated manager is usually fair, not because of his Relationships Orientation but because of his lack of it. One way not to get involved is to treat everyone equally. This equality of treatment usually leads to emphasis on seniority rather than on ability.

MANAGING WITHIN CHANGE

The separated manager tends to drop in effectiveness as the amount of change required increases. He prefers specific instructions for each new situation, and until he gets them, he is against stretching rules just enough to keep all of them applicable. Clearly, the separated style of management is highly inappropriate among key managers in a rapidly changing situation. A few separated managers as accountants or lawyers, perhaps, may be of help in that situation, but most of the key figures cannot be separated because change will not take place. The separated manager has an overwhelming need for symmetry and order. He wants all the pieces to come together, all the numbers to be in place, and all the evaluations to be neatly tabulated. This is his bastion against change.

Increasing output, as such, does not really interest the separated manager. He prefers to decrease costs rather than increase profit. This is one of many reasons why he is attracted to lower levels of the government service.

More so than with other basic styles the separated manager wants others who are separated as subordinates. These managers will be tuned in to the same things as himself, will add stability to his department, and will lower the impact of a changing environment. The separated superior influences and controls in the name of procedures and existing system demands. He wants subordinates to follow duties, not to follow the situation or him. He abhors strong personal leadership or example. The active, innovative subordinate will not work well with a separated superior. His superior rewards him only for staying in line, yet many acts of innovation require straying from the system or at least testing it.

Committees, but certainly not project teams, are much used by the separated manager. Committees are impersonal and appear to be founded on the rational principle that several heads are better than one. The use of committees leads to orderly changes in power structure, in decision responsibility, and in systems and procedure. Committee members are chosen for the power position they represent rather than for their ability to solve the problem. A deserter would use committees to induce rigidity rather than order and to diffuse or disguise responsibility rather than to share or concentrate it.

SEPARATED AUTHORITY

The separated manager believes he owes personal obedience to no one, and no one owes it to him. Authority is impersonal. Obedience is based squarely on established procedures, regulations, and managerial position. The separated manager does not like his decisions to be questioned. He sees himself as autonomous within the sphere of his position description. This helps explain why the bureaucrat is sometimes called an "autocrat." He places the rules so far ahead of the individual that he is sometimes seen as being unnecessarily nasty. The separated manager usually prefers that managerial levels be clearly distinguished by status devices, such as desks, offices, and carpets. To some extent such devices are always present in large organizations, but the separated manager can carry them to extremes.

THE SEPARATED MANAGER AS A PERSON

The separated manager wants the system to control him. Most children learn, and then accept as their own, social regulations, values, and attitudes. By doing this, they know that society then will not hurt them and, in fact, will value their behavior. (Rule following can be likened to a desire to be loved by a powerful yet detached figure.) The separated manager usually very much wants to become part of the whole. He may want, in effect, to marry the organization. As an extreme, he may be an aging bachelor with no life outside the organization, or he may be anyone with little effective involvement with other people who still wants to get involved somehow yet on an impersonal basis.

"Identification" is the name given to the process of obtaining personal satisfaction through the existence and activities of something or someone other than oneself. The identification may be with the organization and its rules, superiors, coworkers, or subordinates or the work technology. The separated manager identifies with the organization and its rules. Sherlock Holmes' brother, Mycroft, identified with Sherlock Holmes in much the same way.

Within fairly narrow limits, we all have to make our peace with the standards that society imposes. Some learn to do this easily in childhood, while others do not. Those who do not may use a great deal of energy in fighting the standards, and those who do, like the separated manager, may embrace the rules and become "true believers." This latter form can be a satisfactory adjustment because no longer is society or the organization giving orders to us; instead, we are giving orders to ourselves which can serve to lower the tensions that some feel at being ordered around.

The Deserter Manager

DESERTER INDICATORS
>   Works to rules—minimum output—gives up
>   Avoids involvement—responsibility—commitment
>   Gives few useful opinions—suggestions
>   Uncreative—unoriginal—narrow-minded
>   Hinders others—makes things difficult
>   Resists change—uncooperative—uncommunicative

The deserter manager is essentially a separated manager in the wrong situation. He is seen as one who often shows his lack of interest in both task and relationships. He is less effective not only because of his lack of interest but also because of his effect on morale. He may be seen not only as shirking his own duties but also as hindering the performance of others through intervention or by withholding information.

In its refined form and in modern organizations, desertion is likely to reveal itself in resistance to change or in accepting change and then quietly sabotaging it. Making all things difficult, withholding information up or down, aiming for minimum output, impeding others, and lowering morale—the deserter manager uses the whole range. Desertion is to be found more often in the large than in the small company. It is the scar tissue on the human fabric of the organization.

Organization life can be seen as a game, and as in games, people sometimes get hurt. Some are hurt deliberately and some accidentally; sometimes no one else knows it; sometimes the hurt is imaginary. The deserter manager is often one who feels he has been hurt and has never gotten over it. He may be a result of change that was clumsily introduced. He may be a man kicked aside, kicked downstairs, or just ignored. No matter what the case, the important thing is that he thinks he has been treated unfairly. He has decided that he will try to ignore the demands of the organization as much as possible. His avoidance of Task and Relationships is often handled in highly sophisticated ways so that only close observation will disclose it.

Deserters are more to be pitied than anything else because they have usually been made deserters by a major management error. People do not come to organizations acting this way. They are driven to it. The issue for managers is not only how to change the style of deserters but also to prevent more deserters from being created.

Deserter behavior is often a general example of displaced aggression which is turned toward an essentially innocent party. In its simplest form, it is the manager who would like to have a shouting match with his superior but instead has one with a subordinate. This unjustified attack is certainly being nasty, but it is not autocracy since no Task Orientation is involved. It is best called desertion. Aggression may be turned toward oneself so that the person may become accident-prone in the physical or administrative sense.

Such displacement helps the manager using it but seldom helps the organization. It is of considerable value to the manager because it enables him to express aggression without incurring retaliation from the individual whom he really fears. Displacement is essentially desertion because the real problem is not faced. In addition, the displacement may become so deviant that the deserter's action leads to direct harm to the organization.

AVOIDS RESPONSIBILITY

The deserter manager aims for output just high enough to keep people from bothering him. He remains uninvolved by pleading insufficient information. He follows up very slowly, likes to send things to committees in order to bury them, and wants minimum involvement. He develops a wondrous array of techniques to accomplish this. As he does not do too much anyway, and often enjoys his desertion, he has the time and inclination to invent creative ways to inhibit change.

The deserter manager is skilled at avoiding responsibility. He knows how to use separated techniques as tools to slow things down, sometimes to a halt. He will use the "letter" rather than the "spirit" of the regulations. Often he will point to the rules to prove he cannot make a decision. He knows how to use the system to pass the buck and to avoid sticking his neck out. He limits his discretionary powers to a vanishing point. Those subjected to this behavior call it "red tape."

He may ask whether the approval to initiate the task has been fully cleared. He may ask whether the project is fully defined. If he thinks he is in a strong enough position, he will simply turn it down, perhaps on the grounds that it is against his principles or simply is not his job. He may do all this in a forthright and even aggressive way to mask his underlying desertion.

If a decision is likely to be a particularly sticky or complex one, the deserter manager will postpone action on it. At the extreme this may take the ostrich approach of head in the sand—believing that to ignore a problem is likely to send it way. More often his action will be to pass the file to others, pigeonhole it, or raise complex procedural questions concerning it. By these devices the deserter buys time but may pay for it with interest when the decision has to be confronted. Small problems when delayed sometimes go away; they also sometimes magnify.

The separated manager can easily revert to desertion by using the organization's rules against itself. A popular worker parallel to this form of sabotage is the "work-to-rule" strategy of unions. By following all procedures to the letter, slowdowns inevitably result: managers sometimes have sophisticated "work to rule" programs of their own. They may be ingenious and disguised, but the effects are the same.

The deserter has the amazing ability to act as a computer at the most inopportune time. He can rattle off detailed facts and arguments to prove that a particular plan is unworkable. He knows all the reasons why things cannot be done. This may often be facilitated by a high verbal fluency and an intellectual camouflage. The deserter who can use statistics well is often hard to spot for what he is and sometimes hard to stop.

SUICIDAL DESERTION

If inappropriate deserter behavior is prolonged, a manager can actually come to find it satisfying to obstruct and resist others. He may be quite willing to endure discomfort, himself, for the pleasure of maintaining his negative stand. A very clear example of this is the person who pursues a course of action knowing that it will eventually lead to his exclusion from the group or the company. To maintain this immature behavior, a face-saving device is essential. It is usually some principle, some rule, or set of procedures which the deserter claims are inviolate.

The deserter manager can make deserters of his subordinates. Less experienced subordinates may be led to believe that desertion is a reasonable response to the organization so long as they do not get caught. Others may move to desertion in disgust at their superior's behavior and in their knowledge that they may have no power to change the situation. There is usually no incentive to work effectively for a deserter superior because the rewards and recognition may be low or even in the wrong direction.

USING FILES AND RULES AS WEAPONRY

The deserter manager generally prefers to avoid loose, open, unstructured personal conflict so, instead, uses the files or rules as weapons. These may be used to attack just as surely as the sword. He usually likes to keep a copy of every memo he sends and uses them as "alibi papers" to prove he took action. The deserter will often resist, inhibit, or even prevent major change by using outdated but unreplaced rules.

THE AMBITIOUS DESERTER

The ambitious deserter manager can exist in an organization with poor control techniques and a poor reward-and-punishment system. This manager usually develops skills in personal effectiveness and apparent effectiveness but is not directly concerned with his managerial effectiveness.

Some deserters are ambitious, and in a company with poor managerial-measurement devices they may well advance. Many problems can be avoided for years, such as the low-performing subordinate, the major restructuring of a policy or procedure, the extensive survey of markets, customers, or technologies, and the provision for management succession. A deserter may lead a quiet, cordial life putting off all these problems for his successor. He keeps the lid on until he has gone. The crisis is his successor's problem, not his. Incompetent senior management may not spot this desertion for years and may think the deserter's successor is incompetent because he seems to have so many new problems with which to deal.

A deserter may become so concerned over status rather than managerial effectiveness that he becomes an empire builder. He is interested in increasing his personal effectiveness by enlarging his apparent importance. He will spend an inordinate amount of time in scheming to obtain more subordinates, more space, and more power. All this may have no real relationship to the actual demands of his position. He is interested in make-work projects which will add subordinates, more or less permanently.

THE MANAGERIAL RECLUSE

Some forms of desertion are founded in avoidance behavior designed to protect the manager from threatening situations. Some deserters are simply scared. They say, "No!" or are stubborn because to do otherwise might expose them, they believe, to situations difficult to face.

Some emotionally immature managers resort to what is essentially childish behavior in an attempt to solve their adult problems. Their behavior might be the equivalent of a temper tantrum or sulking. The psychologists call this "regression." The particular form it takes depends on what behavior was successful for the manager during his early development. Normal amounts of regression are apparent when men revert to adolescent behavior at conventions and reunions. Abnormal amounts lead to desertion.

These managers have not had an opportunity to grow up. Like the spoiled boy who finds things different at boarding school, the deserter decides to withdraw and so inhibits the development of his own social maturity. In boys' schools, as in organizations, we see those who have psychologically fled from their surroundings. They are quiet, friendless, unnoticed, little respected. The rituals of the institution carry them on, beginning with the 8:00 A.M. chapel or the opening of the mail, but they might as well not be there.

The Bureaucrat Manager

BUREAUCRAT INDICATORS
Follows orders—rules—procedures
Reliable—dependable
Maintains system and going concern
Watches details—efficient
Rational—logical—self-controlled
Fair—just—equitable

The bureaucrat style is simply the separated style used appropriately. The bureaucrat manager is essentially one who uses separated behavior in a separated situation. The bureaucrat is not overly interested in either task or relationships. He is effective, however, in that his position, or situation, does not require this sort of interest. He succeeds because he follows the company rules, maintains an air of interest, and gets less personally involved with the problems of others.

The bureaucrat manager is efficient. He goes through the right channels, is a stickler for detail, and follows orders exactly. His orientation is to the rules of the game. If he is a manager, he sees standard operating procedures in the same light. For him, existing and past practice are the guidelines to follow. The true bureaucrat is a highly useful organizational member. He keeps the going concern in order. The rules, none of which he may have established, he follows.

"Bureaucrat" has unfortunately become a negative term in most management literature. Many people do not appear to recognize or accept the fact that the bureaucrat style is a key style in maintaining the effectiveness of modern organizations. Rules are needed to harness the efforts of more than a small face-to-face group. A device is also needed to see that all know the rules and follow them. The bureaucrat is often this device.

While effective in following the rules, the bureaucrat manager produces few ideas, does not push for production, and does a poor job of developing his subordinates. Either his job does not require these qualities or it requires them to a minimal degree.

Bureaucrats and even deserters are sometimes incorrectly appraised as autocrats. All three of these styles have a low Relationships Orientation, but only autocrat has a high Task Orientation. What some people mistake for Task Orientation is often adherence to outmoded rules at a heavy expense to the individuals involved. This behavior is simply being nasty.

This chapter has outlined the general nature of a basic style, separated, and its two associated managerial styles, deserter and bureaucrat. At the heart of the two managerial styles is the basic style. To understand the two managerial styles, it is best to study the basic style as well.

The average human being learns, under proper conditions, not only to accept but to seek responsibility.

DOUGLAS McGREGOR

Man's capacities have never been measured; nor are we to judge of what he can do by any precedents, so little has been tried.

H. D. THOREAU

People need people. Laurie was about three when one night she requested my aid in getting undressed. I was downstairs and she was upstairs, and . . . well "you know how to undress yourself," I reminded. "Yes," she explained, "but sometimes people need people anyway, even if they do know how to do things by theirselves." As I slowly lowered the newspaper a strong feeling came over me, a mixture of delight, embarrassment, and pride; delight in the realization that what I had just heard crystallized many stray thoughts of interpersonal behavior, anger because Laurie stated so effortlessly what I had been struggling with for months, and pride because, after all, she is my daughter.

W. C. SCHUTZ

Chapter Sixteen

RELATED—MISSIONARY—
DEVELOPER

The Related Manager

RELATED INDICATORS
> People come first
> Emphasizes personal development
> Informal—quiet—unnoticed
> Long conversations
> Sympathetic—approving—accepting—friendly
> Creates secure atmosphere

The related manager is basically oriented to other people. Effective managers with a related basic style are often found in personnel, training, research management, and sometimes in managing large clerical offices. They may sometimes be the top man in a division or company paired with a key immediate subordinate with a dedicated style.

The related manager can produce a work atmosphere of security and acceptance. Subordinates will then feel free to contribute in every way they can or think they can. They will be willing to participate in a variety of tasks, even those which do not directly affect them. In a flexible, loose structure, where subordinates know more about some things than their

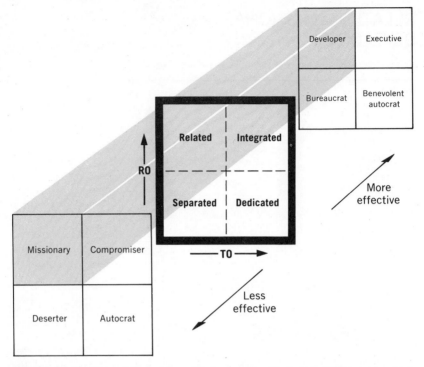

Exhibit 16–1   The related styles. All have a low Task Orientation and a high Relationships Orientation.

superior, this style can lead to effectiveness. In a formal, continuous-flow production process, it might not.

The related manager identifies with his subordinates and through them fulfills his needs. The process is much the same as the way in which college students identify with their football team and parents with their children. This identification can center on the subordinates' growth leading to the developer style or center on the subordinates' personal needs leading to the missionary style.

Subordinates are usually attracted to the related manager. As in the family situation, he represents a needed source of support and affection. However the rivalry over who should get his attention can create problems. The little direction he offers leaves much unsaid. This ambiguity may create tension, or it may lead to the solution of otherwise difficult problems.

The related manager uses friendship and understanding to influence others. He is reluctant to use his authority, and prefers to see good points. The related manager is usually aware of his own attitudes and assumptions about himself, other individuals, and groups. He knows when to look inward to find an explanation or solution rather than outward. By being open to this kind of inquiry, he is a careful listener to the views of others. In addition, he is skillful in making his point of view or feelings known.

The related manager is more sensitive to the demands of the human system than the demands of the technical system. As long as directions are not needed and personal subordinate involvement is essential, the style can be an effective one.

An interest in participative management does not necessarily indicate a related style. Some managers use so-called "related techniques" to bypass people who should be in on the decision making, but with whom they disagree. A superior may suggest, for instance, that participation be applied two levels down. He thus could manipulate the intermediate level out of its legitimate part in the decision-making process. High-sounding labels may be given to such schemes, such as "democratic leadership," but it may be manipulation just the same.

The Missionary Manager

MISSIONARY INDICATORS
    Avoids conflict
    Pleasant—kind—warm
    Seeks acceptance of himself—dependent
    Makes things easier
    Avoids initiation—passive—gives no direction
    Unconcerned with output—standards—controls

The missionary manager is one using the related style in a situation in which it is inappropriate. The missionary manager is basically a kindly soul who puts happy relationships above all other considerations. He is ineffective because his desire to see himself and be seen as a "good person" prevents him from risking even mild disagreement in order to improve production.

The missionary manager believes that happy people produce more. He attempts to run his department like a social club because he believes that production is less important than good fellowship. He strives to create a warm, pleasant, social atmosphere where an easygoing work tempo may be maintained. Kind and pleasant to everyone, he never wants to rock the boat for fear that someone may get upset.

The missionary manager spends much of his time trying to find ways to make things easier for his people. If they want one man, he would give them two; if they want to exceed their budget, he would immediately consent. His attitude toward conflict leads to poor management and low output. He thinks that conflict is out of place in an industrial organization, that no good ideas are developed by an argument, and that mature people never argue. When conflict arises, he smothers it with concern for the feelings involved. He deals with hot issues by waiting for them to cool down. He is a master at pouring oil on troubled waters and so avoids dealing with the problems beneath.

The missionary's management style is less effective because he always puts human problems first in situations where they may not really demand priority. He avoids those who argue and prefers that difficult human problems be solved by transfer, promotion, or pay raises.

He naturally discusses all issues with the staff. He is willing to change his mind to keep the peace. What is worse, he thinks this is always the best thing to do.

The missionary manager carries identification too far and for the wrong reasons. He may identify so strongly with his subordinates and their personal needs that he essentially joins them. He gives up his role as manager.

The Developer Manager

DEVELOPER INDICATORS
  Maintains open communication channels—listens
  Develops talents of others—coaches
  Understands others—supports
  Works well with others—cooperates
  Trusted by others—trusts

The developer style arises when the related style is being used inappropriately. The developer manager is generally seen as one who places implicit trust in people. This is the effective version of the related style. The main difference between the missionary and the developer is that the latter is effective in motivating and working with people in a situation that requires him to do so. He sees his job as primarily concerned with developing the talents of others and of providing a work atmosphere conducive to his subordinates' commitment to both himself and the job.

General Electric Company invited outside interviewers to ask 300 of its managers what had been most important in their development. Ninety percent answered in terms of working for a particular superior at some point in their career.

In most organizations, the developer manager has very low visibility. He just sits there turning engineers into general managers, and no one knows it until he has gone. His job is seen by all as a very pleasant one because there is usually so much cooperation in his and associated departments. His skill in creating such a condition often goes unnoticed.

He spends a lot of time with his subordinates. He gives them as many new responsibilities as he can. He knows that the average person in industry is producing far below his capacity, but he also knows how to motivate them to produce more.

The developer is seen as having some interesting assumptions about work. He believes that work is as natural as play or rest, that men want to exercise self-direction and self-control, and that they seek responsibility. He believes what is hard for many managers to believe: that intelligence, imagination, creativity, are widely distributed in the population and are not possessed solely by senior managers.

The developer manager can motivate others to long-term peak performance because subordinates see themselves doing it for him and with him. The developer tends to produce a creative atmosphere. He deliberately weakens the impact of the existing organization or job structure, and this allows his individual subordinates more freedom to think of new ideas. His openness to novelty and his genuine interest in subordinate self-expression fosters creativity even more.

One ought to be both feared and loved, but as it is difficult for the two to go together, it is much safer to be feared than loved, if one of the two has to be wanting. For it may be said of men in general that they are ungrateful, voluble, dissemblers, anxious to avoid danger, and covetous of gains; as long as you benefit them, they are entirely yours; they offer you their blood, their goods, their life, and their children, as I have said before, when the necessity is remote; but when it approaches, they revolt. And men have less scruple in offending one who makes himself loved than one who makes himself feared; for love is held by a chain of obligation which, men being selfish, is broken whenever it serves their purpose; but fear is maintained by a dread of punishment which never fails.

MACHIAVELLI

Chapter Seventeen

DEDICATED—AUTOCRAT—
BENEVOLENT AUTOCRAT

The Dedicated Manager

DEDICATED INDICATORS
> Determined—aggressive—confident
> Busy—driving—initiating
> Sets individual tasks—responsibilities—standards
> Self-reliant—independent—ambitious
> Uses rewards—punishments—controls
> Task comes first

The dedicated manager basically directs the work of others. Effective managers with a dedicated basic style are often found in production work, at the top of firms built by themselves, and in senior line jobs.

DEDICATED TECHNOLOGY

Work technology may demand the use of the dedicated style. Time pressures may be high, emergencies may often arise, the work may be dangerous or intrinsically uninteresting, group problem solving may be unimportant, and quality and quantity may be easily measurable. Even

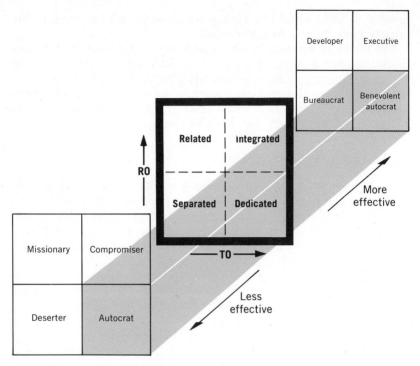

Exhibit 17–1   The dedicated styles. All have a high Task Orientation and a low Relationships Orientation.

if the technology does not demand dedicated behavior, the manager who is characteristically dedicated identifies with, and is heavily influenced by, it rather than by any other situational element.

The dedicated manager knows a great deal about his job. He has to, or he cannot operate in the style he has chosen. In relying less on subordinates for information, he must rely more on himself. He alone tends to define the problem and the route to solutions. This style, then, is often used effectively when there is a wide experience range between levels.

There is much confusion over the potential effectiveness of the dedicated style. A large number of management writers, suggesting that it is generally less effective, call the style "autocrat" and leave it at that. Yet most managers know that it is this style which is often the most effective, in both the short and long run, within their own company.

A man who drives himself but does not drive others cannot be called a "dedicated" manager. Managing involves others, and one's orientation with respect to them is the important consideration. A manager who works ten hours a day in his office and ignores his subordinates obviously works hard, but as a manager, he may be a deserter or bureaucrat. If he is a scientist or other essentially solitary worker whose position requires him to work alone, he may be a bureaucrat.

The dedicated manager is most useful when much must be done very quickly or when a profound change of any kind is needed. If a firm hand and clear direction are essential, virtually all other basic styles will lead to less effectiveness. The dedicated manager seldom flounders. He makes decisions quickly. He has a single direction which he maintains. Not all will agree on the direction, but it will be clearly established.

THE DEDICATED ORGANIZATION

Some types of organization philosophy may be characterized as dedicated and thus support the use of the dedicated style even in some positions where, in other firms, another style might be appropriate. This type of organization is not too difficult to identify: the top manager, himself, is often dedicated; managers most likely to be promoted are dedicated; the general orientation is task first and people second.

The dedicated style is very likely to be effective if most managers in a company use it. This structures the expectations of all subordinates toward it and thus increases their acceptance of it.

DEDICATED SUBORDINATES

Under some conditions, the nature of the subordinates, themselves, will suggest the use of the dedicated style. They may simply expect to be managed that way because of either prior experience or training. The subordinates may lack decision skills or be quite willing to obey, may fear punishment or overvalue rewards, and may lack knowledge or be simply insecure.

The dedicated style is appealing to those subordinates who are not frightened by it and who also agree on the direction taken. It is disliked intensely by separated subordinates who prefer to be left alone or by those who have their own independent ideas on policy. The style is more effective in crisis situations and less effective in administration, research, or educational settings, except by top managers. Many good college presidents, especially those facilitating and managing change, are seen as autocrats, yet any objective appraisal would suggest benevolent autocrat or even executive as closer to the truth.

The dedicated manager is likely to cast up grand programs by himself and then spend time to reshape the organization to see that the programs are followed. He shows that he means business, and the implicit message he sends to subordinates is either get on or get off. If his subordinates are highly mobile, as are many professional workers, they are likely to leave him. Partly because of this easy mobility, the dedicated style is often inappropriate with professional workers.

The dedicated manager prefers one-to-one management decision making. He deals with subordinates as individuals and makes each directly accountable to him for a specific set of responsibilities. There is seldom the problem of overlapping of responsibilities, but lack of work integration can occur.

The dedicated style may or may not lead to sound management development. Its effectiveness in development depends on the time length of the control loop. A dedicated manager who checks daily on subordinate performance and corrects it may inhibit, rather than foster, development. The manager, with still the same emphasis on performance, who checks monthly will get better results. It is becoming clear that a superb management-development device for new managers is to give them a series of difficult jobs with tough effectiveness standards associated with each. The dedicated idea of "perform or else" is still clearly present, but the manager is not actually breathing down a subordinate's neck.

The dedicated manager prefers to influence his subordinates through his own dedication to hard work. He prefers to motivate by various types of incentive plans based on quantity or quality. He knows the workings and limits of the firm's reward-and-punishment system, and he uses it.

The Autocrat Manager

AUTOCRAT INDICATORS
  Critical—threatening
  Makes all decisions
  Demands obedience—suppresses conflict
  Wants action—results immediately
  Downward communication only—acts without consultation
  Feared—disliked

The autocrat arises when dedicated behavior is used inappropriately. The autocrat manager is usually perceived as one who puts the immediate task above all other considerations. He is ineffective in that he makes it obvious that he has no concern for relationships and has little confidence in other people. While many fear him, they also dislike him and are thus motivated to work only when he applies direct pressure. The autocrat manager cannot understand why so many people are uncooperative. He does not fully realize that cooperation, to him, means doing it his way. The autocrat overvalues such control devices as appraisal, merit rating, efficiency reporting, and piecework.

The autocrat manager is perceived as one who believes that the average human being has an inherent dislike for work and will avoid it if he can and that most people must be coerced, controlled, directed, and threatened with punishment before they will produce. He also believes that the average human being prefers to be directed, wishes to avoid responsibility, has relatively little ambition, and wants security above all. The autocrat manager thus does not fully utilize the capabilities of others. Part of his own low effectiveness is explained by his underutilization of human resources.

With assumptions like these, it is easy to see that he gets into trouble.

> Not too long ago a Canadian organization decided to install a computer. The executive committee made the error of giving the job to an autocrat manager who introduced the computer with a crash program. He had decided in effect that the best approach was to thrust the computer down everyone's throat. He was completely unaware of the social cost involved as he concentrated solely on the task and ignored the fact that it is human beings who run organizations.
>
> After a few months some managers would, literally, not speak to him. At times he had to obtain signed orders from the company president in order to get procedures changed. Yes, the computer was installed—any child or autocrat could do that. But what was the cost? The long-term damage done to the relationships in that organization and the number of managers pushed toward desertion, will haunt that company for years to come.

On occasions like this, the autocrat manager is "lucky." He is now capable of tracing undesirable effects directly to his own behavior. Too many autocrats go through their entire working life bemoaning the fact that people are so uncooperative, never dreaming that they themselves caused most of the problems.

The autocrat manager sees workers solely as extensions of machines. A subordinate's job is to follow orders, nothing more. The job of the boss is to plan in detail every aspect of his subordinate's job. The autocrat does not know what "motivate" means. His view of work is simple: some people order and others obey. He thinks that the best committee is the one-man committee, that people work best alone, and that his job is to generate fear and immediate action. He provides no way to be imaginative. He does not understand man's need for recognition.

He handles conflict by suppressing it. If he faces disagreement from a subordinate, he makes it clear that he sees it only as a challenge to his authority. And he does not forgive easily. The autocrat manager has a powerful effect on the organization and does not know it. He helps to produce grapevines, cliques, troublemakers, and deserters. At best, he gets blind obedience; at worst, he gets desertion. The autocrat believes that threats motivate. He might be the sales manager who says, "if you get to meet your quota, you get to keep your job," or, in a lighter vein, when asked whether he believes in clubs for employees replies, "'I do believe in clubs for employees but I would only club them if kindness fails."

The autocrat manager will get work accomplished, of course. The accomplishments, however, will be far short of potential. In addition, this style does not provide for a solid foundation of continued performance, and it certainly provides no lasting satisfaction for subordinates.

Subordinates tend to withdraw from the autocrat manager, and this can lead to further aggressive behavior on his part. He wants to bridge the gap but has no means for doing so, except by using more controls. His notion of closeness is agreement on the demands of the technological system, not the human system.

In many ways the autocrat is simply not in the picture. He wants to use more power than his position has, he is more task-oriented than the technology demands, and he is less sensitive to relationships than he should be.

The Benevolent Autocrat Manager

BENEVOLENT AUTOCRAT INDICATORS
  Decisive—shows initiative
  Industrious—energetic
  Finisher—committed
  Evaluative of quantity—quality—waste—time
  Cost—profit—sales conscious
  Obtains results

The benevolent autocrat manager is usually perceived as one who places implicit trust in himself and in his own way of doing things. He is concerned about, and effective in, obtaining high production in both the short and long run. His main skill is in getting other people to do what he wants them to do, without creating undue resentment. He is seen as having much of the orientation of the autocrat but as a bit smoother.

This style is a popular one in industry today. It often characterizes managers who have worked up through the company ranks and who have attempted to improve their skill by learning from their errors. The benevolent autocrat, or "ben. auto." as it is often reduced to in the heat of a Managerial Effectiveness Seminar, is usually somewhat ambitious, knows the company methods very well, stays on top of his job, and gets the job done.

The benevolent autocrat in top management has little sympathy with participation or bottom-up management. He will sometimes use a participative approach before reaching his decision but not after it. He knows that allowing subordinates to comment beforehand may produce a good idea, will alert him to problems he must deal with, and almost always will reduce resistance to change.

The dedicated style is likely to be effective when the manager has responsibility, effective power, and a reward-and-punishment system; when he has to give orders for the system to work, and when he has more knowledge than his subordinates. It is facilitated further if the subordinates expect to be managed in a dedicated fashion and if they lack knowledge or decision-making capability.

The benevolent autocrat manager can be compared to the team sport captain. He does not ask the players which play to use next. He tells them. Here is autocracy with volunteers, yet it is accepted and effective. The work technology demands it, the subordinuates', or players', expectations allow it, and the organization, or game history, and philosophy support it. All this leads to the dedicated style being effective.

Some men through charm, a long-run view, obvious competence, or personal example can make the dedicated style effective in many quite different situations. What happens, in fact, is that subordinates accept the style as appropriate for the manager. They may still call him "hard-nosed" and a "driver" but nevertheless will be committed to him and his plans.

There is nothing in the world more pitiable than an irreso-lute man, vascillating between two feelings, who would willingly unite the two, and who does not perceive that nothing can unite them.

GOETHE

Chapter Eighteen

INTEGRATED—COMPROMISER—
EXECUTIVE

The Integrated Manager

INTEGRATED INDICATORS
    Derives authority from aims—ideals—goals—policies
    Integrates individual with organization
    Wants participation—low power differences
    Prefers shared objectives—responsibilities
    Interested in motivational techniques

The integrated manager always uses both Task and Relationships Orientation. Almost all such behavior involves either motivational techniques or the setting of overall aims and ideals. Effective managers who are integrated are often found supervising other managers who have to interact in making decisions. The integrated manager wishes to structure things so there is a highly cooperative approach toward the achievement of organizational goals. He develops skills in what are essentially personal motivational techniques. He uses a maximum of Task Orientation and Relationships Orientation to produce effectiveness. The integrated manager uses a variety of participative techniques. Through them he attempts to flatten his power differential with respect to subordinates, make his

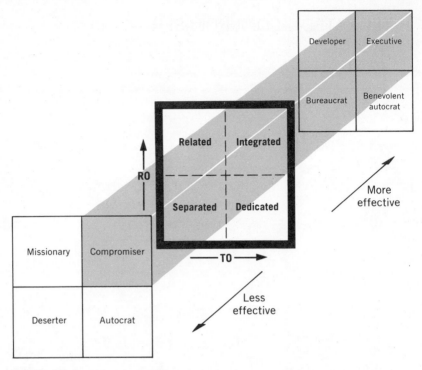

Exhibit 18–1   The integrated styles. All have a high Task Orientation and a high Relationships Orientation.

authority less personal, and obtain his subordinates' commitment to decisions and changes.

The integrated manager goes, at some lengths, to make sure his subordinates understand why they are being asked to do something. This will usually go quite a bit beyond advising them of a reason for a change— an act which even a dedicated manager might do. The integrated manager wants them to accept the reasons for the change and will use a variety of devices to facilitate such acceptance. Clearly this approach might be very appropriate for a senior manager but considerably less appropriate for a foreman, especially if he is faced with union militancy.

The integrated manager wants to depersonalize authority. To be successful in this he must substitute ideals, aims, goals, or policies, in the name of which certain responses are expected. This ideal may be simply "for the good of the firm," Theory Y, or 9.9. If subordinates can be taught to respond appropriately to one or another of these, they may be used as impersonal control devices. Although few would salute two flags, many are prepared to die for one.

Clearly the integrated approach is based on the idea that subordinates must be "turned on" in order for effectiveness to be achieved. Its use suggests that unless certain ideals or end results are jointly accepted, subordinates will not put forth their best efforts.

The integrated manager wants to integrate the needs of the individual with the needs of the organization. He wants to align personal goals with organizational goals. To do this requires a sound understanding of the subordinate as an individual and, usually, a longer time period over which changes are to be made. Clearly a blanket use of this style is based on an idealistic view of all situations and men in all organizations.

MISUNDERSTANDINGS OF INTEGRATED STYLE

One problem in being objective about the integrated style is that many managers see themselves as integrated when in fact they are not. There is little doubt that the integrated style is an attractive one and is often appropriate. But there is also little doubt that its very attractiveness may lead to its being used in situations where it is inappropriate.

Those who persistently misuse the integrated style usually have serious distortions of the nature of human motivation or simply do not understand the superior-subordinate contract. In its simplest form the contract is pay in return for obedience and effort. This is honorable enough although many managers feel guilty about it (195) and thus overuse various motivational or participative techniques.

Some managers claim that the integrated style is a "fuzzy beast," that they do not understand it, and that they have no idea of how to use it. They ask how a manager can use high TO and RO at the same time. Those that ask this question are very often those who currently encounter a situation in which it cannot be used but, perhaps, have been told in the past they should use it. Not knowing what the style really is may simply mean that in his career, so far, the manager has not encountered a situation where it is clearly appropriate.

This integrated style is close to the ideal management style proposed by several university professors: McGregor's Theory Y (140), Likert's System 4 (120), and Blake's 9.9 (23).

The Compromiser Manager

COMPROMISER INDICATORS
   Overuses participation
   Yielding—weak
   Avoids decisions—produces grey acceptable decisions
   Emphasizes task and relationships when inappropriate
   Idealist—ambiguous—distrusted

The compromiser manager is essentially one who sees advantage in being oriented to both task and relationships but who is in a job where only one or the other or neither is needed or who is incapable or unwilling to integrate these ideas and to make sound decisions. Ambivalence and compromise are seen to be his stock in trade. The strongest influence in his decision-making process tends to be the most recent or heaviest pressure. He tries to minimize immediate problems rather than maximize long-term production.

The compromiser, as the name suggests, never does anything well. He pushes, but not too hard. Whereas he would not condone very poor performance, he shows that he does not expect high performance. The compromiser manager is convinced that optimum production is a dream, thinks that any plan must be a series of compromises, and thus looks only for what will work.

Managers sometimes use participative techniques when they are clearly inappropriate. It may be that the decision is already made, that the decision to be made is trite, or that the subordinates are in no mood because of expectations or skill to engage in participation. Under such circumstances, the decision will almost certainly be poorer than the one the manager might have made on his own. It is likely to be a compromise decision which optimized and resolved nothing.

The compromiser is likely to ask his subordinates to participate in a decision which has only a single good solution. He may already know of the solution, or skilled staff could have advised him of it if they had been consulted. The solution that comes out of such use of participation may be the single good solution in which case the time spent was wasted. Increased motivation could hardly arise unless the subordinates were so dim as not to see that only one solution was possible and that management must or should have known it. If the single good solution is not forthcoming, then a compromise would be produced. This would be some kind of balance between what one or more subordinates need and what the organization needs. This poorer grey decision, to which no one is likely to be truly committed, is a direct result of the inappropriate use of an integrated approach.

Good decision making often leads to the production of sets of quite different solutions to problems. Any one set alone could lead to success, whereas a combination of two or more could lead to failure. The compromiser manager, not wanting to make a decision, attempts to satisfy several alternatives at once and becomes even less effective. As an example, managers are sometimes faced with two different alternative methods of solving a particular problem involving people and the organization. It may be that one method essentially favors the organization and the task side of things, and the other favors people and the relationships side of things. Either could be effective if used alone and would lead to the benevolent autocrat or developer style. The compromiser manager, however, would attempt to satisfy both alternative solutions rather than one or the other.

The compromiser manager avoids conflict by using participation. With strong subordinates this approach can lead to executive infighting among them so that two distinct antagonistic camps develop.

A university administrator, internationally known for his leanings toward participative management, did not use his personal influence to deal with a distinct ideological rift in his department. Ph.D. students found they had to pick one side or the other and to cling for dear life if they wanted their Ph.D. on time. The administrator's unexpected departure led to one side emerging as dominant and to key members of the other side leaving the institution which set some Ph.D. students awash unless they cared to follow suit.

This department needed leadership but got participation.

The compromiser has a devastating effect on a subordinate who prefers to work from a clear plan. The manager's vacillating approach leads to poor goal setting by subordinates because they have no way of predicting the future course of events in their department.

The Executive Manager

EXECUTIVE INDICATORS
   Uses teamwork in decision making
   Uses participation appropriately
   Induces commitment to objectives
   Encourages higher performance
   Coordinates others in work

The executive style is usually reflected in the behavior of the manager who sees his job as effectively maximizing the effort of others in relation to both the short- and long-run task. He sets high standards for production and performance but recognizes that because of individual differences, he will have to treat everyone a little differently. He is effective in that his commitment to both Task and Relationships is evident to all and acts as a powerful motivating force.

The executive manager welcomes disagreement and conflict over task problems. He sees such behavior as necessary, normal, and appropriate. He does not suppress, deny, or avoid conflict. He believes that differences can be worked through, that conflict can be solved, and that commitment will result when both are done.

He is not just a morale builder, although the morale of his team is high. He does not run a sweatshop, but his team works hard. He does not want mistakes buried by a team decision since the team feels intimately involved in both failures and successes.

The executive manager knows his own job and wants others to know theirs. He creates a situation where the job demands do not blind a manager to the needs of others.

TEAMWORK

Executive management is often team management. The executive manager believes in the interdependence of job functions and works to produce a smoothly functioning, efficiently working team. He initiates many things by group action. Often he is seen as creative and as an innovator, but, in fact, it is his team that produces the ideas owing to the climate he has induced.

He arouses participation and by it, obtains commitment. He strives to obtain involvement in planning and to obtain the best thinking possible. He knows that any mature person has a need for both dependence and independence and that individual needs and organizational goals can be meshed.

Although the executive is a good manager, he has an essentially colleague or coworker orientation. He works particularly well when there are no power differences between himself and others—when only expertise has influence. He wants to respond to the actual demands of the sociotechnical system in which he finds himself. He does not want to be bothered with what he sees as artificial elements such as power differences.

The executive manager prefers equality in management to differences of status and power. He leads by inducing his subordinates to commit themselves to common objectives rather than to him or to their own duties.

The executive manager builds loyalty among his subordinates. In doing so, he develops in all of them a keen sense of self-respect which they are reluctant to lose. This, itself, adds another strong tie to the service of organizational objectives.

The executive manager is seen by his subordinates as being personally interested in them and as wanting to improve their effectiveness. They have confidence in him and see him as attempting to build an effective organization.

Clearly, the executive style is needed in managing interacting managers. Its use is virtually demanded when managers must decide on the optimum distribution of scarce resources among them. Creating a marketing team from such managers is a good example of using the executive style.

Chapter Nineteen

THE MANAGEMENT–
STYLE–DIAGNOSIS TEST

To make a theory operational, measuring instruments must be constructed. One of the most important measures developed for the 3-D Theory is the *management-style-diagnosis test*. This test was developed to identify styles of managers and of organizations (Exhibit 19.1). It is designed primarily for use as a training instrument, not as an appraisal test. Although it does have validity in identifying styles, its primary use is as a device for raising some questions about style rather than providing all the answers. It consists of sixty-four pairs of statements. The manager is asked to pick one from each pair which best describes the way he behaves in the job he now has.

Through an analysis of the answers he selects from the MSDT questionnaire (Exhibit 19.2), the test measures a manager's perception of his management style in his present job. The test does not tell a manager he is an autocrat or some other style—only that he, himself, describes his behavior that way. Managers who change their jobs and take the test again usually score differently. Since the job demands have changed, so has the style to deal with them.

STYLE PROFILE

The management-style-diagnosis test provides the manager with his *style profile*. This is essentially a description of the extent to which he uses each

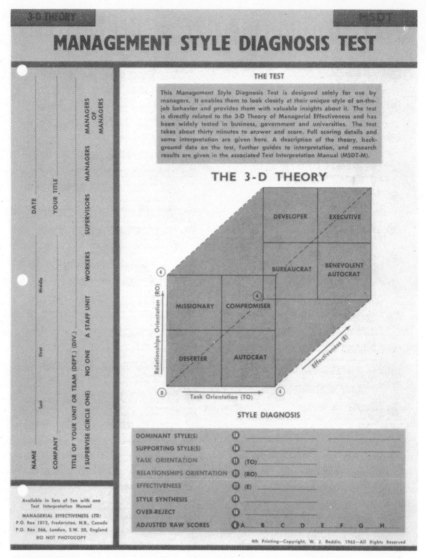

Exhibit 19–1 Management-style-diagnosis test. This test provides a manager with a diagnosis of the style he uses in the position he currently occupies.

managerial style. The profile is in the form of a vertical-bar chart as in Exhibit 19.3.

Plotted on this chart is the score obtained for each of the eight styles. These scores show to what extent each style is exhibited in the behavior of the manager compared to the average manager. The average score for

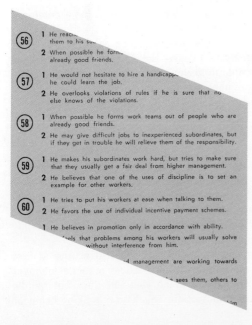

56
1 He reach... them to his su...
2 When possible he form... already good friends.

57
1 He would not hesitate to hire a handicapp... he could learn the job.
2 He overlooks violations of rules if he is sure that no... else knows of the violations.

58
1 When possible he forms work teams out of people who are already good friends.
2 He may give difficult jobs to inexperienced subordinates, but if they get in trouble he will relieve them of the responsibility.

59
1 He makes his subordinates work hard, but tries to make sure that they usually get a fair deal from higher management.
2 He believes that one of the uses of discipline is to set an example for other workers.

60
1 He tries to put his workers at ease when talking to them.
2 He favors the use of individual incentive payment schemes.

1 He believes in promotion only in accordance with ability.
...els that problems among his workers will usually solve without interference from him.

...d management are working towards

... sees them, others to

Exhibit 19–2 MSDT questionnaire. The MSDT has sixty-four pairs of questions which compare one style to another.

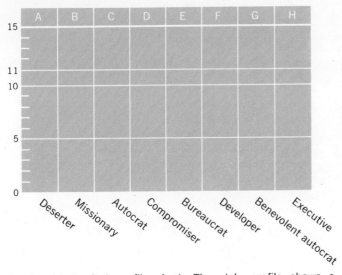

Exhibit 19–3 Style-profile chart. The style profile shows a manager the mix of styles he is using. Scores of 11 and above are dominant.

any style is approximately 8. A score of 11, or above, indicates a dominant style; a score of 10 indicates a supporting style.

For 70 percent of the managers, the test produces a single dominant style and a single supporting style. Twenty-four percent have a double dominant style. A few, 6 percent, in having many styles with the same score, reveal no discernible dominant style at all.

ILLUSTRATIVE STYLE PROFILES

For the individual manager, the style profile contains the most useful information of the test. The manager charted in Exhibit 19.4 has a double dominant style of missionary and developer with a supporting style of executive. This profile with a high degree of RO and effectiveness occurs often for managers in training functions. The benevolent autocrat style is used very little, probably because the job does not demand it but possibly because the manager himself has difficulty in using it.

A dominant style of deserter and a supporting style of executive at first seems strange, but it does occur (Exhibit 19.5). It could reflect a manager who works at optimum when things are going well but does not handle roadblocks too well and so moves to desertion. This kind of sulking behavior is learned as a child.

Two or more dominant less effective styles may be an indicator of low situational sensitivity (Exhibit 19.6). This manager can behave in either a TO or RO manner, but when he does, he is less effective. This suggests

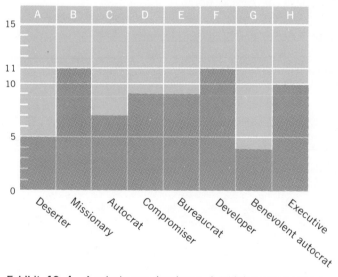

Exhibit 19–4   A missionary-developer. A training manager profile.

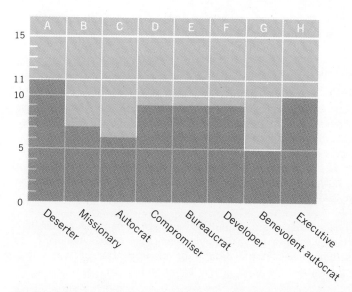

Exhibit 19–5 A deserter-executive. A good man, sometimes.

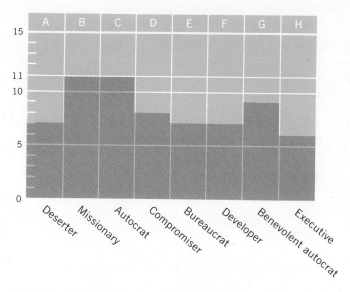

Exhibit 19–6 A missionary-autocrat. Low situational sensitivity can be inferred from this profile.

that he reads situations incorrectly and that he is perhaps more tuned into his own needs than into those of the situation.

STYLE SYNTHESIS

In addition to the style profile, the test produces three diagnostic measures: Task Orientation, Relationships Orientation, and Effectiveness level. These measures can be scored from 0 to 4 (Exhibit 19.7). When combined, these three produce the *style synthesis.*

Style synthesis is an average style based on a manager's overall behavior. The synthesis is not necessarily the same as the dominant style. It might be the same, however, if the dominant style were highly dominant and the supporting style a more effective or less effective version of the dominant style.

Because style synthesis is essentially an average, it can hide rather than reveal important elements in an individual manager's style behavior. Its particular usefulness lies in the description of an average manager in a particular organization. It then gives some indication of organization philosophy.

Organization-Philosophy Profile

When the style synthesis of a group of managers is analyzed, much important information can be obtained about the group as a whole, and if from a single company, about its organization philosophy.

MIDDLE-MANAGER SEMINAR   The MSDT was given to 236 middle managers who attended four different one- to three-week management courses at Queens University in Canada. The percentage of occurrence of each style synthesis was calculated. In reviewing these percentages (Exhibit 19.8), consider that the test was constructed to produce about an equal percentage, 12½ percent, of each style on the style synthesis. Notice that 25 percent of the managers had a style synthesis of executive. This

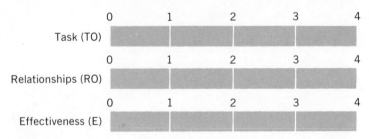

Exhibit 19–7   TO, RO, and E scores. The test provides the manager with a rating of his Task Orientation, Relationships Orientation, and Effectiveness.

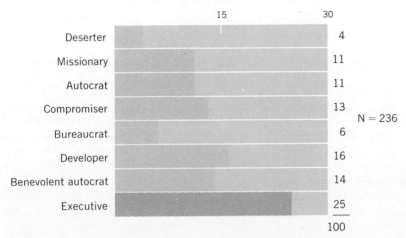

Exhibit 19–8   Middle-manager profile. Most styles are about equally repre-sented except many executive and few bureaucrat and deserter.

is twice as high as an average management population. Both deserter, with 4 percent, and bureaucrat, with 6 percent, are low. The other five styles fall close to the average, or between 11 and 16 percent. This distribution fits closely the expectations that are held about selected managers who attend university seminars.

HEADS OF VOLUNTARY AGENCIES   Unlike managers, the heads of voluntary agencies do most of their work with people who have equal if not more power than they. In addition, the technology is usually related. All this tends to make a high RO style more effective. Thus the developer style is widely used. One group containing heads of voluntary agencies such as Blue-Cross, Red Feather, etc., had the distribution of style synthesis shown in Exhibit 19.9. Notice that 41 percent had a developer synthesis and the nearest other style had only 11 percent.

PRESIDENTS AND VICE-PRESIDENTS   Thirty-three presidents and vice-presidents of a single international conglomerate of about 100,000 employees had the distribution of style synthesis shown in Exhibit 19.10. Notice that 49 percent had an executive synthesis. Presidents and vice-presidents are likely to be effective and usually supervise managers who interact. Their technology is integrated which if handled effectively produces the executive style. The conglomerate is well known for its autocratic man-agement and this too is illustrated in the distribution. Fifteen percent were autocrat, and 12 percent were benevolent autocrat.

R & D MANAGERS   Sixty-two R & D managers participated in a three-week seminar jointly sponsored by Ohio University and Battelle Labo-

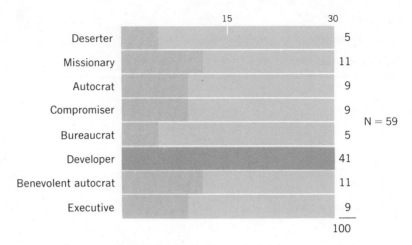

Exhibit 19–9 Heads of voluntary agencies profile. Forty-one percent are developer.

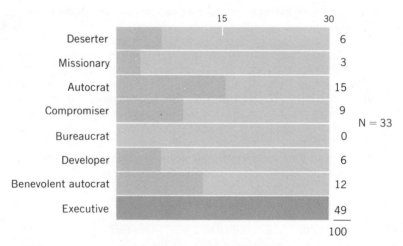

Exhibit 19–10 Presidents and vice-presidents profile. Forty-nine percent are executive.

ratory. Most were scientists and about half had a science Ph.D. As shown in Exhibit 19.11, the only effective management style produced, to any extent, was developer. All four less effective styles were used to an equal degree. Notable is the 15 percent deserters. The managing of researchers is a difficult job at the best of times, and the related style is the most effective. Since scientists typically have a strong loyalty outside the firm to their professional association, this influence rather than the superior provides them with a degree of direction, supervision, and standards. The

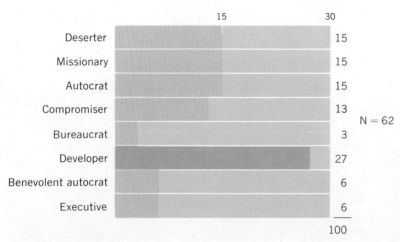

Exhibit 19–11   Research and development managers profile. Twenty-seven percent are developer.

research manager, so-called, often has little to manage which may explain the many less effective styles.

MIDDLE MANAGERS: PULP AND PAPER (A)   Individual companies, whatever their technology, may display a distinct organization philosophy. This may be a long shadow of the top man or founder who might be dead. This style is expressed clearly in the distribution of style synthesis among sixteen middle managers of a 15,000-employee pulp and paper company who were given the test (Exhibit 19.12). Thirty-seven percent of them had

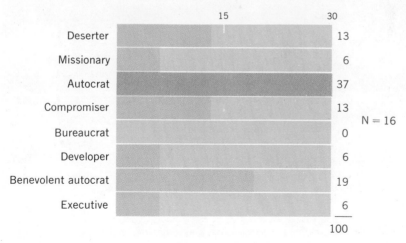

Exhibit 19–12   Middle managers: pulp and paper (A). In this company 56 percent are autocrat or benevolent autocrat.

a style synthesis of autocrat and 19 percent of benevolent autocrat. The company is well known in the industry for what is described as its "toughness." Although confidentiality is respected, industry insiders have little difficulty in identifying this company.

MIDDLE MANAGERS: PULP AND PAPER (B)   Another company of the same size in the same industry had a markedly different profile, which is shown in Exhibit 19.13. In this company 28 percent had a style synthesis of missionary and 24 percent of developer. The managers agreed that this profile described their organization philosophy. The firm had been consistently in the lower half of the financial ratios of the industry for some years. It was founded by a very related manager whose imprint was still clearly present.

MILITARY OFFICERS: CAPTAIN RANK   At the midpoint of a year-long training course, ninety officers of the three armed services with a captain rank equivalent took the test (Exhibit 19.14). Thirty-two percent had a style synthesis of benevolent autocrat and 28 percent had executive. Notably low were deserter, bureaucrat, and missionary. All this fits the picture we have of young military officers specially selected for advanced training.

MILITARY OFFICERS: LIEUTENANT COLONEL RANK   During three different ten-day refresher courses, a total of seventy-three officers of equivalent lieutenant colonel rank from all three services took the test (Exhibit 19.15). Thirty-two percent had a style synthesis of executive, and like the captains, very few scored deserter or missionary. An important

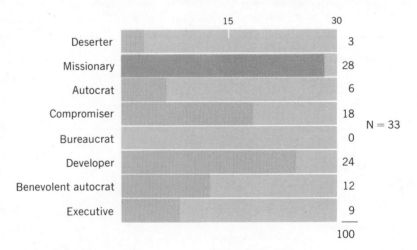

Exhibit 19–13   Middle managers; pulp and paper (B). But in this company 52 percent are missionary or developer.

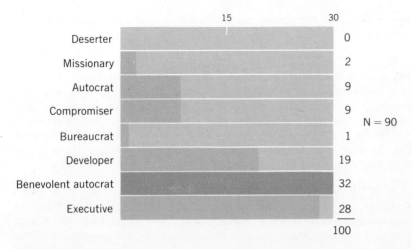

Exhibit 19–14 Military officers: army captain equivalent. A very effective profile with a slight edge of benevolent autocrat over executive.

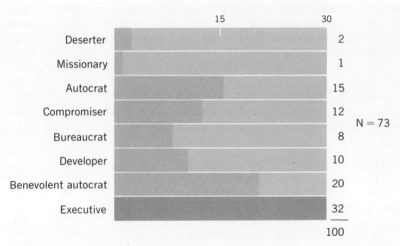

Exhibit 19–15 Military officers: army lieutenant colonel equivalent. More executive but more autocrat as well.

distinction to note is the higher percentage of less effective styles, particularly autocrats and compromisers, than the captains. This may be explained on the basis of the technology associated with their position, but more probably is explained in terms of their earlier experience. All had participated in World War II and some in the pre-World War II military whereas few of the captains had done either. The single deserter approached the test administrator informally, revealed his score, and said he agreed that it described his current style and that he had been seeking an early retirement.

MANAGERS OF INDUSTRIAL RELATIONS UNITS   Queen's University in Canada conducts an annual five-day seminar in industrial relations. The seventy-eight industrial relations managers who attended one year produced the distribution shown in Exhibit 19.16. The seventy-six managers who attended the following year produced the distribution shown in Exhibit 19.17. There was no overlap in attendance. The similarity between the two style distributions of presumably matched groups attests to the reliability of the test on a group basis.

A COMPANY IN DESERTION   The top 175 managers of a single Canadian company produced the results in Exhibit 19.18. The 25 percent deserter score is obviously a serious problem and its identification, in part, triggered the executives' decision to implement withspread changes. They accepted the fact that managers do not join organizations as deserters; they are driven to it. Consequently they focused more on style and procedure modifications than on extensive personnel changes. About another company in the United Kingdom a consultant wrote to the author: "It was my unfortunate experience to work for twelve months with an organization that was completely deserter oriented. Every single suggestion put forward for change was blocked, and indeed any action which would have led to the survival of the organization was also blocked as the main driving force was for each manager to obtain a greater share of a smaller cake as the income of the organization dropped."

The deserter philosophy can pervade a whole organization and can even impede change that is designed to ensure survival.

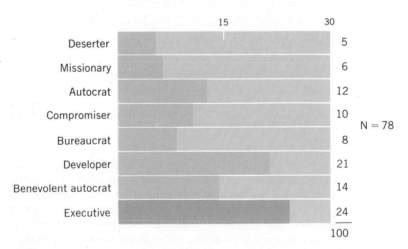

Exhibit 19–16 Industrial relations managers (A). Very high on executive and developer.

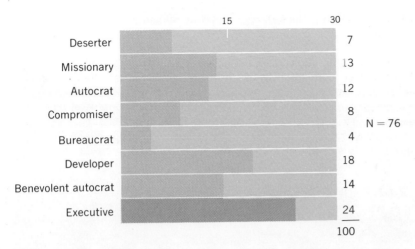

	15	30	
Deserter			7
Missionary			13
Autocrat			12
Compromiser			8
Bureaucrat			4
Developer			18
Benevolent autocrat			14
Executive			24

N = 76

100

Exhibit 19–17   Industrial relations managers (B). A matched group to (A) a year later with similar profile.

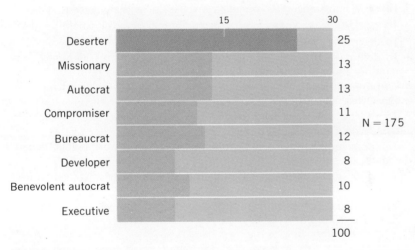

	15	30	
Deserter			25
Missionary			13
Autocrat			13
Compromiser			11
Bureaucrat			12
Developer			8
Benevolent autocrat			10
Executive			8

N = 175

100

Exhibit 19–18   A company in desertion. Managers do not come to organizations acting this way. They are driven to it.

DIVISIONAL ANALYSIS   The test is useful to diagnose style profiles of particular divisions as well as of a company as a whole. In a public utility of five divisions, each division had a style profile reflecting its technology and to some extent the style of its top man. The production division had a benevolent autocrat dominant style and an autocrat supporting style; the design division had a bureaucrat dominant style and an autocrat supporting style; the systems operation division had an executive dominant style with no single supporting style; the distribution division had a missionary dominant style with no supporting style; and the accounting division had an autocrat dominant style with no supporting style.

CROSS-CULTURAL USE   The test has been translated into French and Japanese. Using North American adjustment factors, a high proportion of less effective styles, especially autocrat, are produced on each of the above-mentioned versions. This diagnosis holds for the English version used in India but not for the same version in the United Kingdom, Australia, New Zealand, and South Africa where normal distributions are obtained.

USING THE MSDT

The management-style-diagnosis test is used by organizational training specialists for these purposes:

To create awareness of, and interest in, management styles.
To unfreeze managers, prior to individual or team training programs.
To personalize and thus stimulate discussion on management style.
To establish a readiness to experience a personal development program.
To determine development and training needs.
To determine the stylistic features of an organization's hierarchy, preparatory to an organization change program.
To provide the individual manager with a reasonably objective report of the styles he uses.
To provide a starting point for coaching between associates or superior-subordinate pairs.
To appraise important stylistic differences between work teams, departments, or companies.
To appraise the nature of individual or company style modification over time.
To corroborate or invalidate information about his style that a manager has received from other sources.

New Concepts Introduced

STYLE PROFILE
STYLE SYNTHESIS

Style Profile   A bar chart showing the degree to which a manager uses each of the managerial styles.
Style Synthesis   An average basic or managerial style based on all styles used.

Part 4
FLEX

Management must develop as broad a horizon as possible for every position, with guide posts along the way rather than rigid fences that hem the individual into a completely preplanned . . . existence.

EDWARD C. SCHLEH

People move in the course of their daily work from a role in one system to a different role in another system; and it is essential that this be recognized and that behaviour appropriate to the role be adopted if trouble is to be avoided.

WILFRED BROWN

Chapter Twenty

HIGH FLEX—FLEXIBILITY—DRIFT

The manager with high style flex has a wider range of behavior than most managers. This high flex can be more or less effective depending upon the situation in which it is used. If his high flex is appropriate and therefore leads to increased managerial effectiveness, the term "style flexibility" is used; if the high flex is inappropriate and therefore less effective, the term "style drift" is used instead. Both of these terms can describe identical behavior. It is the situation in which the behavior is used, not the behavior alone, which determines effectiveness. The four personality characteristics which underlie most high-flex behavior are:

High ambiguity tolerance (comfortable in unstructured situations)
Power insensitivity (not control-oriented)
Open-belief system (few fixed ideas)
Other-directed (interested in others)

HIGH AMBIGUITY TOLERANCE (COMFORTABLE IN UNSTRUCTURED SITUATIONS)

The high-flex type has a high tolerance for ambiguity. He is comfortable in an unstructured situation where one or more of the past, present, or future are ill-defined. He is not too threatened by rapid, unexpected changes. He is not one for paperwork as he sees this as unnecessarily structuring a situation best kept loose. He favors short reports, loose ground rules, and open-ended planning and scheduling. It is important to him to maintain a friendly, easy atmosphere where the "old boy" approach is used more than "standard operating procedures." Approaches that could be characterized as "right or wrong," "black or white," "go-no-go," and "win-lose" are foreign to the high-flex manager.

POWER INSENSITIVITY (NOT CONTROL-ORIENTED)

Being insensitive to power often leads the high-flex manager to listen more to subordinates than to his superior. He generally favors flattening the status and power differences between levels and usually avoids displays of status symbols. He is in favor of most forms of participation. The high-flex manager is sensitive to the way things are. He sees good management as the art of the possible. He would prefer to have things develop and flow naturally rather than go one step at a time or be dramatically restructured.

OPEN-BELIEF SYSTEM (FEW FIXED IDEAS)

The high-flex manager is open-minded. He is ready to see new points of view and to expose himself to influence. He could easily hold a particular view on one day and change his mind, in the light of new evidence, a day later. He is more concerned with full knowledge than in having his prior beliefs confirmed. He is less likely than others to take extreme positions for or against anything. He has a capacity to accommodate a wide range of viewpoints and does not feel he must make a successful synthesis of them.

Even when unable to accept another point of view, he will always listen to it, usually contemplate it seriously, and often live comfortably with it although it may be contradictory to his existing belief system. He is usually open to new inputs from any source. He is on a continuing search for maximum contact with his environment and is thus open to influence. This openness leads him to drop prior methods with ease. Not tending to hold extreme, fixed views, he argues less vehemently than others. He is tolerant of others holding opposite views. If he has to change his mind, he can do so easily. He is, therefore, as much interested in hearing other views as in pushing his own.

To have high flex, a manager must have few, if any, intrusive personal needs. He must not have a need to do things in one way, to have a particular relationship with others, to live according to a particular ideology, or to accomplish a particular thing.

OTHER-DIRECTED (INTERESTED IN OTHERS)

His openness to influence and his unconcern with power make the high-flex type a team member. He wants to be involved in analysis, planning, and decision making with others. He seeks collaboration with his coworkers and is willing to accommodate a group view rather than maintain his own. He thus is usually more prepared to work for a consensus decision than for a vote. He looks for that creative solution or synthesis that everyone will accept. He, in fact, finds it a challenge to work for such a solution which combines all views, even though the final decision may have some ambiguous elements.

The high-flex manager tends to get involved with people as individuals, not just as subordinates or coworkers. He does not see others as bounded by their role. He is sensitive to individual differences and wants to respond to them. He sometimes finds himself involved with another manager's home problems. He does this not because he is inquisitive or has high RO but because he is interested in a variety of inputs and thus looks at the total person rather than at a human frame bounded by a job description.

Both high- and low-flex types can be seen as fair to others but for different reasons. The high-flex type is fair owing to his willingness to consider all points of view. The low-flex type is fair because he wants to treat everyone equally and because he wants to lower the ambiguity of the situation. The high-flex type is generally more concerned with fairness to the individual, the low-flex type with fairness to a particular social system as a whole. The high-flex type tends to be sentitive to the RO elements in a situation, the low-flex type to the TO elements.

HIGH-FLEX DEMANDS

Some managerial positions make high demands on flex so that a variety of basic styles must be used to produce effectiveness.

> The creative director of an advertising agency has to deal with a creative staff, the agency management, and an account executive. With a creative staff, he must provide a supportive climate; with the account executive, he must act like a salesman and push for his ideas; with the management, he is expected to take a rational, hardheaded approach with costs, profits, planning, and running a department. Small wonder that low-flex, creative directors are thought to be excitable and tend to develop ulcers rapidly.

Job characteristics which usually demand high flex include:

High-level management
Loose procedures
Unstructured tasks
Nonroutine decision making
Rapid environmental change
Manager without complete power
Many interdependent coworkers

Very few jobs possess all of the above-mentioned characteristics, but the following positions having one or more of them tend to make higher than average demands on flex:

Senior manager
Personnel manager
Service-function coordinator
Research administrator
Manager of staff department
General foreman
University principal

The more senior the manager, the more important high flex is likely to be. No administrative problem repeats itself in every detail. The higher the level, the more complex and diverse successive problems are likely to be. In many policy issues, the personality of the shaper has an enormous influence. It is then that flex can be of the utmost importance. The senior executive is continually encountering exceptional circumstances which fall outside established patterns of solutions. It is how he handles these situations that most determines his overall effectiveness.

The high-flex manager in a low-flex organization may not be allowed to manage effectively, and if he does, he could get fired.

> Joe Stokes is a general manager of a 500-man detached plant. He is what everyone would call a "great guy"—except the president who is his immediate superior. His superior, a bureaucrat, wants Joe to pay more attention to detail, stay within his budget, make sure salesmen send in reports weekly, and stay closer to his phone. At one point, he was seriously thinking of firing Joe even though, by any standard of managerial effectiveness, Joe was an outstanding performer. He had doubled profit in three years and far outstripped head-office projections of sales and profits. He ultimately left and immediately doubled his salary.

Style Flexibility

"Style flexibility" is the term used to describe the behavior and effectiveness of a high-flex manager in a high-flex situation.

The flexible manager is perceived as having few personal needs or biases which might lead him to interpret wrongly the real world. He is reality-oriented, and this reality guides his action. He is not led to analyze a situation in terms of how he thinks things should be. Rather he reads a situation for what it is and for what can reasonably be accomplished. He is seldom identified with lost causes but more often with objectives being achieved. The flexible manager is essentially an optimist about himself and about the situation. Often he sees things he does not care for but knows that with time and appropriate behavior, the situation can be changed.

Because the flexible manager recognizes that he lives in a complex world, he is aware that a wide range of responses are necessary in order to be effective in it. The flexible manager is very sensitive to other people. He is not only sensitive to their differences but accepts the differences as normal, appropriate, and even necessary. He is trusted, and all believe that his proposals for change are based on improving overall effectiveness and are not intended simply to satisfy his own needs in some way.

The flexible manager spends more time in making decisions and less time in implementing them. He is concerned with method of introduction, timing, rate of introduction, and probable responses and resistances. In spending more time on deciding how to implement decisions, the implementation period is shortened considerably. Snap decisions are seldom made. The flexible manager uses team management when appropriate. This gives him an ideal opportunity to use his flexibility.

Rapid change does not make him unduly anxious. It brings temporary ambiguity which the flexible manager can tolerate easily. He is likely to be willing to experiment with changes that have only a moderate chance of success. He knows the world is complex and recognizes that any change may bring unanticipated consequences so he is prepared to test a large number of ideas.

He is willing to accept a variety of styles of management, varying degrees of participation, and an assortment of control techniques. Appropriateness is his only test.

MILITARY LEADERSHIP AND FLEXIBILITY   The outsider's view of the military, especially in most British Commonwealth countries, is that the only possible style is dedicated. It is refreshing to see this advice given by a Canadian brigadier (173) to the lieutenant colonels of the Canada Defence Force.

> Acceptance of the leader-follower-situation concept of leadership, and realization that the circumstances of the followers and the situation are variables, brings us to the conclusion that to achieve success the style of the leader must also be a variable. Clearly there can be no best style except in terms of the aim and the inter-action of leader, followers, and the situation.

So what style to adopt? We can consider some guidelines:

1. A leader must work through his own personality. Each, through personal characteristics, training, and experience, has an individual style, a dominant style, of leadership. Better results will accrue from following natural instincts of style than by affecting a style used successfully by a chosen hero.
2. As a leader senses shortcomings in one aspect of his leadership activities he may exaggerate other aspects in order to compensate.

3. The need for leadership to be dynamic should be interpreted as a need to be active rather than static. Leadership does not have to be explosive; one can be forceful in one's own way.

4. Any individual is capable of only limited flexibility in style—he has only a finite set of responses to deal with infinite demands and pressures. However, through techniques of leadership, the manner of performance in relation to practical details (as distinct from the general style or effect), or, if you like, through varying his behaviour he can exert varied influence within his general style.

5. By application of judgment and logic to his knowledge of himself, his subordinates, and his situation, he devises, or selects, and adopts these leadership courses of action which are most likely to achieve his goals.

6. Whereas there can be no style or technique which is universally applicable to all men in all situations, the successful leader will develop a repertoire of behaviour within his capability to apply to different situations as he recognizes the need. Changes of style to fit the challenge of the moment may take place habitually or consciously. Adjustment sub-consciously may indicate a natural or instinctive leader; adjustment consciously to meet the circumstances indicates a planned flexibility. However arrived at, adjustment is an essential ingredient of success.

In the course of a few hours, the flexible manager may have used a variety of basic styles. He adapts his style to what is then demanded. He uses participation at times, and at other times he does not.

Style flexibility checklist	
Reality-oriented	Colleague orientation
Optimistic	Fair
Objective	Situationist (looks outward)
Other-directed	Adaptive
Sensitive	Open-minded
Collaborator	Socially adjusted
Tolerant	Experimental
Interdependent	Participator at times
Involved	Uses all basic styles
Team player	Practical

Style Drift

Style drift describes the behavior and lack of effectiveness of a high-flex manager in a low-flex situation.

The drift manager is perceived as having no mind of his own. He is accused of immaturity, of having a fuzzy self-concept, and of not having decided what kind of manager he is. He is seen as the servant rather than the master of the situation he is in. Each small change may cause an overreaction. The drift manager is tuned in to the situation but overreacts to it. Having no identity himself, the situation and its changes influence him unduly.

The drift manager wants people to respond positively to him. He becomes so sensitive to what other people think that he reacts poorly to being rejected. All managers undergo some form of rejection at times. Usually it is of their ideas but sometimes it goes deeper. Most managers handle rejection moderately well, and after a while, their own self-esteem and identity carry them through. This is not so for the drift manager. Being sensitive to rejection gives him a reluctance to disagree with or to reject others' ideas, even if they are poor ones.

The problem compounds itself. His unwillingness to say, "No," leads him to accept projects which cannot be completed on time. The incomplete projects grow in number so that they hinder him even more.

Wishing to avoid adversity yet being unable to control his environment, leads him to commit himself to plans he cannot follow, to goals he cannot achieve, and to assume responsibilities he cannot fulfill. He then misses deadlines and acts as if promises are only talking points rather than guarantees.

The drift manager is open to exploitation by others. He is dependent and even appears helpless, at times, to do his job. He is yielding, conforming, and compliant. He is not this way because he likes people but because he wants others to like him.

Nothing ever gets pinned down for the drift manager. His subordinates know that a decision once made will be made several times again—but differently—since it is influenced by the most recent minor events.

The drift manager fails to organize his situation or his response to it. He allows change to overwhelm him. Although open to it, he cannot handle it.

Style drift checklist	
Uncommitted	Many promises
Procrastinator	Dependent
Disorganized	No self
"Yes" not "no"	Compliant
Indecisive	Conforming
Yielding	Unpredictable
Inconsistent	Erratic
Misses deadlines	Helpless
Avoids adversity	Too sensitive
Gives lip service	Avoids rejection

Life always gets harder toward the summit—the cold increases, responsibility increases.

FRIEDRICH NIETZSCHE
The Antichrist Aphorism

No Utopia, nothing but bedlam, will automatically emerge from a regime of unbridled individualism, be it ever so rugged.

LEARNED HAND
QUOTED BY JUSTICE FRANKFURTER
The New York Times Magazine, 1954

The fundamental qualities for good execution of a plan are, first, naturally, intelligence; then discernment and judgment, which enable one to recognize the best methods to attain it; then singleness of purpose; and, lastly, what is most essential of all, will—stubborn will.

MARSHAL FOCH

Chapter Twenty-one

LOW FLEX—RESILIENCE—RIGIDITY

The manager with low flex can be more or less effective depending upon the situation. If his low flex is appropriate and therefore leads to increased managerial effectiveness, the term "style resilience" is used to describe his behavior and its effects. If the low flex is inappropriate and therefore less effective, the term "style rigidity" is used instead. Both of these terms, then, can describe identical behavior because it is the situation in which the behavior is used, not the behavior alone, that determines effectiveness.

The personality characteristics producing low flex and high flex can be sharply differentiated as opposites. The four characteristics underlying low flex are:

Low ambiguity tolerance (comfortable in structured situations)
Power sensitivity (control-oriented)
Firm-belief system (fixed ideas)
Inner-directed (interested in self)

All these low-flex characteristics could be appropriate in some managerial situations and inappropriate in others.

LOW AMBIGUITY TOLERANCE (COMFORTABLE IN STRUCTURED SITUATIONS)

Above all, the low-flex manager wants to organize his environment. He has a low tolerance for ambiguity and so works best when things are clear to him and, preferably, clear to others. To keep the situation organized, he will often employ compulsive work habits which might take the form of orderliness, precise hours, long hours, neatness, and tight schedules. This may lead to a high production of paperwork that is used as a means to control the total situation in which he is working. He wants to be free of the need to be flexible.

He likes to establish operating ground rules, preferably elaborate standard operating procedures. Naturally the low-flex type is attracted to systems design work as this is an excellent opportunity for creating order out of what he might see as disorder or even chaos.

He naturally seeks and attempts to produce situations which have clarity, consistency, and agreement. He does not want to be confused. He prefers the tasks he is given to be clear. He believes that rush leads to errors: "If you must rush, do it in an orderly way but avoid rushing at all if you can."

If he has power to do it, the low-flex manager will go to great lengths to organize his physical environment. Offices, desks, curtains, even buildings will sometimes be designed according to a single pattern.

POWER SENSITIVITY (CONTROL-ORIENTED)

The low-flex manager is often very sensitive to power differentials and is far more responsive to a superior than to subordinates. He is quick to notice small changes in status, power, and prestige. Being so power sensitive, he often makes a good master or servant but not as good a colleague. He puts great value on his relationship with his superior. In situations where following commands promptly is a virtue, he will be effective.

It is very important for him to be sure of his relationship with his superior. While good if it is amicable, it is more important that it be clear. If it starts to become vague, the low-flex manager will become anxious and his effectiveness will often decrease.

> A retired army officer working as an administrator in a university setting was not accustomed to his ambiguous status and power position, especially with respect to professors. To structure things, somewhat, he grew a mustache which he did not have in the military. He then assumed a gruff mien. To all except his superior, he initially refused the requests of those whom he saw as having a less equal or ambiguous power relationship with him. At each such confrontation he later became amicable but, as he saw it, on his terms. He did not mind doing things for others but wanted to know whether he was doing it as a master or servant. The military had taught him the importance of this distinction, but the university structurally did not provide it so he, to some extent unwittingly, provided it for himself.

Low tolerance for ambiguity and power sensitivity taken together lead to some other important characteristics. The low-flex manager is often highly committed to the organization, his superior, his job, and his responsibilities. He needs so much to be part of the structure that he makes it part of himself. He identifies with his role so much that he often becomes it.

The low-flex manager wants to be guided. The guides might be anything from an ideology or theory favoring human relations to a complex system of rules and procedures. In spite of the fact that the effects might be different, the important thing is that he wants guides to control him.

Wanting to control or be controlled, strangely enough, makes the low-flex manager less subject to informal influence. An equal-power coworker situation is full of problems for him. The ambiguity is higher, power relations are diffuse, and no one is in control—a kind of situation the low-flex manager wants to avoid.

The low-flex manager even with a low RO can be charming to subordinates or peers. He accommodates them not because he thinks they deserve it but because he has decided that if he wants to control them, it is the best way to act.

FIRM-BELIEF SYSTEM (FIXED IDEAS)

The low-flex manager has a firm-belief system. It may be expressed in terms of something as simple as the five steps to follow in making a decision or in terms of something as complex as a comprehensive integrated theory of the firm in its environment. He prefers black or white to grey. He prefers to have a single, clear cognitive frame through which to see the world. He wants to know in advance whether something is right or wrong and wants his actions to be evaluated in the same terms. Although his values might be of any type, he has clear and strong ones. On a variety of measures he might be termed a "conservative" or "radical" but never "slightly left or right of center." In essence he has a low tolerance for intellectual ambiguity in himself. His value and belief system acts as a superb intellectual gyroscope to provide stability.

His simple belief system gives him a clear point of view of the way things should be. He has an opinion, not always given to his superior, about what is wrong and what constitutes an ideal state. Naturally he is interested in obtaining perfection since he knows what it is.

INNER-DIRECTED (INTERESTED IN SELF)

A central feature of the low-flex type is that he is inner-directed. He resists new inputs from his environment. Although he must exist in it, he does not want to be affected too much by it. He prefers to be independent or to relate to others in formal ways. Being this way generally leads to a narrow range of interests and possibly to a single hobby pursued intensively, even compulsively. The hobby could be his work. If not, the hobby would more likely be a solitary one than one involving other people.

The low-flex type, being inner-directed, has a high degree of self-control which can lead to patience and diplomacy. This is not in the name of RO but in the name of stability and structure.

LOW-FLEX DEMANDS

Some jobs make low demands on flex. As an extreme case, consider a low-level managerial job requiring the supervision of workers who are doing routine, highly repetitive work on a demand basis. Sorting mail is an example and so is processing simple claims. A manager supervising work like this would usually need only a very low Task and Relationships Orientation and low flex in order to perform effectively.

Position characteristics which usually have low-flex demands include:

Low-level management
Tight procedures
Established tasks
Routine, automated decision making
Little environmental change
Manager with complete power
Few interdependent coworkers

Positions with one or more of the above-mentioned dominant characteristics include:

Accountant
Economic analyst
Work-study engineer
Inspection foreman
Clerical supervisor
Plant engineer
Systems analyst

These lists are general guides at best.

Consider, for instance, the foreman of a production unit. Does he need high or low flex? One might say that he can maintain the same style with whomever he works. He may be the "bull of the woods" both up and down or, for that matter, act toward everyone in a rational, cost-conscious manner. He can be solely task-oriented in everything he does. This behavior, however, assumes his relative independence of other systems in the plant. One asks, must he resolve conflicting demands for output made by his superior and for standards made by the quality-control department? Has he any real power? Must he interact with other foremen at his level and persuade them even though he has no power? It is clear that although a particular job may suggest high or low flex, it is best to look at the underlying demands rather than at the job title, itself.

HIGH POWER AND FLEX

As a manager's power increases, his need for being flexible decreases. He may still be somewhat more effective by being flexible, but a high level of effectiveness does not depend on it. With high power, one simply changes the elements in the situation to suit one's particular style and flex. One military officer reports (173):

> I came across an interesting comparative study of three unnamed, but reportedly highly successful, senior officers. The study pointed out how their viewpoints and attitudes were dissimilar, how the means they employed were strikingly and startlingly different, how the ends obtained were not uniform but were uniformly outstanding. The author, who served each of these three officers in turn, described this experience as a 'revelation in the complexities and mutations of ability and personality in similarly trained officers with generally comparable backgrounds and experience.'
>
> Each had a technique for achieving his aim and each of these techniques, geared to the total personality of the officer concerned, was different. In generally similar circumstances, in a difficult leadership situation, one would employ delay and thorough preparation, the second would employ his skill at presentation and the persuasiveness of his personality and presence, and the third plowed the difficulties under and steamrollered forward.

Style Resilience

Style Resilience is used to describe the behavior and effectiveness of a low-flex manager in a low-flex situation.

HIGH TOLERANCE FOR STRESS

The resilient manager reacts well to moderate amounts of stress and even thrives on it. He has a well-integrated set of internal standards and has, over the years, built strong intellectual and emotional defences to maintain them. He is self-confident and emotionally stable. The resilient manager with emotional disturbances has found ways to keep them under control and even to put them to good use.

RATHER RIGHT THAN PLEASANT

The resilient manager is often found in situations where unpleasant decisions must be made. These are often positions of high power at the top of a major organizational unit, such as a managing director, a military commander, or a cabinet minister. As he would rather be right than pleasant, he is also found in positions where his job requires him to say, "No," to what appears to be reasonable requests. Examples of the latter are budget officers, controllers, systems designers, and those charged with rationing scare resources, such as food, freedom, or any kind of aid.

Sometimes the resilient manager is seen as the rugged individualist. He ignores what he sees as trivia and proceeds directly toward the task. Very often his individuality is based not so much on violating the rules as on following them closely.

It is obvious that the resilient manager knows his own mind and knows what he wants and how to get it. He is persistent in his pursuit of goals and has little doubt that he will achieve them. He is disciplined, decisive, and tough-minded, and carries through with plans to which he is personally committed, even against extreme difficulties.

SOCIALLY ASSERTIVE

He is socially assertive, and to the extent that he can, attempts to be one-up in all social interactions. He makes a good superior or subordinate however as long as both sides can agree on the aim and he is allowed to get on with it. With coworkers he tends to take a dominant position, if he can, in order to enlist their aid in achieving his aim.

Although not liking ambiguity, the resilient manager is prepared to make necessary decisions based on little data. His decisions tend to be quick ones which of themselves restructure the situation for him. His need to restructure gives him the appearance of being headstrong and of having much will power.

INTEGRATES SITUATION

In his passion for order and good form, the resilient manager learns quickly how to simplify problems as they arrive. He refuses to be confused by situational complexities. He extracts the core issues and deals with them. He copes best with stability and strives to continually create it by dealing with intrusive elements.

He copes so well with a stable situation that he strives to create one out of the current circumstances. When a routine is well tested, it is formalized. When an organization structure is well tested, it is approved and formally distributed. Any success experience is ritualized, if possible, to increase the possibility of its continuous occurrence.

Style resilience checklist	
Will power	Firm superior
Tough-minded	Tolerates stress
Headstrong	Makes quick decisions
Simplifies issues	Follows orders
Self-confident	Stable
Clear goals	Systematic
Individualist	Disciplined
Orderly	Decisive
Persistent	Reliable
Good subordinate	Fulfills commitments

Style Rigidity

Style rigidity is used to describe the behavior and lack of effectiveness of a low-flex manager in a high-flex situation.

Low-flex types can resist personal change so effectively (92) that it has been proposed (124) that theory and research within management development should be centered on what is known about resistance to change. One study (77) of the effects of a management development program showed that those less likely to benefit are those who are very sure of themselves, are unconcerned with their own and others' motives, and prefer to remain aloof.

It is difficult to present new evidence to a rigid manager. He has a closed mind or, at least, is a poor listener. He is intolerant of most ideas except his own and these can lead to what are essentially prejudiced, narrow, and even mean actions. He goes to great lengths and uses much energy in being dogmatic. He often uses his intelligence to get involved in arguments of such generality that they barely touch the issue at hand. At times he finds ways to be logical at the expense of being rational.

His rigidity is most evident when he is presented with clear evidence refuting his beliefs. He simply discards, denies, or forgets the valid evidence. To be rigid, one must learn to maintain beliefs in the face of clearly contrary evidence.

The rigid manager, then, has a narrow range of intellectual responses. He has a perfect solution in his head and usually believes there is a perfect way to implement it. He may do this by using high RO, high TO, developing elaborate plans, by setting objectives. All these can be useful at times, but the rigid manager tends to select one method and use it even when inappropriate. After a short while, subordinates know what his response to their problems will be, so they stop asking him.

Jack Brown's job title was service department coordinator. He had a M.Sc. in physics and was highly intelligent. His actual job was to implement control techniques for top management who had experienced difficulty in doing it through the line. He was given no power but was expected to produce results with an essentially hostile group of middle managers. His job clearly demanded a great deal of style flex which he did not have. Within a few months he had two serious so-called "personality conflicts" with managers with whom he was supposed to work. He insisted his way was best—which it often was—but was unwilling to consider modifying his sophisticated systems designs to accommodate even minor changes. During one critical period, he actually developed a fantasy about the job he had been given. He believed and stated publicly that the president had given him great powers to implement an involved control-technique system. The president told him he had not, but he continued to believe it. He acted as if he were leading a crusade. He lost about 30 pounds, started drinking heavily, and eventually the company dismissed him.

PERSONAL PRIORITIES

The rigid manager is more concerned with himself than with the situation he is in. He puts personal priorities for order and consistency above the situational priorities. He often has an airtight ideology of some kind which prevents him from even comprehending new ideas.

The rigid manager's emphasis on self and not on reality leads him to attempt to build departmental empires in his own image. He has many pet projects and methods and is continually petting them. He ignores new technologies or management advances of any sort, if they do not fit into the narrow methods he prefers.

Although capable of a moderate amount of charm when necessary, the rigid manager is often unsociable toward those who have different views on how to run things. He sharply rejects ideas with which he does not agree. Being so emotionally involved, he sees such disagreement as a rejection of himself as a person.

> Tom Smith was a low-flex manager. He worked first as a foreman, then as a technical trainer, and then as a systems analyst. As a foreman, he was highly conscientious, not well liked, and had many labor problems. As a technical trainer, he did an outstanding job and was well known even outside his firm for his innovation in training aids and for his clarity of presentation. Although relatively junior, he served successfully on a national committee and ended up by taking and fulfilling responsibilty for drafting a comprehensive set of standards for a technical trade. He became head of a systems department and started running into problems again. He designed comprehensive systems but had difficulty in introducing them. He was frequently called "stubborn" and "rigid," and he obviously was. His new job was a low-power situation, yet he had responsibility for implementing change. He started to have increasing difficulty. At the managerial effectiveness seminar he was rated autocrat by his team and given a flex rating of 1. At the seminar he was virtually always the last to change his mind even about unimportant items. Tom Smith died on the job at fifty-six. It is impossible to tell but a higher flex might have made his work less stressful and his life longer.

OVERVALUES POWER

The rigid manager overvalues and pays too much attention to authority, power, and hierarchy. He overvalues suggestions from his superior and undervalues those from his coworkers or subordinates. He is the antithesis of the team manager.

Sensitivity to what superiors want can lead to taking on more than can be effectively accomplished. This role overload is assumed, however, to please the superior and to keep the total system under better control.

The rigid manager often has harmonious relations with his superior so long as the superior's power over him seems legal and legitimate. Rigid managers prefer to be controlled by the system, the rule books, and also their superiors. The rigid manager is often a "true believer" in a particular ideology which his boss also shares. If they both had had the same professional training in engineering, work study, accountancy, or even psychology, this is even more likely to occur.

If the rigid manager feels he is rejected by his superior, he is thrown into a turmoil. To whom should he relate? One common response is counter-dependency wherein the rigid manager reverses himself, rejects his superior, and accepts his subordinates. To his superior he is then seen as an autocrat or maverick, but his subordinates see him as a developer.

The rigid manager, naturally enough, becomes very concerned over the prospect of a new superior. Next to moving to another organization, this is the source of greatest possible change.

CANNOT RESPOND TO CHANGE

It is in a changing situation that the rigid manager most dramatically is less effective because he would rather be consistent than responsive. It is in a high-stress, high-change situation that the rigid manager is most likely to encounter difficulties. Many rigid managers can maintain a minimum effectiveness as long as they can control a slowly changing environment. With a major change, such as a new boss, they often temporarily become of little use to the company or themselves.

The rigid manager's response to stress may be to limit his range of behavior even more than previously. He may insist on everything in writing, insist on signing all letters from the department, or insist on exhaustive, unnecessary, almost interminable meetings to decide minor issues. Not able to control the situation, he overuses one technique, useful and well learned in the past. Now he is actually using it to control himself.

> Jim Brien was a graduate engineer heading a simple, continuous-flow production process. He was quiet and well liked. His two technical subordinates looked after the minor problems that arose while Jim continued to improve the production process. His job required low flex, and as it turned out, Jim had only low flex. He was promoted to manager of a larger operating unit which involved directing interacting managers. His job demands changed dramatically, but not Jim. He was unable to deal with the rapidly changing situation in which he found himself.

The rigid manager, like glass, is brittle. Through moderate stress, glass is a superb material. Unfortunately, like the rigid manager, it has a "go-no-go" quality which leads to its sudden, complete uselessness in times of high stress.

Parkinson (158) has pointed out that the last act of a dying organization is the preparation of a revised and greatly enlarged rule book. What this rule book may be is a last ditch attempt by a low-flex senior manager to control a high-flex situation rapidly getting out of his hands. The rule book grants him a reprieve but that only.

CAREER CRISIS   Changing organizational ground rules, like other changes, sometimes lead managers to experience a career crisis. This is a period of high and even overwhelming anxiety centered on current or future performance. Moderate amounts of anxiety usually improve performance, but extreme amounts do not. At the root of the crisis is anticipated low effectiveness (which finally may be actual or imagined) caused by the manager's knowledge of his inability to satisfy the changed demands of situational elements. The crisis is most likely to occur among middle managers of low flex who are about to be moved to a completely different kind of job. The more flexible a manager is, the less likely such a crisis will occur or the better it can be handled.

RELATIONSHIPS RIGIDITY   Rigidity is often wrongly associated solely with the autocrat style, but it is equally likely to occur with the missionary or remaining less effective styles. In the same way that some managers cannot move from a dedicated basic style, others cannot move from a related basic style, even when the situation demands it. The latter managers are often well liked, but unless they are employed as human relations trainers or in other high RO jobs, they are not likely to be effective.

Rigidity is often confused with autocracy. There is a difference between being autocratic and being nasty. To be labeled an "autocrat," a manager must have high TO and low RO in a situation that does not require this dedicated behavior. The rigid manager with power may desire to maintain a situation just as it is, using no TO or RO. He may be disliked by subordinates who want change, but he is not an autocrat in the high TO sense. Rather he is a bureaucrat or deserter.

RIGIDITY INDUCTION   Some organizations train men to be rigid rather than to be flexible. They in effect train them to decrease rather than increase their range of basic-style behavior.

The results of a learning experiment using a fish (Exhibit 22.1) make the process clear. The experimenter obtained a glass tank of water with a glass partition in its center and put a fish on one side and minnows on the other. After a while, the lone fish became hungry and tried to eat the minnows. The invisible glass partition stopped him. After bumping himself a few hundred times, he stopped trying to eat the minnows. Then the glass partition was removed, the minnows surrounded the fish but it had learned not to eat them and so died of starvation. It learned too well what ultimately became inappropriate behavior.

This experiment has relevance for explaining the problems of middle managers in an organizational change program. It is clear why this group,

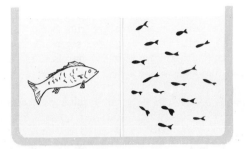

Exhibit 21–1 Rigidity induction. A fish can be taught to starve to death. Do managers sometimes learn the wrong things as well?

more than others, resists change. Like the fish, they have learned the old methods too well. Forces shaped them, some of which they were only dimly aware. Suddenly, without notice, top management changes these forces, or ground rules, by removing the "glass partition" and says, "Become more creative, risk-taking, profit-centered"—or something else. The managers hear, but they do not believe. They have difficulty in unlearning what are now inappropriate responses. They cannot unlearn what is not so any longer. They are naturally seen as rigid, and in terms of the new organization philosophy, they are. It is easy to see that a major focus of many management development programs might well be making sure that managers get a better understanding of what they know which is not so any longer.

Junior managers will not resist change as much as the middle managers since they have not bumped themselves so often against invisible barriers. They have less to unlearn. Senior managers, also, have little difficulty in changing since they have spent months or years deciding to change the rules—to take out the "glass partition" that previously blocked the middle manager's way.

Style rigidity checklist	
Status oriented	Resists change
Authority-oriented	Unresponsive
Control-oriented	Poor coworker
Prejudiced	Brittle
Closed mind	Limited responses
Intolerant	Overcontrolled
Inhibited	Unsociable
Poor listener	Rejects subordinates
Dogmatic	Self first not reality
Low self-insight	Personal blockages

Part 5

MANAGERIAL EFFECTIVENESS

The great end in life is not knowledge but action.

T. H. HUXLEY

Chapter Twenty-two

HOW TO SET OBJECTIVES

A focus on managerial effectiveness leads directly to an interest in management by objectives. "MBO," as it is referred to, is a system of managing which focuses on the outputs of managerial positions. The heart of MBO is the establishment of effectiveness standards for a managerial position and then a periodic conversion of them into objectives. The ideas behind MBO were popularized by Peter Drucker in two books (47, 48). Currently, the name most associated with MBO in the United States is George Odiorne (155) and in the United Kingdom, John Humble (94, 95, 96).

FROM APPRAISAL TO OBJECTIVE SETTING

Like Scrooge's ghosts, effectiveness has its past, present, and future. Management systems can be designed around any one or any combination of the perspectives of Exhibit 22.1. An emphasis on the past is known as appraisal, an emphasis on the present is coaching, and an emphasis on the future is MBO. Elements of appraisal and coaching are still part of MBO, but the emphasis is on planning for the immediate future, not analyzing the present or past.

The introduction of MBO is usually welcomed by all managers. Through it, a manager knows what is expected of him; he has agreed on a concrete method of measuring his performance; and his authority and responsibility

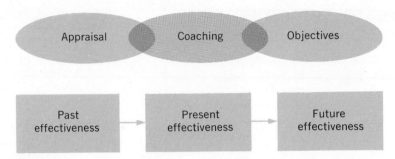

Exhibit 22–1   From appraisal to objective setting. MBO gets managers to look forward rather than backward.

are clarified. All this leads directly to increased job satisfaction and, eventually, to reward which is related to effort and success.

EFFECTIVENESS STANDARDS AND OBJECTIVES COMPARED

Effectiveness standards and objectives are directly related to each other. Effectiveness standards are the general output requirements of a managerial position, whereas objectives are the specific output requirements. Effectiveness standards for a position may remain unchanged year after year, whereas the objectives based on them will be changed, usually annually. In brief, effectiveness standards define the function of the position, and objectives indicate what a manager is going to do about it.

An effectiveness standard might read: "Improve profitability on product A." And the associated objectives for a particular year might read:

1. Increase sales of product A to $A during . . .
2. Increase gross margin of product A to Y percent by decreasing distribution cost to $2 per unit during . . .
3. Increase profitability of product A to $2X during . . .

Preparing Effectiveness Standards and Objectives

In order to prepare effectiveness standards and objectives for his position, a manager should understand:

Levels of effectiveness standards
Bases of effectiveness standards
Frames for objectives
Who drafts objectives?
Sound objectives
Unsatisfactory objectives
Classes of objectives
Errors to avoid

LEVELS OF EFFECTIVENESS STANDARDS

There are three general levels of effectiveness standards: corporate, departmental, and managerial.

Corporate standards are concerned with the enterprise as a whole and are established by the top team. The standards tend to be long-term and five-year although one-year standards are also common. The corporate standards may refer to:

Return on assets
Profitability
Competitive position
Growth—expansion
Productivity
Flexibility
Technological position
Employee development
Employee relations
Public responsibility
Governmental relationships

Departmental or divisional standards are concerned with the particular contribution a subunit of an organization can make to the organization as a whole. They fall between the breadth of corporate standards and the specificity of managerial standards. They may be concerned with profit contribution, meeting production or service demands, and the integration of the department's role and its standards with those of other departments or of the corporation as a whole.

Managerial standards are directly concerned with the outputs of a particular managerial position. They are the direct concern of this chapter.

BASES OF EFFECTIVENESS STANDARDS

There are numerous standards on which the outputs of managerial positions may be based. Many are directly measurable using existing data-generating devices such as accounting or reporting systems. In most firms some systems redesign is necessary to produce the data required. The total cost of measurement must be weighed against the use that will be made of the data and the expected benefits of an MBO program.

A few, but by no means all, major areas in which managers set effectiveness standards and objectives are:

Profitability
Sales
Materials

PROFITABILITY STANDARDS   Some managers head profit-or-loss margin centers, and they can use profitability as a measure of their performance. Typical measures include:

Net profit
Rate of profit change
Profit percent sales
Profit percent capital
Profit by line or department

Even this kind of measure is never perfect, but it, nevertheless, is a very good one if available.

SALES STANDARDS   Marketing departments and retail stores have had what amounts to MBO for years. This is based, in part, on the clarity of their effectiveness standards and the ease of measurement. Typical measures include:

Net sales
Rate of sales change
Market share
Sales/product
Sales/area
New customers

Many measures such as these depend on competitors' actions just as they do on one's own. However, implicit in setting such objectives is taking these actions into account.

MATERIAL STANDARDS   Material standards are directly useful to those involved in the production process, and they include:

Unit cost reductions
Unit cost handling
Scrap
Rejects
Inventory level
Inventory ratio
Model change time

Many of these will be applied to individual products or product lines. A few can apply to the total material handled.

SELECTING EFFECTIVENESS STANDARDS   Using this information, a competent manager can now select the effectiveness standards which most directly apply to his position. Some will be identical to those listed, some considerably modified or refined by specific products, and some, perhaps, will not have been mentioned.

FRAMES FOR OBJECTIVES

Once effectiveness standards are set, they are converted into objectives. Within every objective, whether explicitly stated or not, one thing, state, condition, or amount is compared to some base. Examples of the many possible bases which can be selected for an objective are:

Past period (X above 197–)
Units processed (X percent of those handled)
Units available (X percent of those available)
Own forecast (X units)
Competitors results (percent of market)
Market statistics (percent of disposable income)

Another important element within an objective may be time. If so, such wording as "starting on," "completed by," "during," may be used.

Another common element within an objective may be in terms of deviations from something else. Such wording as "within," "not outside," and "with (+), (−), X percent of," may be common. This kind of wording is often used with standard costs, deadlines, targets, budgets, PERT and CPM networks.

WHO DRAFTS OBJECTIVES?

Managerial objectives may be drafted in one of four ways:

1. Superior
2. Superior←——————————→Subordinate
3. Superior←———Staff———→Superior
   Subordinate←———   ———→Subordinate
4. Subordinate←——————————→Superior

One method is for the superior to draft them for the subordinate. This, at first, seems the obvious way to do things and is still used by some. The problem is that it is not very different from giving a more specific order than usual. It certainly does not contain all the elements of planning, involvement, commitment, and measurement implied by MBO. A major weakness of this method is that it does not tap the subordinate's ideas and certainly does not get him involved.

The second method involves the superior setting the objectives and then discussing them with the subordinate. The idea is that all objectives are tentative and thus open for change and discussion. This method is better than the first, but the weakness is that the superior quickly finds himself defending what have become his objectives rather than the subordinate's. Also, the good ideas of the subordinate are not best tapped. Commitment again is unlikely to result.

The third method is widely used to establish objectives. It consists of a third party, an internal or external consultant, who meets both privately and jointly with the superior and subordinate and engineers their agreement to a set of objectives and measurements. Some advantages of using a third party is his added experience, his perceived impartiality, and the tendency for objectives to get established because a man has been hired to see to it. A primary disadvantage of this method is the cost. A second disadvantage is that the initial set of objectives tend to be far more sophisticated and complicated than either superior or subordinate can handle initially. A third disadvantage is that the subordinate knows who is paying the staff man and sometimes sees the meeting as a two-against-one proposition. Rather than eliciting spontaneous involvement from the subordinate, suppressed hostility or passive acceptance is more likely. The subordinate rightly feels he is being got at and thus wants to protect himself. One purpose of MBO is to strengthen the superior-subordinate relationship. A third party can inhibit this. Consultants experienced at installing MBO programs this way all run into the same central problem. A subordinate does not get committed to the objectives that are set.

The fourth and recommended method is for the subordinate to draft a set of proposed objectives and over a series of several meetings, work out with his superior what his objectives should be. This is the design of the third stage of the 3-D organizational development program. By this method, both sides contribute evenly to the objectives and both develop a thorough understanding of what they mean. Because of inexperience on both sides, the initial objectives so drafted will not be perfect but, most important, will be an acceptable and understood starting point.

SOUND OBJECTIVES

Sound objectives can be easily distinguished from unsound ones.

SOUND	PROBABLY UNSOUND
Measurable	Nonmeasurable
Quantitative	Qualitative
Specific	General
Results-centered	Activity-centered
Individual	Shared
Realistic	Optimistic or pessimistic
Time-bounded	Time-extended

Many factors on this list overlap somewhat, but taken together or separately, they serve to identify clearly the characteristics of desirable sound objectives.

A sound objective must be *measurable;* without this quality, its achievement cannot be established. It should be *quantitative* so that clear cut values can be placed on it. It should be *specific* rather than general so that what is being measured is unambiguous. "Most product lines," is not as good a statement as "product lines A, C, and S." It should focus on *results* rather than activities; that is, it should focus on what a manager achieves rather than on what he simply does. "Implement budget control," is not as good a statement as "have budget control system in full operation." It should be an *individual* rather than a shared objective. Some shared objectives are necessary in certain positions but it is better to tie objectives to individual, not shared, performance. It should be seen as a *realistic* objective to both the superior and subordinate rather than as a *minimum* objective that would be met anyway. It should be *time-bounded* with clear time limits for completion rather than be time-extended.

UNSATISFACTORY OBJECTIVES

Using the paired list as a guide, it is an easy matter to detect unsatisfactory objectives. Without training, managers sometimes propose such objectives as:

Satisfy my superior
Keep my subordinates happy
Keep in-basket clear
Maintain sound communication
Continue cost-saving investigation

One manager proposed the following as a complete set of objectives for his position:

1. When authority and accountability for execution are defined.
2. When effective control is available to measure action.
3. When motivating forces in department are positive.
4. When effective communication is maintained with others from the top down.

While all these may be desirable conditions, they are clearly unsatisfactory as objectives or even as statements on which measurable objectives could be based.

CLASSES OF OBJECTIVES

There are three classes of objectives: *standard, special,* and *developmental.*

Standard objectives are those based directly on the established effectiveness standards of the position. As such they are by far the most important and are the focus of this chapter.

Special objectives refer to feasibility studies which explore new areas, trial applications of—as yet untested—new systems, and other more creative and different areas. Special objectives typically have a far lower priority than standard objectives and, of course, may vary widely from year to year. Successful developments in special objectives may become standard objectives later on.

Developmental objectives are primarily concerned with the development of the manager's professional competence. They may be concerned with taking courses, visiting plants, joining associations, attending conferences, or reading books and journals.

ERRORS TO AVOID

In casting up their objectives, managers should be wary of the following errors that frequently occur:

Objectives too high (overload)
Objectives too low (underload)
Objectives not measurable
Cost measurement too high
Too many objectives
Too complex or elegant objectives
Too long time period
Too short time period
Imbalanced emphasis

Most of these are self-explanatory and have been discussed earlier.

Although opinions differ, more than eight or ten objectives probably indicate a fragmentation of the job rather than a cohesive whole. Complex objectives tend to be produced as hedges against unsatisfactory performance; hidden in them are "ifs" and "buts." Except for the top team, objectives need not usually cover more than a year whereas less than a three-month time period is usually considered too short. Imbalanced emphasis would occur if there are five objectives covering 20 percent of the effectiveness standards of the position and one for the other 80 percent.

Managers should expect that they and their subordinates will make all these errors at least once or twice in the introductory stages of installing an MBO system.

Objectives Record Form

As a superior-and-subordinate pair agree on the objectives for the subordinate, they are recorded on a form with these seven headings:

Effectiveness standard
Serial
Objective
Priority
Measurement method
Program
Actual performance

One copy of the completed form is kept by the superior and one by the subordinate. There are no other copies.

EFFECTIVENESS STANDARD   An effectiveness standard is a general output requirement of a managerial position which remains basically unchanged from year to year.

SERIAL   A serial is a numerical reference for each objective. Too few serials may indicate that goal setting is being avoided, is too broad, or is too shallow. Too many serials indicate planning is too detailed. The appropriate number varies widely from position to position and with the concept the manager has of his position.

OBJECTIVE   What the manager plans to accomplish, stated as clearly and specifically as possible, are his objectives. There may be more than one objective for a particular effectiveness standard. Essentially, an objective is an effectiveness standard, or part of one, which is as specific, as time-bounded, and as measurable as possible.

PRIORITY   Each objective is assigned a priority of 1, 2, or 3 to indicate its relative importance. The highest priority is 1. More than one objective can be assigned this or any other priority.

MEASUREMENT METHOD   A measurement method is a clear statement of how the attainment of the objective is to be measured. If no measurement method is available, a note is made on the steps being taken to provide one, or if not, some expression such as "subjective judgment" is added. Try and avoid this.

PROGRAM   The program is the specific activities the subordinate will undertake as steps toward achieving the objective. These are essentially inputs, and care must be taken that they are not seen as substitutes for, or supplementary to, the objectives. Some will have a heavy task and others a heavy relationships component. This column is used solely to assist with planning. The superior takes no responsibility that the program proposed will lead to the attainment of the objectives.

ACTUAL PERFORMANCE   The actual performance is a record of the extent to which the objective, not the program, was actually achieved within the time period and by the established measurement method. This is worded in a similar fashion to the objective so that comparisons may be made. In addition, it includes a statement of whether the objective was overachieved, achieved, or underachieved. If underachieved, a clear and accurate explanation should be given.

EFFECTIVENESS IS MULTIDIMENSIONAL

Managerial effectiveness can seldom be obtained by achieving a single objective, no matter how broadly it is written. Profit, for instance, may be obtained at the risk of losing customers or by sacrificing human resources (119, 120). Any manager who sees his effectiveness criteria in simple black-and-white terms may perform well in the short run but may not in the long run.

LONG-RUN EFFECTIVENESS

The battle does not win the war, nor the sale win the customer forever. Managerial effectiveness is not solely concerned with the present, or short run, but the future, or long run, as well. Objectives, although set for one-year time periods, can still reflect an understanding of the future.

SUCCESSFUL IMPLEMENTATION OF MBO

A strength and weakness of MBO is that it appears to be so obvious and simple to introduce. In spite of the fact that there have been many successful introductions, by far the majority of attempts end in failure. Many firms in the United States, United Kingdom, and Canada claim to be using MBO when insiders could tell another story.

Implementation is a problem because MBO is so powerful that it must lead directly to change to be truly successful. MBO is a good tool to identify waste and inefficiency, and unless a method exists to remove this waste and inefficiency, then MBO cannot properly be implemented. MBO demands organizational and managerial flexibility and a low resistance to change. Unless these conditions exist initially or are created, then MBO is difficult to implement.

THE 3-D PROGRAM AND MBO   The 3-D organizational effectiveness program (Chapter 24) is often used to implement MBO. It is particularly applicable because of the emphasis it places on flexibility and effectiveness. The four stages that are used are shown in Exhibit 22.2. Before objectives for managers can be set, overall corporate strategy is decided upon at a corporate strategy laboratory, pages 304–305. Next is the managerial effectiveness seminar, pages 301–302, which teaches man-

Exhibit 22–2

Four stages to MBO			
PROGRAM	OBJECTIVE	WHO	LENGTH
Corporate strategy laboratory	Organizational policies and design	Top team only once	Three days
Managerial effectiveness seminar	Managerial effectiveness	All managers once in stranger teams	Five days
Team role laboratory	Team role structure	All managers twice in work teams, once as subordinate then as superior	Three days
Managerial effectiveness conference	Managerial objective setting	All managers twice in superior-subordinate pairs, once as subordinate then as superior	Half-day

agers the meaning of effectiveness, enables them to make what is essentially a value analysis of themselves, and produces a readiness for change. The team role laboratory, pages 302–303 is next because change is more likely to occur and be maintained if fastened to a group than to an individual, and the best way to sort out individual managerial objectives is in a frank discussion of them with all coworkers and the superior. This is followed by each manager establishing his objectives and discussing them with his superior in a managerial effectiveness conference, pages 303–304. This may seem like a long way around to implementing MBO, but in most organizations, it is the shortest route to success.

New Concepts Introduced

EFFECTIVENESS STANDARDS
OBJECTIVES

Effectiveness Standards   General output requirements of a managerial position.
Objectives   Effectiveness standards which are as specific, as time-bounded, and as measurable as possible.

If a man has a talent and cannot use it, he has failed. If he has a talent and uses one half of it, he has partly failed. If he has a talent and learns somehow to use the whole of it, he has gloriously succeeded and won a satisfaction and triumph few men will know.

THOMAS WOLFE

Tomorrow is the first day of the rest of your life.

UNKNOWN

Chapter Twenty-three

HOW TO BECOME MORE EFFECTIVE

The principles of managerial effectiveness can be learned from a book. But the manager, himself, must make the decision that he wants to put them into practice. He must first decide that he, in fact, wants to become more effective. Once this is done, it is but a simple step to translate ideas into action.

The actions he is to take will arise from the answers a manager gives to these fifteen questions.

Do I want to become more effective?
What is my potential contribution?
What are my effectiveness standards?
What are my objectives?
What does it take to be effective here?
What needs changing?
What is the organization's philosophy?
How can I improve my superior's effectiveness?
How can I improve my coworkers' effectiveness?
How can I improve my subordinates' effectiveness?
How can I change the technology?
Should I change my job?
What is my future?

What will the future demand?
What can I do now?

Do I Want to Become More Effective?

It is natural for a manager to say, "Of course, I want to become more effective; every manager does," but in practice, every manager is not always prepared to make the effort to become more effective. One manager may simply want to mark time until retirement. Another may be in the completely wrong job for him, and any additional involvement would be unpleasant. Some are simply lazy and not inclined to do their best in contributing what they can. A manager must be sure that he really wants to become more effective before he reads about how to do so. Have you as a manager, decided?

What Is My Potential Contribution?

Once a manager has decided he wants to become effective, he should initially focus on how he could contribute more or at least more effectively than he is now doing. Some managers have narrow views of their jobs. What they do, they may do well, but what they leave undone is enormous. Some managers let the in-tray define their potential contribution, and the clock its limit. One manager might view his contribution as simply that of managing a going concern and keeping it on an even keel. Whereas another might see the same job as having large components of subordinate development and creative problem solving in it. Still another might see his position primarily as a link with other parts of the firm and, thus, take a wider view of his responsibility.

Specialists seldom focus on contributions. They often see themselves simply as a knowledge bank: "I am not paid for what I do but what I know." This view can and does insulate the specialist from the firm, the professor from the student, and the university from society.

Job descriptions seldom focus on contributions and if followed too closely, may discourage contributions from being made. Too often job descriptions look downward, not outward. They focus on activities a manager must perform and not on the method by which his effectiveness may be increased.

Contributions can seldom be expressed or seen in terms of maintenance of a system. Where possible, contribution should be expressed through effectiveness standards in terms of growth, profitability, and innovation.

What Are My Effectiveness Standards?

The contribution possible from a managerial position is reflected in the effectiveness standards for that position. Clearly, an early step in becoming effective is to establish effectiveness standards and then objectives. At any level, they must be worked out with the superior or they may be meaningless, unacceptable, incorrect, or difficult to apply. Some managers, particularly those at the top of an organization, find that their standards could take a number of different forms, indicating the inherent *flex* in the top man's job. Setting such standards, then, becomes making a decision about what kind of contribution can best be made.

What Are My Objectives?

Effectiveness standards are converted to annual objectives. These are the specific, measurable, time-bounded contributions the manager plans to make. The superior must always agree to them, coworkers should have an opportunity to comment on them, and subordinates be at least aware of them.

Objectives which are set for the first time are seldom met. This may reflect the substitution of hope for reality or simply lack of skill. Management by objectives, like most other skills, requires coaching, training, practice, and feedback on results.

What Does It Take to Be Effective Here?

Once objectives are set then comes the crucial question: "What must be done to achieve the objectives?" It may be time reallocation, making more decisions, patching up a problem with another division, or changing a superior's view of his job. The objectives state only what is to be achieved, not how to achieve them. Objectives without plans are dreams. Plans must be made and this usually means change.

What Needs Changing?

There are five areas a manager can think of changing:

    Organization philosophy
    Superior
    Coworkers
    Subordinates
    Technology

Not all of these can be changed in the short or long run by every manager, but each should be at least considered as a target of change so that managerial effectiveness is increased.

What Is the Organization's Philosophy?

To be effective a manager must understand the existing organization philosophy, and the direction in which it seems to be going. He should also know what makes for success in the company as a whole. The organization philosophy of a particular company is not deducible from a study of the technology. A pulp and paper company, for instance, may have a dedicated, related, or some other basic philosophy as, for instance, may a government department.

But the decision to change organization philosophy can be made only at the top level. Without such a decision at that level and without a commitment and a plan, no change is possible. Managers below the top level are obligated to understand, support, and eventually implement the existing policy or the proposed change.

A manager can find himself in the wrong sort of organization. For instance, he may be basically related while the organization philosophy is dedicated. In some fields such as accounting, marketing, or public relations such differences may amount to little. In many line positions, however, the differences may be very important indeed.

How Can I Improve My Superior's Effectiveness?

Most managers would like to be able to influence their superior in some way. There is no better way for a manager to gain such influence than by amply satisfying his superior's expectations. This usually directly involves the manager in becoming effective and, at the same time, making the superior more effective.

If the manager's subordinates could take actions to improve his effectiveness, then presumably the manager can do the same for his superior. The manager is unlikely to do much in the way of changing his style, but he can make him more effective. This is particularly possible if the status and power differential between the two is low. Also, if the superior's job is much interwoven with the manager's, he is, therefore, dependent on the manager.

A superior may also be influenced by using an indirect approach. In effect the manager gets someone else to tell him. This influence may be exerted by another manager, a book or article, a consultant, or a course. The written word is a much underused influence device, yet it is particularly helpful in the low-power situation a subordinate usually finds himself in.

How Can I Improve My Coworkers' Effectiveness?

Coworkers are often more open to influence at committee meetings which they attend with the managers. Managers should, therefore, think of starting meetings with one of these kind of questions: "What is the objective of this meeting?" "How will we know if it has been successful?" "What are its effectiveness standards?" "Do we need it?" "Can we conclude it in fifteen minutes?" To ask questions out of the blue is not always to be recommended, but managers should get around to it as soon as they can.

Over a period of time, it is a relatively simple matter for an effective manager to raise the aspiration level of his coworkers. He shares with them the past successes and failures; he can state things as they really are; he can suggest that standards could be much higher, and by personal example, shows that this is what he intends to do.

How Can I Improve My Subordinates' Effectiveness?

By improving his subordinates' effectiveness, a manager also improves his own effectiveness. Perhaps the single, best test of a manager is the effectiveness of his subordinates. As a minimum, this would be expressed by the capacity for one or two of the subordinates to step into the manager's shoes.

The most effective way of making subordinates more effective is by giving them challenging responsibilities early in their career. The more challenging the responsibilities, the more effective a subordinate is likely to become. Also, clear effectiveness standards for subordinates are obviously crucial.

While the development of managers can be furthered by formal courses, 95 percent of all real management development goes on in the context of the superior-subordinate relationship. The quality of this relationship determines effectiveness. The superior has, by far, the most influence in structuring it.

A subordinate does not have to model his superior in order to become effective. The younger ones tend to do so, though, especially if the superior appears to be effective, has upward influence, and gives them support. Managers usually accept or even welcome such modeling. But a manager's real skill is in recognizing, accepting, and managing differences, and he can be effective in varying ways. Thus, to force a subordinate into his manager's mold may not work or be necessary. A superior is not running a game called, "How to be more like me." He must demonstrate to his subordinates that they should meet their effectiveness standards, not to please him but to answer their position demands.

How Can I Change the Technology?

If a manager can add a new subordinate and can define the new subordinate's effectiveness standards, then his own effectiveness standards, as influenced by technology, are capable of wide variation. Within limits, he is able to change the things he does or, at least, the things he places emphasis on. This presents him with one of his most important opportunities to improve effectiveness. Some freedom is needed to do this, of course, and it is more likely to be found in managers at the top of the organization or in firms which have a deliberate policy of job flexibility.

Effectiveness standards are particularly susceptible to change when the job is new or the manager is new in it, when some kind of crisis situation has developed, or when managers operate as a team and are thus willing to engage in flexible job trading. Some of the many alternatives which a manager can consider when modifying his effectiveness standards are: emphasizing either task or relationships; emphasizing one of planning, directing, or administering; being either basically an inside or outside man for his department; and working with more or fewer subordinates.

WHO ELSE COULD DO THIS?

An effective manager asks of every piece of work that comes before him, "Who below me could do this?" He does not work himself out of a job this way; he works himself into his rightful job. He may well work himself out of routine administration and into long-range planning, liaison with other divisions, or the more effective development of his subordinates.

HOW CAN I MANAGE TIME?

Time, as the economists might put it, is an inelastic resource. You cannot stretch it out. It appears to exist in unlimited quantities in the future, but reaching into the future for it means delay. Time management, perhaps more than anything, is the one skill a manager needs to learn.

Time management starts with a heightened awareness of time; how much time is available, and how is it being spent. Some managers have found it useful to undertake a study of their own time utilization. They are almost invariably surprised at the results and the lack of effective time management displayed.

Effective managers need to learn how to create massed undisturbed time and distributed undisturbed time. Massed undisturbed time is particularly useful for projects that involve thinking sequentially, such as writing a report, developing a plan, or reading a report or book. Small blocks of distributed undisturbed time are useful for clearing the desk of the accumulation of notices, memos, and travel claims to sign.

An easy, short-term way to create mass undisturbed time is by coming in three hours early or doing work at home. This may lower effectiveness in the long run, however, so other methods may have to be used. One such method, and there are practical limits in many jobs, is simply to make oneself unavailable on certain days or between certain hours. Most daily interruptions, for many managers, are on relatively trivial matters. As each interruption occurs, a manager should ask himself, "How could this have been avoided?" and then should modify the company decision or information system so that such interruptions either do not occur or, at least, are minimized.

AM I MAKING DECISIONS?

Effectiveness can never be brought about unless the right decisions are made. Decisions are a manager's stock-in-trade. A lack of decision making can lead to prolonged low effectiveness.

Managers, in reviewing their decisions, often find that most could have been made months or years before. Timing is obviously as important as accuracy.

At any one point in time, a manager usually has several important decisions he should make. On some, action is postponed for good reason; on others, it is postponed for perhaps no reason at all. There is no value in making decisions hastily or too far in advance, but there is often no point in postponing them for too long either. Many managers avoid making difficult decisions and let the situation take care of itself over time.

Managers might well prepare a list of all the decisions facing them. This is not the usual list of things to do. Rather, it contains each item on which a decision has to be made. The list should have the most pressing decision, which is not necessarily the most important, at the top. This list can be used as a guide to action. With such a list, there is a great temptation to make it and then ignore it, or make it and then start with the easiest decision rather than with the most pressing one.

Any decision involving people has basic style elements in it. However the central elements in decision making are judgment and timeliness. Style is no substitute for judgment.

Should I Change My Job?

Once they have looked closely at what a job really demands, some managers decide that they are in the wrong job. Sometimes everyone knows it, and sometimes no one does. There is a big difference between having or not having daily deadlines, between supervising professionals and supervising hourly paid workers, between systems management and selling. It may be that the job is too demanding, not demanding enough, too boring, or involving a manager in things he would simply rather not do.

When one has seen hundreds of managers at work, it takes very little skill to pick out the ones who are in the wrong job. They simply are not with it; they get no pleasure out of it. They spend all possible time doing routine work and avoiding decisions. These managers are more to be pitied than blamed, but they cannot be ignored. Perhaps the salary attracted them and that, together with the pension scheme, now has them locked in. Perhaps the job demands changed while they were in it. Perhaps through their own low sensitivity they did not know what they were getting into. Take the case of the professional who gets promoted into managing his fellow professionals or that of the basically separated manager in an integrated situation.

The ideal solution to this problem is obvious. The majority of managers who move from, or are moved from, a position in which they are performing poorly turn out to be more effective and happy in a new position. A clear parallel is the college student who switches from one faculty to another. Prior to the switch, he is in a turmoil of doubt. After it, he wonders how he could have considered anything else.

Perhaps if you are working, you should change your job; not tomorrow but after you have searched around a bit, perhaps in your own division, or perhaps in another company. If you do not get some enjoyment out of going to work and of being there, think about it seriously.

What Is My Future?

Whether or not the organization has a career plan for him, a manager should have one of his own. A manager needs to sit down annually and plan where he expects to be in ten years' time. A good start is to list the ages of the members of his family at that time, his estimated personal holdings, his position, his salary, and his accomplishments. Then he fills in the ten-year gap with what is necessary for him to do in order to achieve his plan. The future can simply occur, or it can be invented. Man can see himself as a cork bobbing on an ocean of fate or as someone with his hand on the tiller facing a fresh breeze. The way the effective manager must see himself is clear if he is to invent his future.

What Will the Future Demand?

All effective managers realize that to stay on top of any management job requires continual learning. If senior managers were formally recognized for their informal educational attainments most would be awarded a Ph.D.

These are a few of the key areas that managers who wish to advance in the future will have to learn to understand.

Managing Professionals: The ratio of "knowledge workers" to others will continue to increase in modern organizations. The route to the top will usually involve a term of managing such men for a few years and will always involve working with them. Quite different skills are involved in this kind of management, and a body of literature is steadily growing on how to do it.

Managing International Operations: Although meeting a mixed reaction, it is becoming apparent that while the biggest industrial power in the world is the United States, the second or third biggest in Europe is the United States. There is no doubt that this trend will continue and that countries other than the United States will start to become more than ever involved internationally. On the one hand, there are some obvious resemblances between managing in one country and another, and on the other, there are usually some important differences as well. These differences may be nothing more than historically different ways of doing business or may instead be reflections of a long-established culture. Although practical experience is obviously the best method of learning about international operation, cultivating foreign friends, traveling, and studying cultural anthropology can also be useful.

Knowing Another Language: When a manager is working in, or selling to, another country, a second or third language becomes almost a necessity. Fortunately with language laboratories, "total immersion" courses, and other advanced techniques, it is becoming easier to learn one. University language departments have, by and large, had no interest or particular competence in language instruction. Fortunately a well-established network of private language schools is growing, and some large and even middle-sized companies are conducting their own training.

Managing Computer-Operations Research: All managers will have to live with the growing impact of the computer and of advanced systems design. To live with them, it is first necessary to understand them. Both computers and systems design are major organizational change devices. If poorly introduced or managed, they lead to an array of unanticipated consequences. Properly introduced and managed, they will quickly separate the firm and the managers who will be most effective from those who will not.

Social Science Sophistication: Much social science application is still in the "witch doctor" stage, but much is excellent and showing concrete benefits. It is not so much the fact that social science application will grow rapidly that managers should take notice of. It is just that up to a few years ago, there was not much being applied at all. The social discipline of the future for managers is clearly sociology. A solid course in organization theory would be more helpful to managers than most university courses they could take.

Current Reading: Any manager who wants to advance must read a great deal. This would be a good daily newspaper and a weekly newsmagazine. In addition, one or two general business newspapers or magazines, the leading technical journals in his field, his key professional journal and the *Harvard Business Review,* and possibly *Scientific American* and *The Economist.* The data on the impact of rapid reading courses are still a bit unclear, but a manager should take a course if he can; yet not wait for it in order to start reading.

What Can I Do Now?

It would be an effective move to take action on this chapter now. The first step for the manager would be to list some actions he is going to take and some decisions he has to make and then to rank them in order of priority. The basis of the priority would be the extent to which each would make him more effective. As a minimum, managers should consider defining their effectiveness standards, establishing their objectives, giving parts of their job to others, and structuring their time use differently.

Part 6
ORGANIZATIONAL EFFECTIVENESS

I hold that that man is right who is most closely in league with the future.

IBSEN

Chapter Twenty-four

HOW TO DEVELOP
ORGANIZATIONAL EFFECTIVENESS

The truly effective company must be capable of making adaptations to changing conditions; it must be flexible when appropriate. A company that can make appropriate changes in its procedures, structure, or products, as they are required, is well equipped for the continuing search for effectiveness. The larger company often has difficulty in maintaining this flexibility. Good ideas are not always accepted or even recognized, and divisional rivalry sometimes impedes change. Emphasis tends to be on operating well today, rather than superbly tomorrow. This situation can be modified so that productive change can be achieved.

Applied behavioral science is now sufficiently sophisticated that its use can increase the effectiveness and flexibility of managers or organizations, or change them in other ways. An extensive program of this sort is often called a "change program." The first extensive account of such a program was published in Britain by a Canadian in 1949 (101). The 3-D organizational effectiveness program is the most recently developed. Such truly large-scale organization-wide programs are rare. Almost all current programs stop at what is essentially individual development and do not move on to organizational development.

The 3-D program has been deliberately designed to provide a way of solving all change problems of an organization-wide nature. It has been used to facilitate the introduction of a computer, to introduce management by objectives, to push decision levels downward, to introduce a marketing orientation, to unfreeze an organization, and to accomplish other specific objectives. The 3-D program makes operational, on an organization-wide basis, all the ideas imbedded in the 3-D Theory of managerial effectiveness. The crux of the 3-D program is that it gives managers an opportunity to utilize their skills in situational sensitivity, style flexibility, and situational management. It provides an opportunity to take an open, honest look at the real situation as it bears on managerial and organizational effectiveness.

HIGHLY FLEXIBLE

The program itself is highly flexible and this greatly contributes to its effectiveness. It has nine different elements or stages which may be used singly or in combination to accomplish particular change objectives. Organizations in the United States, the United Kingdom, Canada, and several Commonwealth countries are now using it.

Of the nine 3-D stages, one focuses on improving the effectiveness of the individual manager, one on the effectiveness of the superior-subordinate manager pair, four on the management department or team, one on the interaction between two teams, and two on the interaction between successive vertical levels of management.

Exhibit 24.1 (page 315) gives in outline form the nature of each of the nine stages. It shows the stage number which is used simply for easy reference, its name, what it is designed to improve, the primary results, its duration, and who attends.

Some of these stages take only half a day to conduct; others take five full days. Prior to each, the managers involved complete a variety of prework assignments which require a minimum of about ten to twenty hours for stages one to four and about five hours for stages five to nine.

These nine stages are really structured meetings. The essence of planned change is nothing more than getting managers together, in what at times may be unusual combinations, to talk about what they should talk about anyway. There is sufficient regularity in the kinds of things to be discussed that makes predesigned stages possible.

INTERNAL CONTROL   A key internal man in the implementation of the 3-D program is the manager of organizational development. He may have been previously a training manager who is capable of handling more responsibility, or he may be a new manager brought in for this particular function. Appointed by the executive committee, he is a member of the organizational effectiveness committee and is responsible for implementing its decisions. Another key man responsible for advising on management by objectives is also sometimes appointed. This committee reports to the executive committee and usually has some members of the executive committee on it. The committee selects which stages to use, the timing, and the sequence.

STAGE ONE: MANAGERIAL EFFECTIVENESS SEMINAR (MES)

The managerial effectiveness seminar focuses on improving the effectiveness of the individual manager. The theme of the five-day seminar is the clarification of a manager's existing effectiveness, his effectiveness standards, and his objectives. In addition to its focus on effectiveness, it teaches the 3-D Theory, improves a manager's situational sensitivity, style flex, and situational management skill. It also gives him skill in appraising the styles of others and sharply increases his awareness of his own style and of how he may work with it to obtain optimum effectiveness.

As the only nonwork stage, it is often conducted off company premises for all managers and supervisors, who usually account for about 12½ to 15 percent of the total work force. One company of 800 employees had 200 of them take the course. Participants are grouped into teams of four to eight. The teams are composed of managers who have no current reporting relationships. About 80 percent of seminar time is spent in these teams working together.

The MES is often used to initiate an organization-wide management-by-objectives program. It is useful here in that it emphasizes effectiveness as the central issue in management. One full day on the seminar is spent solely on each team reaching agreement on the effectiveness standards and appropriate objectives for each team member. Most managers on this day discover that there is more potential for contribution in their job than they had considered.

At the conclusion of the seminar, the manager is usually highly conscious of himself as a key figure in a situation where effectiveness could be increased. The manager then thinks more about the variety of approaches he might use in any particular situation requiring action. He is more open to change. He sees himself, rather than others, as a key to greater effectiveness. He is capable of applying an increased number of sound behavioral-science principles and techniques to achieve effectiveness.

There is little doubt that this stage alone has a profound impact on the organization. When a large number of managers from a single organization have participated, the seminar has a deep unfreezing effect on the organization and considerably increases the readiness for change in the organization as a whole.

The full MES is not necessary for managers with prior experience in a dynamic learning program such as a T-group or grid. For these, a two-and-a-half-day special program is conducted to teach the theory, to establish effectiveness standards for their positions, and to acquaint them with the objectives and methods of the total program.

The president or general manager usually attend all the seminars for a few hours and solicit comments by giving each team the task of identifying major opportunities for effectiveness within the organization. All the comments of all the managerial teams at the seminar are distributed to all the managers of the organization. This feedback produced by the president's session at each seminar is used as raw data for diagnosing the ills and opportunities for effectiveness of the organization in stage four, the corporate strategy laboratory.

The other eight stages, unlike stage one, are all work-related. Only in stage one does a manager participate with others who are not his immediate superior, subordinates, or coworkers. The remaining stages are meetings highly task-oriented, with highly specific and ambitious effectiveness standards associated with each.

The three stages which follow stage one each focus on a different type of managerial unit. Stage two, the team role laboratory, consists solely of a manager and all his subordinates. It is designed to restructure the team if necessary and to improve team effectiveness. Stage three, the managerial effectiveness conference, consists solely of a single manager-subordinate pair and focuses on improving the effectiveness of the individual manager by obtaining his commitment to appropriate objectives. Stage four, the corporate strategy laboratory, is conducted only once per company for the top team, usually called the "executive committee." It is designed to review and possibly restructure the company policies and organization and so improve the effectiveness of the company as a whole.

The time between a manager's attendance at the managerial effectiveness seminar and the team role laboratory, if it is held, is usually three to nine months.

STAGE TWO: TEAM ROLE LABORATORY

Team or departmental training is a relatively new and powerful managerial training technique. In the three-day team role laboratory, a manager and all his subordinate managers discuss and decide how best to improve the way they work together. The team role laboratory, more than any other stage, looks at technology and at the possibilities for modifying it. The team role laboratory has been described as situational management for a team and also as a work-study conference for a team. Each of these descriptions do reflect the essence of the design. The emphasis is not on personality or subordinates' rating of their superior, but on individual and team effectiveness standards; as such, it is conducted easily by company line or staff trainers.

It starts with each team member, including the top man, reading out his effectiveness standards, describing what programs he follows to meet them, and then specifying what each team member could do for him that would enable him to improve his managerial effectiveness. Another key activity is the design of an optimal organization chart for the team or department. This single activity almost always leads to a structural change which is often long overdue and definitely needed before effectiveness can increase.

The team role laboratory leads directly to a clear definition of the team's role in the organization. With this established, team effectiveness standards and team objectives may be prepared. Often the preparation requires some type of team reorganization which the team designs and implements. Flexible job trading usually occurs and leads to the talents of individual managers being better utilized through job enrichment. Needless to say, the enthusiasm and commitment generated by this activity lead to the solution of many problems.

The team role laboratory works best after all team members have participated in the managerial effectiveness seminar. The seminar induces a readiness to change for which the team role laboratory provides the vehicle. Not all companies or all functions should utilize this team training approach. Some management departments do not need teamwork to operate effectively. For them, stage one proceeds directly to stage three.

The elapsed time between the team role laboratory and the managerial effectiveness conference, if it is used, is usually four to eight weeks.

STAGE THREE: MANAGERIAL EFFECTIVENESS CONFERENCE

At least 95 percent of all effective management development takes place in the context of the superior-subordinate relationship which is the focus of stage three. The stage three four-hour managerial effectiveness conference is conducted between a single manager and one of his subordinates. If a manager has five subordinates, he holds five conferences. Its purpose is to establish clear objectives for the subordinate and thus strengthen the relationship between the superior-and-subordinate management pair. This is done in the context of mutual exploration of the job to be done, of the blockages that inhibit optimum performance, of the appropriate objectives for the subordinate over a period of six months to a year, and of the support he needs to obtain them. In effect, this stage introduces management by objectives as a reality. Once well introduced, this stage is usually repeated automatically semiannually or annually.

At the conclusion of the managerial effectiveness conference, a manager has his effectiveness standards established, clear objectives set for each, a measurement method decided upon, a program of activities outlined to achieve each objective, priorities established, and a date set for a review of actual performance.

The managerial effectiveness conference provides an acceptable coaching framework for the superior. Flex maps are often drawn spontaneously as each participant describes the situation and its restraints as he sees it. These flex maps enable an objective and positive appraisal of the total situation to be made.

Some companies, when introducing management by objectives, use outside consultants and a design similar to the 3-D stage three, but they introduce MBO all alone. They find, however, that it is sometimes difficult to produce the required change as the organization is not unfrozen sufficiently for any major change to have any possibility of occurrence. Those who attempt to introduce MBO discover the same problem time after time: the subordinate is not committed to the *objectives*. All the meetings were held, all the paperwork is done, but the degree of improved effectiveness produced is not always clear. MBO can best be introduced as an integrated part of an overall change program, not as a single change program introduced in isolation.

This is why 3-D programs designed to fully implement management by objectives always start with the managerial effectiveness seminar and also why the design of the managerial effectiveness conference, itself, includes an open discussion of blockages to effectiveness before moving toward setting effectiveness standards. The use of 3-D to introduce MBO is outlined on pages 284 and 285.

STAGE FOUR: CORPORATE STATEGY LABORATORY (CSL)

Programs such as 3-D must have the support and participation of the top man and the top executive team of the organization. Without this, in a real sense, programs are not initiated. Making a profound change in a total organization is a big project, and it takes a bold approach from the top to carry it out.

As the top executive team runs the organization, changes proposed by this team have more influence and are more important than those from any other source. This fourth stage, lasting three days, involves the top team of president and vice-presidents or the managing director and other directors in making decisions about such changes.

Some of the decisions made at the corporate strategy laboratory include: philosophy of management, what business the company is in, optimal organization chart, organization development strategy, corporation-government relations, corporate five-year goals, career policy, product policy, top team members' responsibilities, liability-resource inventory, management manpower inventory. The importance of these decisions varies with the organization as does the work already done on each. Through a variety of structured activities and measuring devices, these areas are held up for inspection, and plans are made to modify them if necessary.

Some of the key questions which arise are: Where is our organization today? How has the environment changed? What can be done best? What business are we in? What business should we be in? How do we get there? Any top team has considered these questions previously. The CSL provides a longer period and a freer discussion climate in which to arrive at an optimum solution to which all are committed.

Stage four has a profound impact on the organization because important changes usually follow it. An analysis of such changes has revealed that they are often ones that the executive had wished to make for some time but had neither opportunity nor time to tackle and think through to an agreed decision. This stage frequently leads to the decision to establish a series of management project teams charged with casting optimum policies and procedures for the organization. Stage four is sometimes the first stage an organization uses and is almost always conducted within the first six months or year of the change program.

STAGE FIVE: TEAM EFFECTIVENESS CONFERENCE

Once a team has completed a team role laboratory and the results have been cemented by a managerial objectives conference, the team usually needs a periodic review of its progress toward team objectives. The one-day team effectiveness conference attended by a manager and all of his subordinates accomplishes this review. Some team objectives set in the team role laboratory turn out to be far too ambitious. This is a good sign, of course, provided that they eventually come closer to reality and feasibility.

The design, essentially, consists of a review of the objectives and individual responsibility for each, and of a review of the progress and development of team objectives for the next six months or a year. The knowledge that such a team checkpoint conference is scheduled tends to assist team members in maintaining their efforts directly on the productive changes the team agreed to make. Teams frequently schedule such activities once or twice a year.

STAGE SIX: INTERTEAM EFFECTIVENESS CONFERENCE

A crucial step in most effectiveness programs is the resolution of nonproductive blockages between organization subparts. These subparts may be staff-line, union-management, head office—field, production-sales, or research-production. These blockages usually become more visible and amenable to change during an effectiveness program. The resolution is accomplished by the one-day interteam effectiveness conference attended by the two management teams concerned.

At this conference, each team describes its own objectives and effectiveness and what it sees as the other team's objectives and effectiveness. The customary differences between the two sets of statements lead directly to a discussion which has proved to be extremely effective in resolving blockages.

This interteam activity has been particularly helpful in improving effectiveness of the operations of international affiliates. Intercultural misunderstandings are nothing new, but resolving them through behavioral intervention is.

STAGE SEVEN: DIVISIONAL EFFECTIVENESS CONFERENCE

In most organizations, there are seldom more than two levels present at a decision meeting. For most decisions, this is normal, appropriate, and often necessary. In an effectiveness program or in a flexible organization, however, much benefit can be achieved by holding a meeting at which several levels are present to decide the best way to resolve problems for which cooperation from several levels is essential. The divisional effectiveness conference is a meeting designed to build strong vertical bonds in the organization and to obtain commitment at several levels.

Each level sends its representatives to this one-day conference. Typical decisions would be concerned with the methods to be used in introducing change in a divisional unit or the methods to be used in solving problems that other stages had clearly revealed, such as safety, costs, or productivity.

The conference has a variety of designs to suit particular purposes. One design has five levels represented by only ten people, including a manager and his team, the manager's superior, his superior, and sometimes on up to division manager or president. The formal agenda is a review of the team's objectives set for the coming year. Having a long vertical chain represented at this meeting ensures that all levels are committed to objectives and that troublesome interlevel blockages are ironed out. Some companies hold these annually for every district or department, with perhaps five levels being represented at a single meeting of ten men. The most common agenda is the lower teams' planned objectives and the impact of organizational policies on the likelihood of their being achieved.

STAGE EIGHT: WORK-UNIT IDEA CONFERENCE

The work-unit idea conference is a four-hour meeting conducted by a foreman with his men. It is designed to tap workers' new ideas about improving their jobs. It improves commitment and involvement on both parts, in the context of acceptance of the workers' sound ideas. This particular stage cannot be introduced in all companies overnight. Where there is a militant union, it is sometimes very difficult to introduce at all. The sole focus of this conference is on problems which the work unit, itself, can solve. It is not a gripe session or a bull session, although some items may be passed upward for decision from time to time. Before foremen conduct these meetings, they attend the managerial effectiveness seminar and then a team role laboratory as subordinates.

STAGE NINE: CORPORATE EFFECTIVENESS CONFERENCE

The four-hour corporate effectiveness conference is conducted by the top manager of a profit center or a major unit. He is usually a president, general manager, vice-president of operations, or plant manager. He meets with everyone in his organization, or at least with all managers, to tell them about his method of running a company. He outlines what he believes concerning such things as union-management relations, promotion from within, promotion on merit, community responsibility, etc. This stage is highly useful if timed properly and if the correct topics are chosen. It gives the top man an opportunity to use his personal influence to foster change. It is probably not a good way to start a change program but is a very good way of stabilizing one after a readiness for change or changes, themselves, have been introduced.

Change Strategy

These nine stages may be used in different combinations depending on the fundamental change objective.

OBJECTIVE	STRATEGY
Unfreezing the organization	Managerial effectiveness seminars for all managers is sufficient.
Management revitalization	Managerial effectiveness seminars, followed by a series of corporate effectiveness conferences.
Team building	Managerial effectiveness seminars, followed by team role laboratories and team effectiveness conferences.
Management by objectives	Managerial effectiveness seminars, followed by managerial effectiveness conferences and possibly team role laboratories.
Developing a marketing orientation	Managerial effectiveness seminars for those concerned, followed by a team role laboratory, managerial effectiveness conferences, an interteam effectiveness conference, and then a corporate strategy laboratory.
Merger	An interteam effectiveness conference followed by a corporate strategy laboratory.
Participative management	Managerial effectiveness seminars followed by a series of divisional effectiveness conferences and work-unit idea conferences.

Many other strategies have been used including those for the objectives of centralization, decentralization, and colonizing a new organization.

PROGRAM START-UP

Organization effectiveness programs must have a good working arrangement between the top man, senior managers, senior development staff, and a skilled detached consultant, preferably an outside behavioral scientist. Programs are more likely to be successful when the first step is for ten to fifteen managers to attend a publicly offered managerial effectiveness seminar. Two or more of the executive committee should be among them. The managers then meet as a committee and report to the executive level on the relevance of the program to the company. If the report is favorable, all at the executive level attend a managerial effectiveness seminar. On their return, they appoint the OE (organizational effectiveness) committee composed of both staff and line.

NOT ONLY BIG FIRMS

The 3-D program is not for big firms alone. Some of its notable successes have been with family and single-owner firms of only 200 employees. In one 200-employee firm, the program led to a doubling of the profit in four years, while the sole competitor decreased his profit by about 80 percent in the same period. During this period, there were no changes in the product or the way it was produced. No managers were brought in, and no managers changed their positions. Prior to this change program, the company had the same profit as its sole competitor, and both thought the profit was a good one. The program for this company utilized stages one and three primarily and was designed to build up marketing teams and to introduce a marketing rather than a production orientation.

TIME TAKEN

The time involved for a manager in a full-scale program is about fifteen days over a period of three years, or five days a year. The manager attends the managerial effectiveness seminar for five days, two team role laboratories for three days each—first as a subordinate, then as a superior—a managerial effectiveness conference as subordinate and then perhaps four of the same as a superior for a total of another two and a half days, while other activities average out to about a day and a half. None of this is training downtime. The first five days focus directly on improving the manager's effectiveness, whereas all other stages are highly task-oriented, job-related meetings designed to produce immediate changes.

The overall time taken to complete a total program is usually about two to three years. If all stages are used, some parts of the organization will have completed stages one to three within the first six months and up to stage six within a year, while other parts of the organization will have hardly started stage one. This has many beneficial effects: the program is flexible so that organizational subparts move at a comfortable rate of change for them, and the internal trainers get a rapid exposure to all stages so that they are better prepared for widespread implementation later.

SIMILARITIES BETWEEN THE 3-D AND INSTRUMENTED CHANGE PROGRAMS

The 3-D program has some similarities to other instrumented change programs. These are:

Predesigned training elements
Instrumentation
Sequential approach
Underlying model
Team training

Training sophistication has now reached a point where behavioral training objectives can be made sufficiently clear so that standard designs may be used to achieve them. No longer do we talk simply of "team training" but of training a team to induce a specific change in performance. This might be as fundamental as a complete reorganization of roles and responsibilities or as immediately practical as team objective setting. The 3-D program, in common with other instrumented change programs, has specific predesigned training elements to accomplish such objectives.

Training instrumentation generally refers to a training procedure in which the instructor as a person makes few verbal interventions. Such instrumentation is fundamental to most programmed learning approaches. Instrumentation has now developed to a point where it may be used in more behaviorally oriented courses as well as those designed to teach facts. All 3-D stages are instrumented to a high degree so that mass internal application is feasible.

Some years ago organizational change typically started with a single type of training activity and ended there. Now, with clearer objectives and far more experience, a sequence may be planned in advance. For instance, to actually implement management by objectives, at least four sequential training or decision-making events are required, and correspondingly to facilitate a merger, two or three events are required.

Almost all long-term programs of change have an underlying conceptual model. This model is used to support the values being induced by the program and to provide a common language. There are key differences among the models as some propose an ideal style, others emphasize role behavior, and some stress human relations.

The final similarity of 3-D to other approaches is the emphasis on team training as an anchoring device for change. A fadeout of the effects of training is greatly reduced by involving the team in this way.

UNDERLYING 3-D CHANGE THEORY   There are five theoretical ideas which underlie the 3-D organizational effectiveness program. They are:

"Organizational change is best viewed as a process of getting managers together, in what at times are unusual combinations, to talk about what they should talk about anyway, in an organized way with an atmosphere of trust and an interest in effectiveness."

When organization change is seen this way, much of the mystique disappears, and it is seen for what it really is.

"Managers of organizations rather than outsiders know what direction is best for the organization."

The 3-D program provides no one direction for a firm. It suggests effectiveness as the central value but recognizes that the means to effectiveness may vary widely. In none of the nine stages is the suggestion made that one method of operating or one style is better than another. What it does do, however, is to ask insistently, "What does it take to be effective here?"

"Managers are not applying as much as they already know."

The more senior a manager becomes, the more certain he is that this statement is true. If true, lecture courses providing more information do not get to the problem. The problem can only be solved by giving managers an opportunity to use what they know. This is the condition 3-D attempts to create.

"Change must involve all social units."

An organization consists of individuals, pairs, sets of coworkers, teams, departments, vertical relationships, whole divisions, and other units. For change to affect all of them, they all should be involved in the change process. For this reason 3-D provides its nine different stages for essentially different social units.

"Flexibility precedes change."

Flexibility must be given a positive value, and conditions created for it to occur, if changes are to be made. The 3-D model helps provide the value while the program creates the conditions.

The 3-D organizational effectiveness program improves managerial effectiveness, and through it, improves company profitability. It helps to focus management efforts and turns interdivisional conflict to more productive use by mutual objective setting. It is intended to be a change catalyst for the organization and to be a method of unleashing and then harnessing the tremendous reservoir of potential effectiveness that all top men know exists. The 3-D program provides a vehicle to enable an organization to get where it wants to go. The sole criterion is effectiveness. The 3-D Theory does not suggest one style is best or a single approach is best. Instead, it suggests that whatever leads to effectiveness is best.

The many advantages of the 3-D organizational effectiveness program are that effectiveness is emphasized in every stage, that it is fully flexible in operation and may be easily tailored to meet the particular needs of individual companies, and that if desired, all stages may be conducted internally. Furthermore, the program does not focus unduly on personality and does not require highly personal feedback from a subordinate to his superior. The program is, in part, based on a managerial effectiveness model which is theoretically sound and makes practical sense. And finally, it is important to note that the program is fully tested in both large and small organizations in which all managers were involved over periods usually lasting between two and three years.

THE CHANGE AGENT—CLIENT RELATIONSHIP

The external 3-D expert is often referred to simply as a behavioral consultant, though the more widely used technical term is change agent. The nature of the change agent—client relationship contributes significantly to the success of any change program. It might be said to be one of its most important elements. With 3-D the change agent relationship is always with the top team of the organization. The actual contact time is only for three to five days per year. While short-term relationships of about a year have been successful most extend over a two- to three-year time period. This is, in effect, the only external input other than the designs and materials used. The change agent always makes clear that he expects all members of the top team to participate fully in all key activities. This means that the top team and top man in particular are formally committed. No programs, in fact, are initiated without this understanding. It results in fewer but better programs.

Organizations sometimes prefer all or some of the actual training stages to be carried on by other than organizational members. Then a second relationship may exist between the organization and, most often, the consulting firm they are most familiar with. A third research relationship may be with a university if desired.

The 3-D Program and Organizational Flexibility

The most useful application of the 3-D program is the development and maintenance of organizational flexibility. Like other living things such as plants or animals, organizations have life cycles, and life depends on adequate and appropriate contact with the environment.

The stages of the organization's life cycle are not always clear, but enough is known about them to allow some rough generalizations as depicted in Exhibit 24.2. There are five stages, from formation to achievement, or maturity, after which any one of three long-term trends of flexibility, rigidity, or deterioration become established.

Formation   The initial legal, financial, and social formation of the company. Although this may be well planned, it often initiates no more than a trial run in an untested environment, and can lead in two to three years to a setback.

Setback   The initial organization was not completely suited for the environment, and a setback occurs. This setback may be marked by lower profit, serious internal policy or procedural differences, or good men leaving. Top management realizes that a "shake-up" or "shake-out" which leads to reorganization is needed.

Reorganization   A reorganization period is usually marked by a decrease in profit and a period of lower effectiveness, as the old gives way to the new. The period for large or small organizations lasts one to two years. If the reorganization was designed and implemented effectively it leads to growth.

Growth   The growth stage is marked by an increase in the size of such things as staff and market share. It is also usually marked by stability. Key policies are developed concerning product brands, market penetration, and customer policies which involve service and warranty. This growth stage is, in effect, a period during which the organization fills the market space, an accomplishment justified by its

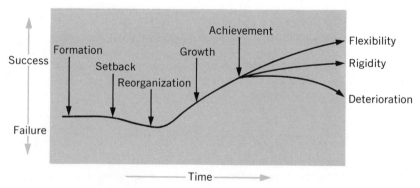

Exhibit 24–2   Organizational life cycle. A very common pattern of early development and the three alternative long-run trends.

policies and products. When this space is filled, the organization is in a state of achievement.

Achievement   At this point the company is seen as having been successful. Somewhat ominously, it might be said, "The organization has the seeds of a great future behind it." Only good organizations get this far, but the future is far from certain. One only has to look at companies steadily tumbling down or moving up on *"Fortune's* 500," a list of the biggest American manufacturing companies, to see that change can occur. Thus, from achievement, the organization can move to one of deterioration, rigidity, or flexibility.

A deteriorating organization is one which has lost its ability to respond to its environment. Profits may remain steady over some years, but the market share is gradually dropping.

A rigid organization is one which has only a single pattern of responses to a changing environment. Profits could be high or even increasing in a static environment, but they would, in fact, be in a long-term decline, relative to competitors, in a changing market.

A flexible organization is obviously the most desirable alternative.

THE FLEXIBLE ORGANIZATION

A flexible organization is one with a range of appropriate responses to a changing environment. Profits are high and probably increasing, with a large amount of the profit coming from products or services not available five years previously. In a government department or other nonprofit concern, the flexibility is shown in the increasing effectiveness of the services provided and in the increasing internal use of advanced organizational and management techniques.

The particular characteristics of a flexible organization, (which the 3-D program can induce), are:

Emphasis on effectiveness—so that this value is the most important consideration in changes affecting individuals, departments, or the organization, itself.

Acceptance of change—so that decisions may be easily implemented at all levels.

Free power flow—so that decisions are more likely to be made in an appropriate area, not simply where they were made before.

Flexible resource allocation—so that men, money, and materials are shifted to where they may do the most good.

Marketing orientation—so that the market defines the organization.

Technological orientation—so that new technological devices are investigated for their appropriateness.

Free information flow—so that within limits imposed by the restraints of commercial intelligence all parts of the organization have a larger frame of reference with which to see their own potential contribution to effectiveness.

Excess managerial capacity—so that new developments may be initiated quickly without damaging the old.

Project teams—so that fresh approaches have a way of being generated.

Focus on outputs—so that the test of a manager's action is not "What did he do?" but "What did he produce?"

A few organizations are moving toward having many or all these conditions now. And most organizations could obtain them.

Exhibit 24–1 The 3-D organizational effectiveness program. (Two parts.) Nine training elements may be used in a variety of combinations to achieve specific objectives.

3-D organizational effectiveness program

STAGE	NAME	DESIGNED TO IMPROVE	PRIMARY RESULTS	DURATION	WHO ATTENDS
1	Managerial effectiveness seminar	Managerial effectiveness	■ Managerial effectiveness improved ■ Flexibility increased ■ Preliminary objectives established	Five days	Each manager from top man down, usually twelve to thirty-six at a time. Managers participate in teams composed of other managers they do not work with.
2	Team role laboratory	Team role structure	■ Team objectives established ■ Team reorganized if necessary ■ Teamwork methods introduced	Three days	Each management team or department consisting of a superior and all of his subordinates who stay together as a team. Most managers go first as a subordinate with their superior and then a second time as a superior.
3	Managerial effectiveness conference	Managerial objective setting	■ Managerial objectives confirmed ■ Superior-subordinate blockages removed ■ Coaching relationship established	Half day	Each superior-subordinate pair alone.
4	Corporate strategy laboratory	Organization policies and design	■ Organization diagnosis made ■ Organization policies reconsidered ■ Organization structure reconsidered	Three days	The executive committee or top team only.
5	Team effectiveness conference	Team objective setting	■ Progress toward team objectives reviewed ■ Additional team objectives set ■ Blockages inhibiting team cleared	One day	Same as team role laboratory.
6	Interteam effectiveness conference	Horizontal team effectiveness	■ Interteam blockages removed ■ Interteam effectiveness standards established ■ Interteam optimum operating arrangements agreed	One day	Two departments, functions, or teams who wish to improve the way they interact.
7	Divisional effectiveness conference	Vertical team effectiveness	■ Multiple levels agree on objectives ■ Vertical information flow increased ■ Resistance to change decreased	One day	A vertical chain of managers with reporting relationships and selected coworkers of one or more of them.
8	Work-unit idea conference	Worker commitment	■ Foreman-worker relationship strengthened ■ Work flows modified ■ Unit output increased	Half day	A foreman and his workers.
9	Corporate effectiveness conference	Organization-wide commitment	■ Corporate objectives and policies clarified ■ Objectives and policies accepted ■ Top man's influence strengthened	Half day	The top man, president, G.M., etc. and all managers, and possibly workers, with a series of groups of various sizes and composition.

If modification of the organization is involved, an under-standing of the structure and dynamics of the thing acted upon is essential so that the chain reaction of change in one part coursing through other parts, can be calculated.

E. WIGHT BAKKE

Chapter Twenty-five

AN ORGANIZATIONAL EFFECTIVENESS PROGRAM

A general manager of an electrical utility describes his organization's experience with the application of the 3-D Theory in a program of organizational effectiveness.

As with many other organizations around the world, we have been searching for methods to improve managerial and organizational effectiveness as well as flexibility. We began one such program a few years ago and have been deeply involved with it and its effects ever since.

The electrical utility of which I am general manager employs over 1,800 persons, of whom approximately one-third are union members. In addition to the head office, there are four regional headquarters. Our fixed assets amount to over $300 million. There are twelve generating stations, and we serve 127,000 direct customers.

Traditional Management Development

Over the past ten years, our supervisory and managerial staff have participated in extensive management development activities of the traditional type. The majority have attended one-week "country house" seminars, where they studied finance and human relations using the case method. Over seventy of our supervisory and managerial force participated in one-week sensitivity training T-groups. In addition, many of our senior management were given an intensive five-week program of case study in general management. These programs were all useful and met their objectives, but we wanted to find more powerful methods of organizational change.

MUCH EXPERIMENTATION

So in the early sixties, we deliberately attempted to sample many of the development programs available. In addition to pure case and pure T-group, we sampled the Blake managerial grid, American Management Association seminars, and many others. For one reason or another, these did not suit our needs fully, although each has been useful in other companies' programs of organizational effectiveness. We believed, however, that some had too little transfer to the work situation, others were too rigid in application, and some were simply too expensive. We were looking for a reasonably priced, well-designed, flexible, and tested program, parts of which could be conducted internally at low cost.

Our Organizational Problems

Like any other organization, ours had some internal problems to solve. In the main, these were caused by very rapid growth and, consequently, unseasoned staff. The key problem was that, as an organization, we had not fully adjusted to the fact that we had suddenly grown. Some problems that arose from this growth were too many managers involved in some decisions and not enough managers involved in others, some interdivisional communication problems, and a need for clear objective setting and management by objectives. We experienced, further, a need for more decision making at lower levels, some resistance to change in the organization, and insufficient emphasis on job performance. These problems are common to many rapidly growing organizations. We wanted to do something about them.

How could we change all this? It is very easy to change an organization by inducing fear. This is done simply by firing a few key people—or demoting them. We are opposed to this idea unless absolutely necessary. We believe that organization life often forces managers and workers into inefficiency so that they, as individuals, are seen as incompetent, when it may not be their fault. Very often they may not have all the resources with which to work, or they may simply be in the wrong job. In other words, it is the situation, not the man, which needs to be changed. The 3-D organizational effectiveness program gave all managers an opportunity to change the situation they were in, provided the change led to greater effectiveness.

The Program

Our change program used all nine different stages of the 3-D organizational effectiveness program which collectively performed the functions of unfreezing the organization, changing it, and then stabilizing it at the new level of flexibility and effectiveness. Exhibit 25.1 shows the stages, which overlap each other in time, and the starting dates for each successive stage.

Exhibit 25–1

Our organizational effectiveness program			
STAGE	DESIGNED TO IMPROVE	PROGRAM	
		LENGTH	START DATE
Managerial effectiveness seminar	Managerial effectiveness	Five days	May, 1963
Team role laboratory	Team role structure	Three days	February, 1965
Managerial effectiveness conference	Managerial objective setting	Half day	April, 1965
Corporate strategy laboratory	Organization policies and design	Three days	September, 1965
Team effectiveness conference	Team objective setting	One day	October, 1965
Work-unit idea conference	Worker commitment	Half day	February, 1966
Interteam effectiveness conference	Horizontal team effectiveness	One day	September, 1966
Divisional effectiveness conference	Vertical team effectiveness	One day	October, 1966
Corporate effectiveness conference	Organization-wide commitment	Half day	Spring, 1967

MANAGERIAL EFFECTIVENESS SEMINAR: MAY 1963

The first stage was the managerial effectiveness seminar. All our 200 managers and supervisors participated in this five-day program, including line crew foremen with an average educational level of nine years. Here we learned the 3-D Theory and its application to organization life. We became acquainted with sound team-work principles, and through management-style-diagnosis tests, we were provided with a direction for optimum style change for our particular jobs. As planned, the main impact of this seminar was a general unfreezing of the organization and of individual managers. There is little doubt that this stage, alone, had a profound impact on the organization and produced a readiness for change.

As the general manager, I attended all but one of the eight seminars for a few hours and discussed with the managers the direction we thought the organization should go. In addition, I solicited their comments by giving each team the task of identifying organizational weak spots and identifying methods of improvement. All the comments of the twenty-eight teams were distributed to the managers in the organization. I cannot say I agreed with all the comments, but I must say that, in aggregate, they exerted a positive shock on the organization.

THE DECISION TO PROCEED

About halfway through this first stage, we decided that the 3-D program had given us a great deal and had still more to offer us. I, therefore, called a planning meeting to chart the direction and timing of the remainder of the program. At that meeting our largest division, the distribution division, volunteered as a pilot group for team training and the subsequent 3-D stages. We wanted a pilot program to make sure we knew what we were getting into. In our pilot division, many changes in procedures and, for that matter, in management philosophy were later introduced. As it happened, an interesting phenomenon then occurred which I call "development by proxy." The pilot division's changes, seen as successful, were picked up by many of the other divisions. This is proof, I think, that once a change in direction is clearly established and appears effective, the whole organization can adopt it or adapt to it.

TEAM ROLE LABORATORY: FEBRUARY 1965

The team role laboratory is the second and, by far, the most important stage in the program. It takes advantage of the unfreezing effect of the managerial effectiveness seminar. It does not focus unduly on style but on the situation, team-member roles, and effectiveness criteria. In effect, it gives an actual management team of a superior and all his subordinates a perfect opportunity to decide just how they intend to work together in the future. One of the key instruments to help the team do this is the team-style-diagnosis test which gives a good reading on how a department is working together.

We decided to go so far as to ask each team to reorganize itself. Many teams did make some long overdue changes. I know of none of these laboratories that did not have a marked influence in making a team more effective. The program we evolved was tested on a senior management team and then conducted on a demand basis in other parts of the organization. Many teams have reconstructed their internal organization after the laboratories, and the methods used to make decisions have also been changed. We involved some unionized employees in this stage, and they also participated, when appropriate, in later stages. One man was employed full time to conduct the team sessions. Several teams have repeated the laboratory when the top man changed or when several team members changed. Our personnel department does not have to encourage teams to repeat the three-day team role laboratory since team members ask for it.

THE DESERTER PROBLEM

The managerial effectiveness seminars and the team-role laboratories had a profound impact on our management force. Withdrawal of involvement and commitment is nothing new in organizations, but changing this condition is. Many of our less involved managers, when confronted with their behavior in the managerial effectiveness seminar, decided to modify it. The team role laboratories gave them the chance to change, and the managerial effectiveness conference helped them still more.

MANAGERIAL EFFECTIVENESS CONFERENCE: APRIL 1965

Through the medium of the four-hour supervisor-subordinate managerial effectiveness conference, we have introduced management by objectives into most parts of the utility. This was introduced with remarkable ease and appears to solve many of our problems concerning both direction and motivation of the managerial and supervisory force. This conference is conducted between a manager and each of his subordinates in turn. It is essentially a formal discussion of roles, effectiveness criteria, and objectives. I think most would agree that the two prior stages were a necessary and useful preparation for introducing management by objectives.

CORPORATE STRATEGY LABORATORY: SEPTEMBER 1965

Shortly after the Managerial Effectiveness Conference had started, we conducted stage four of the program, the corporate strategy laboratory. A three-man top team consisting of myself, the assistant general manager and chief engineer, and the controller met for three days to discuss the organization, its objectives, and its future. In particular, we looked at the internal design of our organization as well as at its comprehensive role in society. We knew we were ready for such a change, and the three days gave us a chance to delve into the new design in some detail. We made many changes which may not seem profound but were significant in their effect on the organization as most represented significant departures from prior practice. These included: introducing a senior engineer into an economic analysis function; collecting several staff departments together in a newly created unit; creating two senior positions for functions not previously distinguished separately; redesigning the composition of the executive committee; and decreasing the number of managers reporting to the general manager. There were many more, of course, but the point is that the strategy seminar was not simply an intellectual exercise. Structural situational changes were made as a direct result of this laboratory.

We also began to produce revised, up-to-date objectives for the utility. These were refined at later meetings of the managers and then introduced to the organization by the ongoing stage three and by stage five, the team effectiveness conference.

TEAM EFFECTIVENESS CONFERENCE: OCTOBER 1965

About this time, several parts of the organization, particularly the distribution division, had been involved in management by objectives for some time. They were discovering that a commitment to the idea is not enough to keep it going. They also found that they needed some direction as to basic corporate philosophy. Some parts of our system had to be modified to suit their needs, and the location of responsibility and control had to be changed completely in other cases. In addition, objective setting as a technique had to be learned, and then feasible objectives set. Many team objectives turned out to be far too ambitious—a good sign, of course, so long as they eventually come closer to reality and feasibility. To tighten and improve objective setting, the team effectiveness conference was introduced. The one-day program was relatively straightforward and consisted of a review of the progress toward objectives and of the situational or personal blockages inhibiting the attainment of some of them. Through this review, an opportunity for further situational management was introduced, and realistic team objective setting became the rule.

WORK-UNIT IDEA CONFERENCE: FEBRUARY 1966

One problem in a geographically decentralized operation such as ours is the difficulty in getting changes introduced in the field. This was facilitated in three ways. One was by bringing into the head office the various groups to discuss proposals for improvement. Another was by going to the field. For me, stage six was a most exciting and personally satisfying part of the program. Our top team sat down with the lowest-level field units, one by one, to discuss their objectives. These small meetings, usually of only ten people, were customarily attended by five levels of an actual superior-subordinate chain. Everyone's superior attended the conference, except my own. The meetings helped to tie the head office and field objectives effectively together and tapped many new ideas. They helped collapse the so-called "executive distance," which tends to blur objectives as they get passed down the line.

INTERTEAM EFFECTIVENESS CONFERENCE: SEPTEMBER 1966

The impact of the effectiveness program was by this time having a profound effect. One outcome was that the various parts of the organization were finding new relationships with other parts. We saw this as a necessary part of growth and adjustment rather than as an unnecessary evil. One major misalignment problem occurred between the staff and the line. This and other similar problems were moved to resolution through stage seven, the interteam effectiveness conference. Here staff and line sat down to hammer out—I think that is the correct expression—their appropriate roles and effectiveness criteria. What resulted was a functional and major redistribution of responsibilities for the good of the organization. Now we see staff more as architects and catalysts than as control or vertical feed-back mechanisms, which to some extent they were before.

DIVISIONAL EFFECTIVENESS CONFERENCE: OCTOBER 1966

Up to this point, the program had concentrated on the manager alone, the vertical relationships, and teams. We next decided to work in similar fashion with a division as the basic unit for change. The distribution division, our largest, decided to hold stage eight, a divisional effectiveness conference with six levels, at one meeting. The enormous number and rapidity of changes being encountered in this division provided a major reason for the program. This was attended by eighty personnel—about a 10 percent representation of all regions and all trades, including linemen and meter readers. It was carefully designed for maximum participation. The objective of this conference was to give the division manager an opportunity to explain his management philosophy and give all present an opportunity to question him in detail on past, present, or future events.

The conference went extremely well and another is planned. An ideal future topic, with enormous payoff, will be one concerning the methods of introducing change. If the division, as a whole, could agree on change-introduction procedures, the productivity potential would be tremendous.

CORPORATE EFFECTIVENESS CONFERENCE: 1967

The design of the last, formal stage of the program is essentially that of the divisional effectiveness conference but organization-wide. A series of formal statements containing what we believe about managerial and corporate life is prepared. To a large extent, these beliefs have shaped and been shaped by the program itself. We hope, by a series of conferences, to induce the reality of unity toward common objectives and a common method of achieving them.

Changes

Training or development is not a profitable proposition unless something happens. I do not think senior managers should be influenced too much by what people simply say about training courses. In fact, I do not know of a training program which is not rated highly by participants, even though it may have been relatively useless in terms of introducing productive changes. The payoff in training is not what people say in answer to researchers. The payoff has to be visible change.

As I have indicated, in the past few years our organization has made several major changes. In the past two years we have reorganized key parts of the management structure with a virtual absence of top-management turnover. Our top ten men are the same men who began the program, although some are in different positions. We have reoriented managers to manage, established a program of management by objectives throughout the company, and pushed decision levels downward so that particular decisions are made at appropriate levels. To point out further examples of change, we have modified procedures so that performance, or output, data are operating as well as input, or control, data; changed the attitude to change itself, so that acceptance of change is becoming the norm; established team-work methods in parts of the organization that could use it and established other methods where team-work was not needed; and introduced the norm of performance measurement, although the reward structure is not yet decided. Thus, the six organizational problems I identified previously have all been substantially eliminated, although I am not suggesting that complete harmony prevails.

It would be quite improper of me to suggest that all managers were delighted or even in favor of the program. Any change, good or poor, has those who support it and those who do not. Change upsets old patterns and makes the future less predictable for a while. Many men are deeply committed to maintaining an organization as it is and believe that the possibility of improvement is not worth the risk inevitably created by change.

COST-BENEFIT ANALYSIS

The total cost of the program, including all materials and consulting advice, was less than $60 per participating manager for each of three years. As we do with most of our engineering projects, we would like to have made a cost-benefit analysis of this program. However, its time scale and its pervasive effects made it difficult. It would be an easy matter to point to sharply decreased labor costs and other such measures which the program undoubtedly influenced greatly, but a rigorous analysis would be difficult indeed.

ANTIFADEOUT

In summary, what has happened is that our organization has succeeded in unfreezing itself, introducing some positive change, and then stabilizing the changes introduced. So many of the changes were structural and procedural rather than simply attitudinal that fadeout is unlikely, if not impossible. Our organization at the end of the program was clearly more effective and more flexible than it was at the beginning.

If a Company Wants to Start

Based on our experience, I would make these suggestions to other top executive managements who are thinking of getting involved in an organizational effectiveness program: obtain top-level involvement from your colleagues; understand the underlying strategy of the various management models and change programs that are current—in particular, 3-D, T-group, and grid; discover the procedures and actual mechanics of the various change programs now available; find an external change agent who you think is competent, has experience, and has or could earn the trust of the top executives; and work with him to develop an organization program to suit your needs. Do not think that your organization will change without top-level support and involvement. Do not rely on a mechanical approach that suggests all companies have the same problems. And do not think that the program will be over in six months.

Is This a Program?

On studying this case history, the reader may get the impression that this organizational effectiveness plan was highly programmed. It was anything but that—development is too important to have it ritualized. As far as it has been feasible, which was practically always, organization subparts could move to the next step as soon as they liked or could wait as long as they liked. As far as I can tell, this improved the reception of the program tremendously and heightened its ultimate impact.

The program, as it evolved, met the needs of the organization, as it evolved. It may be that this nine-stage strategy has general application. I cannot judge that, but it fitted our needs well.

Appendix A.

THE 3-E CONCEPT DICTIONARY

I fear explanations explanatory of things explained.

A. LINCOLN

THE 3-D CONCEPT DICTIONARY

Apparent Effectiveness   The extent to which a manager gives the appearance of being effective (chapter 1).

Area of Effectiveness   The area on a situational flex map where the flex of all the dominant situational elements intersect with the manager's style flex (chapter 10).

Area of Possible Effectiveness   The area on a situational flex map where the flex of all the dominant situational elements intersect (chapter 10).

Autocrat   A manager who is using a high Task Orientation and a low Relationships Orientation in a situation where such behavior is inappropriate and who is, therefore, less effective; perceived as having no confidence in others, as unpleasant, and as interested only in the immediate task (chapter 4).

Basic Style   The way in which a manager behaves as measured by the amount of Task Orientation and Relationships Orientation he uses. The four basic styles are integrated, dedicated, related, and separated (chapter 3).

Basic Style Point (BSP)   A point score for both Task Orientation and Relationships Orientation each scaled from 0 to 4 (chapter 3).

Benevolent Autocrat   A manager who is using a high Task Orientation and a low Relationships Orientation in a situation where such behavior is appropriate and who is, therefore, more effective; perceived as knowing what he wants and how to get it without creating resentment (chapter 4).

Bureaucrat   A manager who is using a low Task Orientation and a low Relationships Orientation in a situation where such behavior is appropriate and who is, therefore, more effective; perceived as being primarily interested in rules and procedures for their own sake, as wanting to control the situation by their use, and as conscientious (chapter 4).

Compromiser   A manager who is using a high Task Orientation and a high Relationships Orientation in a situation that requires a high orientation to only one or neither and who is, therefore, less effective; perceived as being a poor decision maker, as one who allows various pressures in the situation to influence him too much, and as avoiding or minimizing immediate pressures and problems rather than maximizing long-term production (chapter 4).

Coworker   A person with whom a manager works who is neither his superior nor a subordinate (chapter 6).

Dedicated Style   A basic style with more than average Task Orientation and less than average Relationships Orientation (chapter 3).

Demands   See element demands.

Deserter   A manager who is using a low Task Orientation and a low Relationships Orientation in a situation where such behavior is inappropriate and who is therefore less effective; perceived as uninvolved and passive or negative (chapter 4).

Developer   A manager who is using a low Task Orientation and a high Relationships Orientation in a situation where such behavior is appropriate and who is, therefore, more effective; perceived as having implicit trust in people and as being primarily concerned with developing them as individuals (chapter 4).

Dominant Elements   Those elements, in a particular situation, which make the strongest demands on a manager's basic style (chapter 10).

Dominant Style   The basic or managerial style a manager most frequently uses (chapter 4).

Effectiveness Standards   General output requirements of a managerial position (chapter 22).

Element Demands   The basic style required by a situational element in order for it to contribute to effectiveness (chapter 6).

Element Strength   The relative strength of a dominant element in a particular situation expressed as some part of a total of ten points (chapter 10).

Executive   A manager who is using a high Task Orientation and a high Relationships Orientation in a situation where such behavior is appropriate and who is, therefore, more effective; perceived as a good motivating force and manager who sets high standards, treats everyone somewhat differently, and prefers team management (chapter 4).

Flex   See style flex.

Flex Map   See situational flex map.

Integrated Style   A basic style with more than average Task Orientation and more than average Relationships Orientation (chapter 3).

Leader   A person seen by others as being primarily responsible for achieving group objectives (chapter 1).

Leader Effectiveness   The extent to which the leader influences his followers to achieve group objectives (chapter 1).

Manager   A person occupying a position in a formal organization who is responsible for the work of at least one other person and who has formal authority over that person (chapter 3).

Managerial Effectiveness (E)   The extent to which a manager achieves the output requirements of his position. Scaled from 0 to 4 (chapter 1).

Managerial Skills   Three skills required for managerial effectiveness: situational management, situational sensitivity, style flexibility (chapter 10).

Managerial Style   An assessment of the appropriateness and therefore effectiveness of a particular basic style in a situation (chapter 4).

Managerial Style Point (MSP)   A point score for Task Orientation, Relationships Orientation, and managerial effectiveness, each scaled from 0 to 4 (chapter 4).

Missionary   A manager who is using a high Relationships Orientation and a low Task Orientation in a situation where such behavior is inappropriate and who is, therefore, less effective; perceived as being primarily interested in harmony (chapter 4).

Objectives   Effectiveness standards which are as specific, as time-bounded, and as measurable as possible (chapter 22).

Organization   All the factors which influence behavior within a social system that are common to essentially unrelated positions (chapter 6).

Overrejected Style   A basic or managerial style a manager uses far less frequently than the average manager (chapter 4).

Personal Effectiveness   The extent to which a manager achieves his own private objectives (chapter 1).

Related Style   A basic style with less than average Task Orientation and more than average Relationships Orientation (chapter 3).

Relationships Orientation (RO)   The extent to which a manager has personal job relationships; characterized by listening, trusting, and encouraging. Scaled from 0 to 4 (chapter 3).

Separated Style   A basic style with less than average Task Orientation and less than average Relationships Orientation (chapter 3).

Situational Demands   The basic style required by all dominant situational elements in order for managerial effectiveness to be increased (chapter 6).

Situational Elements   Five elements through which all of the situational demands on a manager may be said to be expressed: organization, technology, superior, coworkers, and subordinates (chapter 6).

Situational Flex Map (Flex Map)   A chart depicting the element flex of the dominant situational elements and the basic style of the manager (chapter 10).

Situational Management Skill (SM)   Skill in changing the style demands of one or more situational elements so that managerial effectiveness increases. Scaled from 0 to 4 (chapter 12).

Situational Manipulation   Changing the style demands of one or more situational elements so that personal effectiveness increases (chapter 12).

Situational Sensitivity (SS)   Skill in appraising situational elements in terms of Task-Orientation and Relationships-Orientation demands, flex, and strength. Scaled from 0 to 4 (chapter 11).

Style Appraisal Skill   Ability to appraise another's style correctly (chapter 11).

Style Awareness   Degree to which a manager can appraise his own style correctly (chapter 11).

Style Distortion   Perceiving more or fewer occurrences of a particular style than actually exist (chapter 11).

Style Drift   Varying one's basic-style behavior inappropriately so that managerial effectiveness decreases (chapter 5).

Style Flex (Flex)   The ability to vary one's basic-style behavior. Scaled from 0 to 4 (chapter 5).

Style Flexibility (SF)   Skill in varying one's basic-style behavior appropriately to a changing situation so that managerial effectiveness increases. Scaled from 0 to 4 (chapter 5).

Style Profile   A bar chart showing the degree to which a manager uses each of the managerial styles (chapter 19).

Style Resilience   Maintaining a single appropriate basic style so that managerial effectiveness increases (chapter 5).

Style Rigidity   Maintaining a single inappropriate basic style so that managerial effectiveness decreases (chapter 5).

Style Synthesis   An average basic or managerial style based on all styles used (chapter 19).

Subordinate   A person over whom a manager has authority and for whose work he is responsible (chapter 6).

Superior   A person having authority over a manager and responsibility for his work (chapter 6).

Supporting Style   The basic or managerial style a manager uses next most frequently after the dominant style (chapter 4).

Task Orientation (TO)   The extent to which a manager directs his own and his subordinates' efforts characterized by initiating, organizing, and directing. Scaled from 0 to 4 (chapter 3).

Technology   The way work may be done to achieve managerial effectiveness (chapter 6).

Appendix B

BIBLIOGRAPHY

1 Aitken, H. G. J.: *Taylorism at Watertown Arsenal*, Harvard University Press, Cambridge, Mass., 1960.

2 Allen, L. A.: *The Management Profession*, McGraw-Hill Book Company, New York, 1964.

3 Allport, G. W.: *Personality: A Psychological Interpretation*, Henry Holt and Company, Inc., New York, 1937.

4 Anderson, R. C.: "Learning in Discussions: A Résumé of the Authoritarian-Democratic Studies," *Harvard Educational Review*, vol. 29, pp. 201–215, 1959.

5 Argyris, C.: "T-Groups for Organizational Effectiveness," *Harvard Business Review*, pp. 60–74, March–April, 1964.

6 Argyris, C.: *Interpersonal Competence and Organizational Effectiveness*, Richard D. Irwin, Inc., Homewood, Ill., 1962.

7 Argyris, C.: *Personality and Organization: The Conflict Between System and the Individual*, Harper & Row, Publishers, Incorporated, New York, 1957.

8 Argyris, C.: *Understanding Organizational Behavior*, The Dorsey Press, Homewood, Ill., 1960.

9 Argyle, M., G. Gardner, and F. Cioffi: "Supervisory Methods Related to Productivity, Absenteeism, and Labor Turnover," *Human Relations*, vol. 11, pp. 23–40, 1958.

10 Bales, R. F.: "The Equilibrium Problem in Small Groups," in T. Parsons, R. F. Bales, and E. A. Shills (eds.), *Working Papers in the Theory of Action*, The Free Press of Glencoe, New York, 1933.

11   Barnard, C. I.: *The Functions of the Executive,* Harvard University Press, Cambridge, Mass., 1938.
12   Bassett, G. A.: *Management Styles in Transition,* American Management Association, New York, 1966.
13   Batten, J. D.: *Tough Minded Management,* American Management Association, New York, 1963.
14   Batten, J. D.: *Developing a Tough Minded Climate for Results,* American Management Association, New York, 1965.
15   Batten, J. D.: *Beyond Management by Objectives,* American Management Association, New York, 1966.
16   Bellows, R., T. Q. Gilson, and G. S. Odiorne: *Executive Skills,* Prentice-Hall, Inc., Englewood Cliffs, N.J., 1962.
17   Bennis, W. G.: *The Marked Deck: A Non-objective Playlet for Four Characters,* National Education Association, National Training Laboratories, Subscription Service 2, Washington, D.C., 1963.
18   Bennis, W. G., K. D. Benne, and R. Chin (eds.): *The Planning of Change,* Holt, Rinehart and Winston, Inc., New York, 1961.
19   Bennis, W. G., E. H. Schein, D. E. Berlew, and F. I. Steele: *Interpersonal Dynamics,* Dorsey Press, Homewood, Ill., 1964.
20   Bennis, W. G.: "Leadership Theory and Administrative Behavior: The Problem of Authority," *Administrative Science Quarterly,* vol. 4, pp. 239–301, 1959.
21   Bennett, C. L.: "Defining the Manager's Job," *Manual of Position Descriptions,* American Management Association, New York, 1958.
22   Bird, C.: *Social Psychology,* D. Appleton-Century Company, Inc., New York, 1940.
23   Blake, R. R., and J. S. Mouton: *The Managerial Grid,* Gulf Publishing Company, Houston, 1964.
24   Blake, R. R., and J. S. Mouton: "The Managerial Grid in Three Dimensions," *ASTD Journal,* pp. 2–5, January, 1967.
25   Bolton, W. B.: Proposed the dedicated and related labels during a seminar of the Canadian Dominion Bureau of Statistics, 1966.
26   Boyd, J. A.: *Professional Amateur: The Biography of C. F. Kettering,* E. P. Dutton & Co., Inc., New York, 1951.
27   Bradford, L. P.: "The Case of the Hidden Agenda," *Group Development,* National Education Association, National Training Laboratories, Selected Readings Series, no. 1, Washington, D.C., 1961.
28   Bradford, L. P. (ed.): *Group Development,* National Education Association, National Training Laboratories, Selected Reading Series, no. 1, Washington, D.C., 1961.
29   Bradford, L. P., J. R. Gibb, and K. D. Benne (eds.): *T-Group and Laboratory Method,* John Wiley & Sons, Inc., New York, 1964.
30   Bradford, L. P.: *Explorations in Human Relations Training: An Assessment of Experience, 1947–1953,* National Education Association, National Training Laboratories, Washington, D.C., 1953.
31   Brayfield, A. R., and W. H. Crockett: "Employee Attitudes and Employee Performance," *Psychological Bulletin,* vol. 3, pp. 396–424, 1955.
32   Brown, J. A. C.: *The Social Psychology of Industry,* Penguin Books, Inc., Baltimore, 1954.
33   Brown, W.: *Explorations in Management,* Penguin Books, Inc., Baltimore, 1965.

34   Burgess, E. W.: "Management in France," in F. Harbison and C. A. Myers (eds.), *Management in the Industrial World*, McGraw-Hill Book Company, New York, 1959.

35   Burns, T., and G. M. Stalker: *The Management of Innovation*, Tavistock, 1961.

36   Carnegie, A.: *Autobiography of Andrew Carnegie*, Riverside Press, 1920.

37   Carron, T. J.: "Human Relations Training and Attitude Change: A Vector Analysis," *Personnel Psychology*, vol. 17, pp. 403–424, Winter, 1964.

38   Cassels, L., and R. L. Randall: *The Company Policy Manual: Guide to Efficient Management*, American Management Association, New York, 1960.

39   Cattell, R. B., D. R. Saunders, and G. F. Stive: "The Dimensions of Syntality in Small Groups," *Human Relations*, vol. 6, pp. 331–356, 1953.

40   Coch, L., and J. R. P. French, Jr.: "Overcoming Resistance to Change," *Human Relations*, vol. 1, pp. 512–532, 1947.

41   Dale, E.: *The Great Organizers*, McGraw-Hill Book Company, New York, 1960.

42   Davis, K.: "Evolving Models of Organizational Change," *Academy of Management Journal*, pp. 27–38, March, 1968.

43   Day, R. C., and R. L. Hamblin: "Some Effects of Close and Punitive Styles of Supervision," *Technical Report 8*, Contract N ONR 816(11), Washington University, St. Louis, 1961.

44   DeCharms, R., and W. Bridgeman: "Leadership Compliance and Group Behavior," *Technical Report 9*, Contract N ONR 816(11), Washington University, St. Louis, 1961.

45   Diebold, J.: *Automation*, D. Van Nostrand Company, Inc., Princeton, N.J., 1953.

46   Dill, W. R., T. L. Hilton, and W. R. Reitman: *The New Managers*, Prentice-Hall, Inc., Englewood Cliffs, N.J., 1962.

47   Drucker, P. F.: *The Effective Executive*, Harper & Row, Publishers, Incorporated, New York, 1966.

48   Drucker, P. F.: *The Practice of Management*, Harper & Row, Publishers, Incorporated, New York, 1954.

49   Drucker, P. F.: *Concept of the Corporation*, The John Day Company, Inc., New York, 1946.

50   Drucker, P. F.: *The New Society: The Anatomy of the Industrial Order*, Harper & Row, Publishers, Incorporated, New York, 1950.

51   Dunteman, G., and B. M. Bass: "Supervisory and Engineering Success Associated with Self, Interaction, and Task Orientation Scores," *Personnel Psychology*, vol. 16, pp. 13–21, 1963.

52   Fayol, H.: *Industrial and General Administration*, Pitman Publishing Corporation, New York, 1930.

53   Fiedler, F. E.: *A Theory of Leadership Effectiveness*, McGraw-Hill Book Company, New York, 1966.

54   Fiedler, F. E.: "Leader Attitudes, Group Climate and Group Creativity," *Journal of Abnormal and Social Psychology*, vol. 65, pp. 308–318, 1962.

55   Fiedler, F. E.: "The Influence of Leader-Keyman Relations on Combat Crew Effectiveness," *Journal of Abnormal and Social Psychology*, vol. 51, pp. 227–235, 1955.

56   Fiedler, F. E.: "Leader's Contribution to Task Performance in Cohesive and Uncohesive Groups," *Journal of Abnormal and Social Psychology*, vol. 67, pp. 83–87, 1964.

57   Fiedler, F. E.: "Engineer the Job to Fit the Manager," *Harvard Business Review*, pp. 115–122, September–October, 1965.

58   Fleishman, E. A., and D. R. Peters: "Interpersonal Values, Leadership Attitudes, and Managerial Success," *Personnel Psychology*, vol. 15, pp. 127–143, 1962.

59   Fleishman, E. A.: "The Measurement of Leadership Attitudes in Industry," *Journal of Applied Psychology*, vol. 37, pp. 153–158, 1953.

60   Fleishman, E. A.: "The Leadership Opinion Questionnaire," in R. M. Stogdill, and A. E. Coons (eds.), *Leader Behavior, Its Description and Measurement*, Ohio State University Bureau of Business Research, Columbus, Ohio, 1957.

61   Fleishman, E. A.: *Manual for Administering the Leadership Opinion Questionnaire*, Science Research Associates, Inc., Chicago, 1960.

62   Fleishman, E. A.: *Leadership Climate and Supervisory Behaviour*, Personnel Research Board, Ohio State University, Columbus, Ohio, 1951.

63   Fleishman, E. A., and E. F. Harris: "Patterns of Leadership Behavior Related to Employee Grievances and Turnover," *Personnel Psychology*, vol. 15, pp. 43–56, 1962.

64   Foa, U. G.: "Relation of Worker Expectations to Satisfaction with Supervisor," *Personnel Psychology*, vol. 10, pp. 161–168, 1957.

65   Follett, M. P.: *The New State*, Longmans, Green & Co., Ltd., London, 1920.

66   Follett, M. P.: *Creative Experience*, Longmans, Green & Co., Ltd., London, 1924.

67   Ford, H. (in collaboration with Samuel Crowther): *My Life and Work*, Doubleday & Company, Inc., Garden City, New York, 1926.

68   French, J. R. P., Jr., J. Israel, and A. Dagfinn: "An Experiment on Participation in a Norwegian Factory," *Human Relations*, vol. 13, pp. 3–19, 1960.

69   [French, J. R. P.] and [Coch, L.,] "Overcoming Resistance to Change," *Human Relations*, vol. 1, pp. 512–532, 1947.

70   Freud, S.: *A General Introduction to Psychoanalysis*, Washington Square Press, New York, N.Y., 1952.

71   Gerth, H. H., and C. W. Mills: *Essays in Sociology*, Routledge & Kegan Paul, Ltd., London, 1948.

72   Gibb, C. A.: "Leadership," in G. Lindzey (ed.), *Handbook of Social Psychology*, Addison-Wesley Publishing Company, Inc., Reading, Mass., 1954, pp. 877–920.

73   Gouldner, A. W.: "Cosmopolitan and Locals: Toward an Analysis of Latent Social Roles, Parts 1, 2," *Administrative Science Quarterly*, vol. 2, pp. 281–306, 444–480, 1957.

74   Granger, C. H.: "The Hierarchy of Objectives," *Harvard Business Review*, pp. 63–74, May–June, 1964.

75   Granick, D.: *The Red Executive*, Doubleday & Company, Inc., Garden City. N.Y., 1960.

76   Granick, D.: *The European Executive*, Doubleday & Company, Inc., Garden City, N.Y., 1962.

77   Gruenfeld, L. W.: "Personality Needs and Expected Benefits from a Management Development Program," *Occupation Psychology*, vol. 40, pp. 75–81, 1966.

78   Guetzkow, H. (ed.): *Human Relations Program of the Survey Research*

Center, Carnegie Press, Carnegie Institute of Technology, Pittsburgh, Pa., 1951.

79 Guest, R. H.: *Organizational Change: The Effect of Successful Leadership,* Dorsey Press, Homewood, Ill., 1962.

80 Hall, C. S., and G. Lindzey: *Theories of Personality,* John Wiley & Sons, Inc., New York, 1965.

81 Hall, C. S.: *A Primer of Freudian Psychology,* Harcourt, Brace & World, Inc., New York, 1954.

82 Halpin, A. W., and B. J. Winer: "A Factorial Study of the Leader Behaviour Descriptions," in R. M. Stogdill and A. E. Coons (eds.), *Leader Behaviour: Its Description and Measurement,* Ohio State University Bureau of Business Research Monograph 88, Columbus, Ohio, 1957.

83 Harrell, T. W.: *Managers' Performance and Personality,* South-Western Publishing Company, Cincinnati, 1961.

84 Hemphill, J. K.: "Why People Attempt To Lead," in L. Petrullo (ed.), *Leadership and Interpersonal Behavior,* Holt, Rinehart and Winston, Inc., New York, 1961, pp. 201–215.

85 Herzberg, F., B. Mausner, R. O. Peterson, and D. F. Mapwell: *Job Attitudes: Review of Research and Opinion,* Psychological Service of Pittsburgh, Pittsburgh, 1957.

86 Herzberg, F., B. Mausner, and R. B. Snyderman: *The Motivation To Work,* John Wiley & Sons, Inc., New York, 1959.

87 Herzberg, F.: *Work and the Nature of Man,* The World Publishing Company, Cleveland, 1966.

88 Hobbes, T.: *Body, Man and Citizen,* P. F. Collier & Son Corporation, New York, 1962.

89 Hodgson, R., D. L. Levinson, and A. Zaleznik: *Executive Role Constellation,* Harvard Business School, Division of Research, Boston, 1965.

90 Hoffer, E.: *The True Believer,* Harper & Row, Publishers, Incorporated, New York, 1951.

91 Horney, K.: *Our Inner Conflicts,* W. W. Norton & Company, Inc., New York, 1945.

92 Hovland, C. I., I. L. Janis, and H. H. Kelley: *Communication and Persuasion,* Yale University Press, New Haven, Conn., 1953.

93 Hughes, C. L.: *Goal Setting,* American Management Association, New York, 1965.

94 Humble, J. W.: *Improving Management Performance,* British Institute of Management, London, 1966.

95 Humble, J. W.: *Management by Objectives,* Industrial Education and Research Foundation, London, 1967.

96 Humble, J. W.: *Improving Business Results,* McGraw-Hill Book Company, London, 1968.

97 Hutchins, E. B., and F. E. Fiedler: "Task Oriented and Quasi-therapeutic Role Functions of the Leader in Small Military Groups," *Sociometry,* vol. 23, pp. 393–406, 1960.

98 *Intercollegiate Case Clearing House Catalog,* Harvard Business School, Division of Research, Boston.

99 Indik, B. P., B. S. Georgopoulos, and S. E. Seashore: "Superior-Subordinate Relationships and Performance," *Personnel Psychology,* vol. 14, pp. 357–374, 1961.

100   Jardine, J.: "Style Awareness and Style Awareness Shifts on MES Training," Unpublished manuscript, 1968.
101   Jaques, E.: *The Changing Culture of a Factory*, Tavistock, 1951.
102   Jennings, E. E.: *Anatomy of Leadership*, Harper & Row, Publishers, Incorporated, New York, 1960.
103   Jennings, E. E.: *The Executive*, Harper & Row, Publishers, Incorporated, New York, 1962.
104   Jennings, E. E.: *The Executive in Crisis*, Bureau Business Research Michigan State University Press, 1965.
105   Jennings, E. E.: *Executive Success*, Appleton-Century-Crofts, Inc., New York, 1967.
106   Jennings, E. E.: *The Mobile Manager*, Bureau Business Research, Michigan State University Press, 1967.
107   Kahn, R. L.: "Productivity and Job Satisfaction," *Personnel Psychology*, vol. 13, pp. 275–287, 1960.
108   Kahn, R. L., and D. Katz, "Leadership Practices in Relation to Productivity and Morale," in D. Cartwright and A. Zander (eds.), *Group Dynamics*, Harper & Row, Publishers, Incorporated, New York, 1960, pp. 612–628.
109   Katz, R. L.: "Skills of an Effective Administrator," *Harvard Business Review*, vol. 33, pp. 33–42, January–February, 1955.
110   Kahn, R., D. Wolfe, et al.: *Organizational Stress*, John Wiley & Sons, Inc., New York, 1964.
111   Katona, G.: *Psychological Analysis of Business Behavior*, McGraw-Hill Book Company, New York, 1951.
112   Kelly, G. A.: *The Psychology of Personal Constructs*, W. W. Norton & Company, Inc., New York, 1955.
113   Koontz, H.: "Making Sense of Management Theory," *Harvard Business Review*, pp. 24–46, July–August, 1962.
114   Koontz, H. (ed.): *Toward a Unified Theory of Management*, McGraw-Hill Book Company, New York, 1964.
115   Korman, A. K.: "Consideration, Initiating Structure and Organizational Criteria—A review," *Personnel Psychology*, vol. 19, pp. 349–361, Winter, 1966.
116   Lawrence, L. C., and P. C. Smith: "Group Decision and Employee Participation," *Journal of Applied Psychology*, vol. 39, pp. 334–337, 1955.
117   Levine, J., and J. Butler: "Lecture versus Group Discussion in Changing Behavior," *Journal of Applied Psychology*.
118   Lewin, K., R. Lippitt, and R. K. White: "Patterns of Aggressive Behavior in Experimentally Created Social Climates," *Journal of Social Psychology*, vol. 10, pp. 271–279, 1939.
119   Likert, R.: *New Patterns of Management*, McGraw-Hill Book Company, New York, 1961.
120   Likert, R.: *The Human Organization*, McGraw-Hill Book Company, New York, 1967.
121   Liu, J. T. C.: "Eleventh-century Chinese Bureaucrats: Some Historical Classifications and Behavioral Types," *Administrative Science Quarterly*, vol. 4, pp. 207–226, 1959.
122   Locke, J.: *An Essay Concerning Human Understanding*, Clarendon Press, Oxford, 1928.
123   Machiavelli, N.: *The Prince*, George Routledge & Sons, Ltd., 1886.

124   Mahler, W. R.: "What Is Needed To Improve Management Development Programs?" paper read before A.P.A. Symposium, St. Louis, Sept. 4, 1962.

125   Maier, N. R. F.: "The Quality of Group Decisions as Influenced by the Discussion Leader," *Human Relations*, vol. 3, pp. 155–174, 1950.

126   Mandell, M.: "The Selection of Executives," in M. J. Dooher and E. Marting (eds.), *The Selection of Management Personnel*, American Management Association, New York, 1957.

127   Mandell, M., and D. C. Adkins: "The Validity of Written Tests for the Selection of Administrative Personnel," *Educational and Psychological Measurement*, vol. 6, pp. 293–312, 1946.

128   Mann, F. C., and H. Baumgartel: *Absences and Employee Attitudes in an Electric Power Company*, Institute for Social Research, University of Michigan, Ann Arbor, 1954.

129   Mann, F. C., and H. Baumgartel: *The Supervisor's Views on Costs*, American Management Association, Office Management Series, no. 138, New York, 1954, pp. 3–21.

130   Marquis, J.: *Alfred I. DuPont: The Family Rebel*, The Bobbs-Merrill Company, Inc., Indianapolis, 1941.

131   Marrow, A. J.: *Behind the Executive Mask*, American Management Association, New York, 1964.

132   Marrow, A. J., and J. R. P. French: "Overcoming a Stereotype," *Journal of Social Issues*, vol. 1, pp. 33–37, 1945.

133   Maslow, A. H.: *Motivation and Personality*, Harper & Row, Publishers, Incorporated, New York, 1954.

134   Maslow, A. H.: *Eupsychian Management*, Richard D. Irwin, Inc., Homewood, Ill., 1965, pp. 15–33.

135   Mayo, E.: *The Human Problems of an Industrial Civilization*, Harvard Graduate School of Business Administration, Boston, 1933.

136   Mayo, E.: *The Social Problems of an Industrial Civilization*, Harvard Graduate School of Business Administration, Boston, 1945.

137   McClelland, D. C.: *The Achieving Society*, D. Van Nostrand Company, Inc., Princeton, N.J., 1961.

138   McClelland, D. C.: "Business Drive and National Achievement," *Harvard Business Review*, pp. 99–112, July–August, 1962.

139   McGivering, I. C., D. G. J. Matthews, and W. H. Scott: *Management in Britain*, Liverpool University Press, 1959.

140   McGregor, D. V.: *The Human Side of Enterprise*, McGraw-Hill Book Company, New York, 1960.

141   McGregor, D. V.: *Line Management's Responsibility for Human Relations*, American Management Association, New York, 1953.

142   McNair, M. P.: "What Price Human Relations," *Harvard Business Review*, pp. 15–39; March–April, 1957.

143   McNaughton, J.: Personal communication with author, Fredericton, 1967.

144   Merrill, H. F. (ed.): *Classics in Management*, American Management Association, New York, 1960.

145   Metcalf, H. C., and L. Urwick (eds.): *Dynamic Administration*, Pitman Publishing Corporation, New York, 1941.

146   Miles, M. B.: "Human Relations Training: Current Status," in I. R. Weschler and E. H. Schein (eds.), *Issues in Human Relations Training*,

National Education Association, National Training Laboratories, Selected Reading Series, no. 5, Washington, D.C., 1962.

147 Miles, M. B.: "Human Relations Training: Processes and Outcomes," *Journal of Counseling Psychology,* vol. 7, pp. 301–306, 1960.

148 Miles, M. B.: *Learning To Work in Groups,* Teachers College Press, New York, 1959.

149 Miller, E. C.: *Objectives and Standards,* American Management Association, New York, 1966.

150 Miller, E. J., and A. K. Rice: *The Control of Task and Sentient Boundaries,* Tavistock, 1967.

151 Morse, Nancy C.: *Satisfactions in the White Collar Job,* Institute for Social Research, University of Michigan, Ann Arbor, 1954.

152 Morse, N. C., and E. Reimer: "The Experimental Change of a Major Organizational Variable," *Journal of Abnormal and Social Psychology,* vol. 52, pp. 120–129, 1956.

153 Nash, A. N.: "Vocational Interests of Effective Managers: A Review of the Literature," *Personnel Psychology,* vol. 18, pp. 21–37, 1965.

154 National Industrial Conference Board: "Write Us Some Policies," *The Conference Board Record,* December, 1964.

155 Odiorne, G. S.: *Management by Objectives,* Pitman Publishing Corporation, New York, 1965.

156 Odiorne, G. S.: "The Trouble with Sensitivity Training," *ASTD Journal,* pp. 9–20, October, 1963.

157 Ordway, Tead: *The Art of Administration,* McGraw-Hill Book Company, New York, 1951.

158 Parkinson, C. N.: *Parkinson's Law,* John Murray (Publishers), Ltd., London, 1958.

159 Patchen, M.: "Supervisory Methods and Group Performance Norms," *Administrative Science Quarterly,* vol. 6, pp. 275–294, 1962.

160 Presthus, R. V.: "Toward a Theory of Organizational Behaviour," *Administrative Science Quarterly,* vol. 3, pp. 48–72, 1958.

161 Pugh, D. S., et al.: "A Conceptual Scheme for Organizational Analysis," *Administrative Science Quarterly,* vol. 7, pp. 289–315, 1963.

162 Raskin, A., J. K. Boruchow, and R. Golob: "The Concept of Task Versus Person Orientation in Nursing," *Journal of Applied Psychology,* vol. 49, pp. 182–187, 1965.

163 Reddin, W. J.: "The Tri-dimensional Grid," *The Canadian Personnel and Industrial Relations Journal,* pp. 13–20, January, 1966.

164 Reissman, L.: "A Study of Role Conception in Bureaucracy," *Social Forces,* vol. 27, pp. 305–310, 1941.

165 Reisman, D.: *The Lonely Crowd,* Yale University Press, New Haven, Conn., 1951.

166 Roethlisberger, F. J., and W. J. Dickson: *Management and the Worker,* Harvard University Press, Cambridge, Mass., 1939.

167 Rokeach, M.: *The Open and Closed Mind,* Basic Books, Inc., Publishers, New York, 1960.

168 Sales, S. M.: "Supervisory Style and Productivity: Review and Theory," *Personnel Psychology,* vol. 19, pp. 275–285, 1966.

169 Schachter, S., L. Festinger, B. Willerman, and R. Hyman: "Emotional Disruption and Industrial Productivity," *Journal of Applied Psychology,* vol. 45, pp. 201–213, 1961.

170 Shartle, C. L.: *Executive Performance and Leadership,* Prentice-Hall, Inc., Englewood Cliffs, N.J., 1956.

171 Shaw, M. E.: "Scaling Group Tasks: A Method for Dimensional Analysis," *Technical Report 1*, ONRC NR 170–266 Nonr–580(11), 1963.

172 Sloan, A. J.: *My Years with General Motors*, Doubleday & Company, Inc., Garden City, N.J., 1964.

173 Spencer, Maj. Gen. G. H.: "Leadership Styles in Management," *unpublished manuscript*, 1965.

174 Stogdill, R. M., and A. E. Coons (eds.): *Leader Behavior: Its Description and Measurement*, Ohio State University, Bureau of Business Research, Columbus, Ohio, 1957.

175 Stogdill, R. M.: *Individual Behavior and Group Achievement*, Oxford University Press, Fair Lawn, N.J., 1959.

176 Strong, E. K., Jr.: "Vocational Guidance of Executives," *Journal of Applied Psychology*, vol. 11, pp. 331–347, 1927.

177 Sullivan, H. S.: *The Interpersonal Theory of Psychiatry*, W. W. Norton & Company, Inc., New York, 1953.

178 Tannenbaum, A. S.: "The Relationship between Personality and Group Structure," unpublished doctoral dissertation, Syracuse University, 1954.

179 Taylor, F. W.: *Principles of Scientific Management*, Harper & Row, Publishers, Incorporated, New York, 1947.

180 Turner, A. N., and P. R. Lawrence: *Industrial Jobs and the Worker*, Harvard Business School, Division of Research, Boston, 1965.

181 Urwick, L., and H. C. Metcalf (eds.): *Dynamic Administration*, Pitman Publishing Corporation, New York, 1941.

182 Urwick, L.: *Notes on the Theory of Organization*, American Management Association, New York, 1952.

183 Valentine, R. F.: *Performance Objectives for Managers*, American Management Association, New York, 1966.

184 Vroom, V. H.: *Some Personality Determinants of the Effects of Participation*, Prentice-Hall, Inc., Englewood Cliffs, N.J., 1960.

185 Wager, L. W.: "Leadership Style, Hierarchical Influence and Supervisory Role Obligations," *Administrative Science Quarterly*, vol. 9, pp. 391–420, 1965.

186 Walling, D.: *Summer Institute Notes*, National Training Laboratories, Washington, 1964.

187 Weber, M.: *The Protestant Ethic and the Spirit of Capitalism*, Oxford University Press, Fair Lawn, N.J., 1947.

188 Weber, M.: *The Theory of Social and Economic Organization*, Oxford University Press, Fair Lawn, N.J.: 1947.

189 Whyte, W.: *The Organization Man*, Doubleday & Company, Inc., Garden City, N.Y., 1957.

190 Whyte, W. F., et al.: *Money and Motivation*, Harper & Row, Publishers, Incorporated, New York, chap. 10, 1955.

191 Woodward, J.: *Industrial Organization*, Oxford University Press, Fair Lawn, N.J., 1965.

192 Wickert, F. R., and D. E. McFarland (eds.): *Measuring Executive Effectiveness*, Appleton-Century-Crofts, Inc., New York, p. 199, 1967.

193 Wickert, R.: "Turnover and Employee's Feelings of Ego-involvement in the Day-to-day Operation of a Company," *Personnel Psychology*, vol. 4, pp. 185–197, 1951.

194 Zaleznik, A., and D. Moment: *The Dynamics of Interpersonal Behavior*, John Wiley & Sons, Inc., New York, 1964.

195 Zaleznik, A.: "Management of Disappointment," *Harvard Business Review*, pp. 59–70, November–December, 1967.

Index

Achievement, need for, 194–195
Administration, distinct from management, 160
Ambiguity tolerance:
 high, 253–254
 low, 261–262
Announcements in change, 171–173
Anxiety, 146
Apparent effectiveness:
 defined, 9, 327
 described, 7
Area of effectiveness:
 defined, 136, 327
 described, 129–130
Area of possible effectiveness:
 defined, 136, 327
 described, 130–131
Authoritarian versus democratic leadership, 35–37, 90, 186

Autocrat managerial style:
 defined, 42, 47, 327
 derived, 40
 described, 224–226
 indicators, 224

Bales' leadership research, 22
Basic style(s):
 characteristics, 28–30
 concept introduced, 9
 defined, 33, 327
 derived, 26–27
 how to appraise, 27–30
Basic-style point:
 defined, 33, 327
 described, 25
Behavioral theory (see Theory, behavioral)

Benevolent autocrat managerial
    style:
    defined, 42, 47, 327
    derived, 40
    described, 226–227
    indicators, 226
Blakes' styles and 3-D, 29
Blakes' theory, 194
Blakes' third dimension, 194
Brown's styles and 3-D, 29
BSP (see Basic-style point)
Bureau of Business Research, 20
Bureaucrat managerial style:
    defined, 42, 48, 328
    derived, 40
  ⸝ described, 213
    indicators, 213
    as negative term, 213

Career crisis, 270
Ceremony, use as situational man-
    agement technique, 174–175
Change:
    cannot respond to, 269
    change-acceptance scale, 166
    change-reaction checklist, 163
    change-reaction diagram, 164–
        165
    importance of relationships ori-
        entation in, 161–162
    job, 293–294
    most common errors, 175–176
    rate of: factors, 177
        not introduction of, 177
        rapid, arguments for, 178
        slow, arguments for, 177
    situational management tech-
        niques, 169–177
    suppression of resistance, 176–
        177
    way it affects individual, 162
    what needs changing? 289
    (See also Situational manage-
        ment skill)

Change-acceptance scale, 166
Change agent relationship, 311
Change program, 299–300
    objectives, 299–300, 307
Change-reaction checklist, 163
Change-reaction diagram, 164–165
Compromiser managerial style:
    defined, 41, 48, 328
    derived, 40
    described, 231–233
    indicators, 231
Computer:
    crash introduction, 225
    need for skill in managers, 295
    salesmen, technology demands
        of, 82
Concepts:
    framework of 3-D, 181–184
    as jargon, 184
Conceptual language, lack of, 145
Consideration, Ohio State leader-
    ship factor, 20–21
Contributions, managerial, 288
Corporate effectiveness conference
    case study, 323
    described, 306–307
Corporate strategy laboratory:
    case study, 8, 321
    described, 304–305
Coworker(s):
    assessing demands made, 93–96
    defined, 66, 328
    derived as situational element, 65
    expectations, 90
    explained, 19
    stye, 90
Coworker demands, examples: ac-
        accounting team, 107
    collaborating physical science
        researchers, 108
    head of design, 105
    sales manager, 106

Davis' styles and 3-D, 30

Death, unnoticed, as effectiveness measure, 3–4
Decisions, making, 293
Dedicated basic style:
  capsule descriptions, 31–32
  characteristics, 28–30
  defined, 33, 328
  described, 221–224
  indicators, 221
  technology indicators, 73–74
Defense mechanisms:
  projection, 143–144
  rationalization, 141–143
Demands, element (see Element demands)
Democratic versus authoritarian leadership, 35–37, 90–91, 186
Deserter managerial style:
  defined, 43, 48, 328
  derived, 40
  described, 209–211
  files as weaponry, 211
  indicators, 209
  as recluse, 212
  when ambitious, 211–212
  when suicidal, 211
Desertion, company in, 248
Developer managerial style:
  defined, 42, 48, 328
  derived, 40
  described, 218–219
  indicators, 218
Diagnosis, as situational management technique, 169–170
Distortion, style (see Style distortion)
Divisional effectiveness conference:
  case study, 322–323
  described, 305–306
Domestic argument and flex map, 134
Dominant elements:
  defined, 136, 328
  explained, 128

Dominant style:
  defined, 48, 328
  explained, 46
  on MSDT, 240
Drift, style (see Style drift)

E (see Managerial effectiveness)
Effectiveness:
  area of, 129–130
  area of possible, 130–131
  as central value, 181–182
  rewards, 8
  three kinds, 7–8
  (See also Managerial effectiveness)
Effectiveness improvement:
  coworker's, 290–291
  managerial, 287–296
  subordinate's, 291
  superior's, 290
Effectiveness, leader: defined, 9
  described, 3–8
  (See also Leader effectiveness)
Effectiveness, managerial (see Managerial effectiveness)
Effectiveness standards:
  bases of, 277
  compared to objectives, 276
  defined, 3, 285, 328
  levels, 277
  for material, 278
  preparing, 276
  for profitability, 278
  for sales, 278
  selecting, 278–279
  (See also Management objectives; Objectives)
Efficiency, 5–6
Element demands:
  defined, 66, 328
  explained, 65

Element strength:
  defined, 136, 328
  explained, 128–129
Employee-centered extreme, Michigan studies, 21–22
Executive managerial style:
  defined, 41, 48, 328
  derived, 40
  described, 233–234
  indicators, 233

Family fight and flex map, 134
Fatal flaw, 153
Feedback:
  learning cycle, 154
  loops, 153
  types, 153–154
Fiedler's theory, 199–201
Fish experiment, 270–271
Flex:
  high: demands on, 255–256
    described, 253–255
    high ambiguity tolerance, 253–254
    mistaken view of, 52
    open belief system, 254
    other-directed, 254–255
    power insensitivity, 254
    as role playing, 53–54
  low: demands on, 264
    described, 261–264
    firm belief system, 263
    inner-directed, 263
    low ambiguity tolerance, 261–262
    power sensitivity, 262–263
    as preferred, 54
  style (see Style flex)
  technology (see Technology)
Flex map:
  area of effectiveness, 129–130
  area of possible effectiveness, 130–131
  counselling, 133
Flex map:
  defined, 136, 329
  dominant elements, 128
  element strength, 128–129
  examples: of coworker demands, 105–108
    of manager flex, 55–58
    of organization demands, 96–100
    of subordinate demands, 109–112
    of superior demands, 100–104
    of technology demands, 78–87
  introduction, 115–117
  situational flex form, 131–132
  situational problems, 117–124
  uses, 132–133
Flexibility, style (see Style flexibility)
Flexible organization:
  characteristics, 313–314
  life cycle, 312–313
  and 3-D program, 310–311

Golden handshake, 174
Group dynamics school, 63
Group emphasis, as situational management technique, 171–172

Harvard leadership research, 22
High flex (see Flex, high)
Horney's life styles and 3-D, 30
Human relations school, 62
Herzburg, F., 70, 198–199

Ideal style:
  in behavioral science, 187–188
  is there one, 35–49
  Korman's comprehensive review, 38

Implementation, discussion of, as situational management technique, 173
Information, maximum, as situational management technique, 172–173
Initiating structure, Ohio State leadership factor, 20–21
Integrated basic style:
  capsule description, 32
  characteristics, 28–30
  defined, 33, 328
  described, 229–231
  indicators, 229
  misunderstandings, 231
  technology indicators, 74
Interteam effectiveness conference:
  case study, 322
  described, 305

Jargon, 184
Jennings styles and 3-D, 30
Job descriptions and effectiveness, 5
Johari window, 147–148

Katz' theory, 193–194

Leader, 9
  and followers and situation theory: and military leadership, 257–258
  and 3-D, 193
Leader effectiveness:
  defined, 9
  described, 3–8
  theory, 8
Leadership distinct from management, 160–161
Leadership research:
  integration, 22–25
  surveyed, 20–24

Leadership research:
  two common ideas, 22–23
Likert, 3-D and, 196–197
Low flex (see Flex, low)

McClelland's theory, 194–195
McGregor's theory, 191–193
  styles and 3-D, 29
Management by objectives:
  case study, 317–318
  described, 275
  differentiated from appraisal, 275–276
  implementation, successful, 284
  3-D and, 284–285
  (See also Effectiveness standards; Objectives)
Management distinct from leadership, 160–161
Management style diagnosis test:
  described, 237–242
  divisional analysis, 249–250
  use, 250
  (See also Organizational philosophy profiles; Style profiles)
Manager:
  defined, 19, 33, 329
  not situational element, 66
Managerial effectiveness:
  defined, 3, 9, 329
  increasing, 287–288
  and job descriptions, 5
  long-run, 284
  as multidimensional, 284
  not personality, 3
  and rewards, 8
  scale, 47
  as third dimension, 39–45
Managerial effectiveness conference:
  case study, 321
  described, 303–304
Managerial skills:
  defined, 136, 329
  derived, 135–136

Managerial style:
  defined, 48, 329
  derived, 39–41
Managerial style point:
  defined, 48, 329
  explained, 47
Manipulation, situational, 161
Maslow's theory, 191
MBO (see Management by objectives)
Michigan leadership research,
  21–22
Michigan style continuum, 21–22
Military:
  aircrew commander research, 21
  captain rank style profile,
    246–247
  leadership and flexibility,
    257–258
  lieutenant colonel rank style
    profile, 246–247
  organization philosophy, 91
  organization philosophy demands,
    97–98
  power and flex, 264–265
  retired officer in university, 262
  senior officer as bureaucrat, 6
  superior's demands, 104
Mismatch situation, 116
Missionary managerial style:
  defined, 42, 48, 329
  derived, 40
  described, 217–218
  indicators, 217
Motivation-hygiene theory, 198–199
MSP (see Managerial style point)

Needs:
  achievement, 194–195
  versus expectations, 89
  McClelland's, 194–196
  McGregor's, 191
  Maslow's, 191
Negative adaptation, 144

Normative error:
  in behavioral science, 188–189
  ideal style, 38–39

Objective setting, mutual, as situational management technique,
    170–171
Objectives:
  of change programs, 299–300,
    307
  classes, 281–282
  compared to effectiveness
    standards, 276
  defined, 285, 329
  developmental, 281–282
  drafting, 279–280
  errors to avoid, 282
  frames, 279
  preparing, 276
  record form, 282–283
  refinement, 278–279
  sound, tests of, 281
  special, 281–282
  standard, 281–282
  unsatisfactory, 281
  (See also Effectiveness standards;
    Management by objectives)
Ohio State leadership factors,
    20–21
Organization
  assessing, 93–95
  defined, 66, 329
  derived as situational element, 65
  explained, 91
  influence on, 91–92
  influence on style, 89–112
  manager's, 290
  sensing, 92–93
Organization demands, examples:
    army captain in peacetime,
      98
    internal behavioral consultant,
      100
    personnel manager, 99

Organization demands, examples:
   public servant, 96
   university department heads,
      97
Organization effectiveness program:
   case history, 317–325
   change-agent relationship, 311
   change strategy, 307
   corporate effectiveness confer-
      ence, 306–307, 323
   corporate strategy laboratory,
      304–305, 321
   cost-benefit analysis, 324
   described, 299–309
   divisional effectiveness confer-
      ence, 305–306, 322–323
   flexible organization, 313–314
   internal control, 300
   interteam effectiveness confer-
      ence, 305, 322
   managerial effectiveness confer-
      ence, 303–304, 321
   managerial effectiveness seminar,
      301–302, 319
   objectives, 299–300, 307
   similarities to other programs,
      309
   start-up, 308, 318
   team effectiveness conference,
      305, 321–322
   team role laboratory, 302–303,
      320
   time scale, 308
   underlying theory, 310–311
   work-unit idea conference, 306,
      322
Organization flexibility (see Flexible
   organization)
Organization philosophy profiles:
   company in desertion, 249
   heads of voluntary agencies, 244
   managers of industrial relations
      units, 248–249
   middle managers pulp and
      paper (A), 245

Organization philosophy profiles:
   middle managers pulp and
      paper (B), 246
   middle managers seminar, 243
   military officers captain rank, 247
   military officers lieutenant
      colonel rank, 247
   presidents and vice-presidents,
      244
Organization theory, 64
Overrejected style:
   defined, 48, 329
   explained, 47

Participation:
   inappropriate use, 232
   Norwegian experiment, 36
   pseudoparticipation, 172, 217
   in situational management,
      171–173
   U.S. factory experiment, 35–36
Personal effectiveness:
   defined, 9, 329
   described, 7–8
Personality clash diagnosis,
      144–145
Position descriptions and effective-
      ness, 5–6
Power:
   and flex, 264–265
   insensitivity, 254
   overvalued by rigid, 268–269
   sensitivity, 262–263
Prayer, The Situationists', 136
Production run, impact on tech-
      nology demands, 79
Professional workers:
   coworker's demands, 107, 108
   heads voluntary agencies style
      profile, 244
   managers style profile, 245
   managing, 293
   subordinate demands, 110
   technology demands, 81–87

Projection, as defense mechanism, 143–144

Quotation Test, Style, 151–152

Rate of change, 177–178
Rationality, as 3-D focus, 185
Rationalization, as defense mechanism, 141–143
Recession on flex map, 134
Related basic style:
  capsule description, 31
  characteristics, 28–30
  defined, 33, 329
  described, 215, 217
  indicators, 215
  technology indicators, 73
Relationships orientation:
  defined, 24, 33, 329
  derived, 23
  importance in change, 161–162
  rigidity, 270
  scale, 24–25
  of zero, 25
Relationships rigidity, 270
Research leadership, 20–22
Resilience (see Style resilience)
Resistance to change:
  anticipation, 162–163
  covert signs, 162
  deserter style, 209–212
  interpretation, 175
  Norwegian experiment, 36
  overcoming, 169–178
  scale, 166
  suppression, 176–177
Resistance interpretation, as situational management technique, 175
Resistance suppression, 176–177
Rigid organization, life cycle, 312–313
Rigidity (see Style rigidity)

Rigidity induction, 270–271
Ritual, use of, as situational management technique, 174
Rules, as weaponry, 211

Scales:
  change acceptance, 166
  effectiveness, 47
  relationships orientation, 25
  situational management skill, 166
  situational sensitivity skill, 140
  style flex, 55–56
  style flexibility skill, 55–56
  task orientation, 25
Scientific management, 62
Self-actualization, Maslow's, 191
Separated basic style:
  authority, 208
  capsule description, 30–31
  characteristics, 28–30
  defined, 33, 329
  described, 205–209
  impersonality, 207
  indicators, 205
  as a person, 208–209
  technology indicators, 72–73
Situation feedback loops, 153–154
Situational demands:
  changing, 134
  defined, 66
  derived, 64–66
Situational elements:
  defined, 66, 329
  derived, 61–66
  dominant, 128
  element strength, 128
  explained, 64–66
Situational flex form, 131–132
Situational flex map (see Flex map)
Situational insensitivity factors:
  high levels of anxiety, 146
  lack of conceptual language, 145
  limiting value system, 145–146
  on MSDT, 240–241

Situational insensitivity factors:
  negative adaptation, 144
  projection, 143–144
  rationalization, 141–143
  seven factors, 141
  symptoms for causes, 144–145
Situational management errors:
  human aspects only, 175–176
  no benefits, 175–176
  no information about change,
    175–176
  no planning of introduction,
    175–176
  seen as personal, 175–176
  technical aspects only, 175–176
Situational management skill:
  base in 3-D, 182–183
  defined, 167, 329
  derived, 53–55
  explained, 159–167
  techniques, 169–175
  (See also Change)
Situational management techniques:
  diagnosis, 170
  discussion of implementation,
    173
  group emphasis, 171–172
  maximum information, 172–173
  mutual objective setting,
    170–171
  resistance interpretation, 175
  use of ceremony and ritual,
    174–175
Situational manipulation:
  defined, 167, 330
  explained, 161
Situational problems on flex maps,
  117–124
Situational sensitivity skill:
  appraising, 155–156
  defined, 156, 330
  derived, 53–55
  explained, 139–140
  scale, 140
Situational theory, 64

Socioemotional leader, Bales', 22
Stand-off situation, 117
Structure, Ohio State factor, 20–21
Style appraisal skill, defined,
  156, 330
Style awareness:
  defined, 156, 330
  explained, 147
  Johari Window, 147–148
  questions to ask, 150–151
Style awareness shift:
  example of group of managers,
    150
  example of manager, 149
  explained, 148–149
Style distortion:
  defined, 156, 330
  example, 151
  explained, 151
  measured, 151–152
Style drift:
  defined, 52–53, 58, 330
  derived, 52
  described, 258–259
  differentiated from flexibility, 53
Style flex:
  defined, 58, 330
  explained, 51–52
  four concepts, 52–54
  how to plot, 55–57
  mistaken view, 52
  and power, 264–265
  scale, 54–55
Style flexibility:
  checklist, 258
  defined, 52–53, 58, 330
  derived: as a concept, 52
    as a skill, 55–57
  described, 256–258
  differentiated from drift, 53
  and military leadership, 257–258
  as role playing, 53–54
Style profiles:
  defined, 250, 330
  described, 237–240

Style profiles:
    illustrative, 240–242
    situational insensitivity, 240
    sulking, 240
    in training functions, 240
Style Quotation Test, 151–152
Style resilience:
    checklist, 266
    defined, 53, 58, 330
    derived, 52
    described, 265–266
    differentiated from rigidity, 54
Style rigidity:
    career crisis, 270
    change, cannot respond to,
        269–270
    checklist, 271
    defined, 53, 58, 330
    derived, 52
    described, 267–271
    differentiated from resilience, 54
    induction, 270–271
    overvalues power, 268–269
    personal priorities, 268
    relationships rigidity, 270
Style synthesis:
    defined, 242, 250, 330
    described, 242
Style terminology, 25–26
Style unawareness:
    explained, 147–148
    fatal flaw, 152
Style valences, 43
Subordinate(s):
    assessing demands, 93
    defined, 66, 330
    derived, as situational element,
        65
    expectations, 90–91
    explained, 19
    style, 90–91
Subordinate(s) demands, examples:
    controller by accountant,
        110
    middle manager by MBA, 111

Subordinate(s) demands, examples:
    president by general manager,
        109
    shop foreman by recent immi-
        grant, 112
Sulking behavior, 240
Superior:
    assessing demands, 93
    defined, 66, 330
    derived, as situational element,
        65
    expectations, 89–90
    explained, 19
    style, 89–90
Superior demands, examples: army
        brigade commander, 104
    foreman heavy machinery
        plant, 101
    marketing team member, 102
    work study practitioner, 103
Supporting style:
    defined, 49, 330
    explained, 46
    on MSDT, 240
Symptoms mistaken for causes,
    144–145

Task leader, 22
Task orientation:
    defined, 24, 33, 330
    derived, 22–24
    scale, 24–25
    of zero, 25
Team effectiveness conference:
    case study, 321–322
    described, 305
Team role laboratory:
    case study, 320
    described, 302–303
Technology:
    assessment of demands, 71–75
    changed, 291–292
    classification schemes, 71
    dedicated indicators, 73–74

Technology:
 defined, 66, 330
 demand indicators, 72–74
 derived, as situational element,
  65
 high flex, 78–79
 influence on style, 69
 integrated indicators, 74
 plotting flex, 75
 product not predictor, 81
 redesign, 70–71
 related indicators, 73
 separated indicators, 72–73
Technology demands, examples:
  assembly line management,
   78
  computer salesman management, 82
  encyclopedia salesman management, 83
  interacting division manager
   management, 80
  noninteracting division manager management, 79
  research scientist management, 84
  short and long runs, impact,
   79
  time pressure, impact, 81
  toaster production management, 85–87
  truck drivers, 74
  university department management, 78–79
Terminology, style, 25–26
 letters, 26
 names, 26–27
 numbers, 26
Test (see Management style diagnosis test)
Theory, behavioral: either-or
  approach, 186–187
 ideal style approach, 187–188
 is man a beast approach,
  189–190

Theory, behavioral:
 normative approach, 188–189
 problem areas, 185–189
 psychological approach, 187
 types approach, 186–187
Theory X:
 is man a beast approach,
  189–190
 McGregor's theory, 191–193
Theory Y:
 is man a beast approach,
  189–190
 McGregor's theory, 191–193
Theory Z, 189–190
3-D theory:
 behavioral similarities, 181–182
 characteristics, 181–185
 comprehensive conceptual
  framework, 181, 183
 effectiveness central value,
  181–182
 learning difficulty, 140
 and management by objectives,
  284–285
 organizational effectiveness program, 299–300
 in outline, 11–17
 positive alternatives raised, 185
 practicality, 181–182
 rationality, as focus, 185
 situational management base,
  181–183
 training, as a guide to, 16–17
 two central ideas, 22–24
 underlying change theory,
  310–311
Tightrope situation, 123
Time management, 292–293
Time pressure, impact on technology demands, 81
Trait approach, 3, 20, 188
Truck drivers, technology demands,
  74
Types (typologies) in behavioral
  science, 186–187

Unconscious, 147–148
Unions, militancy on flex map, 133
University:
  organization demands, 97
  technology demands, 78–79

Valences, style, 43
Value system, limiting, 145–146

Walling's styles and 3-D, 30

Work-unit idea conference:
  case study, 322
  described, 306

X, Theory, 189–193

Y, Theory, 189–193

Z, Theory, 189–190
Zaleznik-moment styles and 3-D, 30